D1265324

BLEEDING TALENT

BLEEDING TALENT

HOW THE US MILITARY MISMANAGES GREAT LEADERS AND WHY IT'S TIME FOR A REVOLUTION

TIM KANE

palgrave
macmillan

First published in 2012 by
PALGRAVE MACMILLAN®
in the United States—a division of St. Martin's Press LLC,
175 Fifth Avenue, New York, NY 10010.

Where this book is distributed in the UK, Europe and the rest of the world,
this is by Palgrave Macmillan, a division of Macmillan Publishers Limited,
registered in England, company number 785998, of Houndmills,
Basingstoke, Hampshire RG21 6XS.

Palgrave Macmillan is the global academic imprint of the above companies
and has companies and representatives throughout the world.

Palgrave® and Macmillan® are registered trademarks in the United States,
the United Kingdom, Europe and other countries.

ISBN: 978–0–230–39127–7

Library of Congress Cataloging-in-Publication Data

Kane, Tim.
    Bleeding talent : how the US military mismanages great leaders and
    why it's time for a revolution / Tim Kane.
        p. cm.
    ISBN 978–0–230–39127–7
        1. Command of troops. 2. Leadership—United States. I. Title.

UB210.K363 2012
355.6'80973—dc23   2012021609

A catalogue record of the book is available from the British Library.

Design by Newgen Imaging Systems, (P) Ltd., Chennai, India.

First edition: December 2012

10 9 8 7 6 5 4 3 2

Printed in the United States of America.

To my brothers and sisters from the United States
Air Force Academy, class of Mighty '90

CONTENTS

FIGURES AND TABLES

FIGURES

TABLES

ACKNOWLEDGMENTS

I AM GRATEFUL TO THE MEN AND WOMEN who serve in the US military for sharing their experiences with me, including veterans and active duty service members of all ranks. During a time of war, the sacrifices of our nation's volunteers are humbling, and I hope that my words here are able to fairly represent their diverse views. I would especially like to thank those 250 West Point graduates who responded to the two surveys I conducted in late 2010. I am also thankful to another group of Naval Academy graduates who participated in a similar survey with similar results, but my inability to garner a sufficient sample size precluded publishing the figures here.

In particular, I'd like to thank the many individuals who helped me design the survey questions and think more carefully about the issues at stake. Those include James Carafano, Mike Carter, William Casebeer, Scott Clemenson, Kyle Davis, Joe Deane, Anthony DeToto, Dean Dorman, Jason Dempsey, Nathan Estruth, Guy Filippelli, Alyse Freilich, Scott Halter, Grover Harms, Warren Hearnes, Steve Kiser, Beau Laskey, Robert Litan, Mike Meese, John Nagl, Shawn Olds, Kelly Perdew, Jeff Peterson, Jeff Philippart, Dan Rice, Robert Strom, Troy Thomas, Don Vandergriff, Josh Weed, Russ Laraway, and Elad Yoran. Many of these individuals provided invaluable feedback on early drafts of the manuscript.

I am indebted to the active duty officers in the US Army who advised me while I wrote this book, and who shall remain nameless in order to protect their careers. Many wrote me emails from the battlefield as well as from the Pentagon asking to be anonymous. Some talked to me for hours over the phone and waited for weeks for my slow responses. Thank you for your confidence in me and your patience.

The Ewing Marion Kauffman Foundation was my employer while this book was conceived and written, and I owe a particular debt of gratitude to Bob Litan and Carl Schramm for their support. The Hudson Institute, my current employer, has graciously supported me while I finalized the manuscript and prepared it for publication.

Laurie Harting at Palgrave Macmillan has been a godsend as an editor—patient, smart, and unbelievably supportive. Thank you to all of the folks at Palgrave who guided me through this process, especially Leigh Westerfield for her copyedits. Evelyn Smith and Naoko Funatsu provided excellent support at the Hudson Institute during the final stages of editing. My friend Mindee Forman was just amazing as an editor who made the manuscript so much stronger than the rough text I sent her way for an amazingly fast rewrite. Also, I cannot express enough thanks to Jill Marsal at the Marsal Lyon Literary Agency for taking a risk on me and this project. Thanks as well to the editors at *The Atlantic* for publishing the initial essay that made such a splash. My friend Ben Wildavsky deserves no small amount of credit for making the draft essay twice as good after his magic touch.

My final debt is to my wife, Hiromi, and our four wonderful children, Sean, Naomi, Katherine, and Lauren. Thanks for your love and support.

INTRODUCTION

SUMMER, 1998. JIM COYER AND I ARE SIPPING beers on the patio, overlooking the canyon behind my new house in San Diego. Jim and I had founded NeocorTech four years before, a software company that was more of a hobby than a business, and yet there we were enjoying the benefits of a $1 million dollar cash sale. Jim got a third. I got a third. Our other partners and employees got a third. And, we literally forgot Uncle Sam, who also wanted a third in income taxes. That left my wife and me with just enough of a payoff to justify four years without a salary or health insurance, and it meant that we could buy three things put off for way too long. A new house with a yard, where I could build a sandbox for our two kids. A puppy. And, finally, some new socks and underwear.

That year, we rocketed from the lowest tax bracket to the top (and back the very next year), but I can't begrudge Uncle Sam his cut. It was thanks to the US government that I met Jim when we were cadets at the Air Force Academy. That was a special place for me, a place where I met young men and women who were destined to be more than friends. Brothers and sisters.

Cadet Coyer was a doolie (freshman) in my squadron, and although I basically hazed him for the first year of our acquaintance, I also knew he was one of the smartest, most insightful, and most competitive people I would ever meet. Like most cadets, Coyer and I dreamed of flying space shuttles, leading the nation in battle, pushing the frontiers of science, making the world safe for democracy...little stuff like that. We were cold warriors then, children of Ronald Reagan, getting ready to face off against the Soviets and, in the meantime, sneaking beers and girls into the dorm. Even now, we laugh about boxing classes, obstacle courses, marches to the morning meal, spit-shined combat boots, tours for demerits, spirit cheese, and our ready response for any challenge—one of the seven sentences doolies are permitted to say—"No excuse, sir!"

Fast forward a decade, a company, and many beers, and I couldn't help dreaming new dreams. "You know what's next, don't you?" I said, as Jim and I clinked our Heinekens.

"Another company on your mind already?" Jim asked. He had that big grin on his face, ready to take on the world. And I saw something there that I don't see in many other faces. Trust. This was a guy I would die for, and who would die for me. How can you put a value on trust in business?

"You know it. Internet privacy, it's gonna be big." Jim did the coding. I did the marketing, sales, accounting, legal, taxes, and negotiations. We both did the dreaming, and cofounded enonymous.com a few days later.

Although San Diego isn't nearly the tech mecca that Silicon Valley is, Jim and I had created some buzz in the local venture community. A million dollars isn't huge news, but we had flown under the radar. No investors in our first company. All sweat equity. And it was 1998 after all, so venture money was hungry for new deals, proven entrepreneurs. Within a couple of weeks, Jim was hacking the code, and I was ready to shop the PowerPoint presentation around town.

That's how I met Ted Alexander, and that's where this story begins.

THE NAVY SEAL

Mission Ventures is a small venture capital firm located just north of Sorrento Mesa, based in a modern office park overlooking the coastal merge of two giant California highways and the Pacific Ocean. Word is they just scored a huge deal with an Internet company that is exploding. A friend makes a call. Mission is interested immediately and asks for an introductory meeting. That morning, I decide to wear my lucky shirt, a white polo with the Air Force Academy logo on it. I roll into the parking lot in my beater Saturn (we don't have enough cash for a new car) and am escorted by an attractive blonde woman to an all-glass conference room with a flawless long table and chairs more expensive than my ride. She offers me a drink, helps me set up my laptop, and tells me, "Ted will be with you in just a minute."

I figure Ted Alexander, the junior partner at the firm assigned to hear my pitch, will be fifteen minutes. When you ask for money, they make you wait. It's part of the dance.

A half hour later, in walks this guy wearing the venture capitalist uniform. Expensive khaki slacks. Button-down shirt, with rolled-up sleeves. Light tan. But something is wrong. This guy is too friendly, too trustable, and his haircut is way too short. His jaw is cut from granite and it says, "Sorry for running late." He grins, shakes my hand. Damn it. I feel like I'm looking at Jim.

I go through the pitch. Ted loves it. Brings in the senior partner to meet me. Asks how much money we have, burn rate (I don't know what that means), and if I'd be willing to close a deal soon. They need time to do due diligence (a phrase I've never heard, so I think he says "Doo-doo diligence"). Bottom line, they want to meet up again in a week or two. As we shake hands and part ways, Ted says, "Nice shirt."

Now I get it. When I let go of his hand, I say, "Hey, Ted, what's that?" pointing to the giant ring on his right hand.

He grins like Jim. "Naval Academy. Class of Eighty-eight. You?"

"Air Force. Mighty Ninety."

STRANGERS IN A STRANGE LAND

A year later, Ted Alexander invited me to join a weekend gathering of service academy graduates who had left the military and joined the Internet revolution. Ted was hosting the informal event at the Mission Ventures offices. Attendees were graduates of West Point or Annapolis, had served as Rangers or SEALs, had earned MBAs from Harvard or Wharton, and were working as investors in Silicon Valley or Manhattan. I was tangential in every way: a zoomie, an intelligence officer, still working on a doctoral dissertation in economics, and an entrepreneur. Yet for all our differences, we shared a set of values and experiences alien to many Americans. We were strangers all right: strangers in the strange land of the private sector.

Since that weekend, the group has grown in size and importance to me. These are my best friends and most trusted peers. Dean Dorman, West Point, turnaround CEO. Dan Beldy, F-18 aviator, venture guru. Kelly Perdew, West Point, Trump apprentice. Mike Pompeo, congressman from Kansas. Dawn Dunlop, F-15 squadron commander, White House fellow. Dave McCormick, undersecretary of the Treasury.

But every year, the economist in me looks at this group and is fascinated by a talent paradox: Why did they all leave the military? Why does the US military generate some of the finest, most entrepreneurial leaders in the world, but then mismanage them using the most risk-averse bureaucracy possible? This book explores that question—actually a very old question that has bedeviled Pentagon leaders for generations—with full appreciation that many of our classmates have remained in uniform for full careers. Even among active-duty officers there is recognition that the personnel system bleeds talent, *externally* through attrition and *internally* through misallocation.

PLAN FOR THE BOOK

While the US military is often viewed as a role model for leadership development, *Bleeding Talent* views it as a cautionary tale in talent mismanagement as well as a positive role model in many ways. In this book, I present new evidence that the attrition rate of the "best" officers has become a crisis in the contemporary army. At the same time, I highlight the high quality of officers in the army and its innovative culture at the unit and individual level. In addition, I propose an evolutionary step forward in how the Pentagon manages its leaders, original in some ways yet based in classical economics.

This book will shape the debate on how to save the military from itself. The first part recognizes, indeed celebrates, what the military has done well in attracting and developing leadership talent. The book then examines the causes and consequences of the modern military's stifling personnel system, with a close look at strategic failures in Iraq and Afghanistan. It also details a new survey of active-duty officers (done by the author) that reports what is driving the best and brightest to leave the service in frustration. Solutions round out the book, grounded in an economic emphasis on market forces.

How should a large organization design its organization to promote and engage its leaders? I try to answer that question for the army, navy, air force, Marine Corps, and coast guard by presenting an alternative leadership system, which I call the *Total Volunteer Force*. The *Total Volunteer Force* has at its heart an internal market for officer assignments, matching supply and demand rather than the central planning systems in place today. The new system follows the legacy of the army's adoption of an all-volunteer recruitment policy in 1973 when it abandoned conscription. *Bleeding Talent* will tell the history of the military personnel system, with an emphasis on economists such as Milton Friedman and Walter Oi, who led the charge to end the role of coercion in drafting enlistees. That same choice between coercion and market incentives is what is at stake now.

The research I've done for the book led to a five-page essay in *The Atlantic* (January/February 2011 issue) and a survey of 250 West Point graduates published as an Social Science Research Network (SSRN) paper in January 2011 (the results are highlighted in the appendix). When those were published, they generated a tremendous response. At one point, I was told that every officer in the army had read my article and that it had become part of the curriculum at one of the elite military war colleges. Letters of support flooded in, from enlisted soldiers in Iraq and from World War II veterans. The support was intense among junior officers, but I have yet to hear (formally) from an active-duty general officer, though I've had a few of their emails forwarded to me. I hope this book will change things, because my goal is not to tear down a great institution, but to help it think about the logical next steps it needs to take to get even better.

MY THREE PERSPECTIVES

As a research scholar at the Kauffman Foundation, known as the "Foundation of Entrepreneurship," I've spent a long time pondering this paradox of military entrepreneurship. I combine three personal perspectives in addressing it: my role as a captain in the air force, then as a serial entrepreneur, and now as a professional economist.

First, as a veteran, I witnessed firsthand the dysfunction that drives good people away from the armed forces. An incentive program in the 1990s enticed one of my commanders, beloved in the squadron, to retire early while his risk-averse peers stayed. During interviews and discussions for the *Atlantic* essay, I realized that being a veteran offered me a unique perspective for criticism, which neither an active-duty officer nor a civilian had, as they were constrained (in perception and reality) by being a pure outsider or pure insider. But a larger issue is at stake—the very high esteem in which the public holds the military, which makes it a difficult institution to criticize constructively.

"The military has been No. 1 in Gallup's annual Confidence in Institutions list continuously since 1998, and has ranked No. 1 or No. 2

almost every year since its initial 1975 measure," according to its July 2010 report.[1] The high esteem contrasts with a widening gap between the civilian and military populations, and is actually problematic for the army's ability to evolve. Many observors recognize that the military may be becoming beyond criticism as result. Politicians who oppose the wars in Afghanistan and Iraq go out of their way to praise the troops and military culture. Citizens feel unqualified to challenge a system they know nothing about. The high level of admiration is a meaningful change from the hostility of the early 1970s expressed by antiwar protesters and the media, but some officers worry that the praise can go overboard to the extent that necessary criticism is never made. It's not that the army isn't listening, but rather that the only folks talking about change are insiders with their own experiential blinders. Keep in mind that no American general or admiral has ever worked outside of uniform since the day of his or her commissioning.

My second perspective, as an entrepreneur with a handful of start-up experiences, changed the way I see not only how businesses operate but how efficient organizations operate. Military training emphasizes decisiveness in the fog and friction of war. Entrepreneurship is a very similar environment, where no field manual exists to guide a hundred decisions each day where time is the ultimate constraint. When it comes to personnel, start-ups are ruthless in getting the right people in place and weeding out workers who don't fit. Ironically, the military bureaucracy takes the opposite approach. Officers are almost never fired, and seniority dominates the culture. Consider a question from my survey of West Point graduates: the army was viewed as an 7 on the 10 point seniority-merit scale, in contrast to the private sector, which was viewed as a 4.

The first consequence is that the army is suffering a talent crisis, invisible to the public, but threatening to hollow out its ranks. In fact, the talent drain has been happening since 2001, according to internal army documents. The leakage peaked in 2006 when one-third of West Point grads from the class of 2001 left as soon as their minimum commitment was up. When the army continued to implement a failed strategy for half a decade in Afghanistan and Iraq, it revealed its inner risk-averse bureaucracy at the cost of American lives.

The exodus of talent from the army may be beneficial for the US economy, but the consequences for the military are lost investment and eventually a weaker force that costs lives. While the wars in Iraq and Afghanistan have led to innovations in many areas of the army, the one area that matters most—human capital management—is a quagmire typical of government organizations: opaque, inflexible, dominated by seniority over merit, and hostile to change besides. The army, navy, air force, and Marines make extremely expensive human capital investments in their people, but they are failing to manage that talent.

This leads to my third perspective as a professional economist. In 2005, I published a major study of troop demographics that was cited by every major newspaper in America. Conventional wisdom held that the recruit quality was declining in the wake of the wars in Afghanistan and Iraq. I asked the Pentagon office responsible for manpower for demographic data on every enlistee for the years 1999, 2001, 2002, and 2003, and was able to show the recruit quality had risen, not declined, after 9/11 and the subsequent wars. More to the point, the data proved that recruits came disproportionately from *wealthier* neighborhoods. This evidence was key in disputing the exploitation argument used by advocates of a renewed draft. While this research focused on enlistees, not officers, I have some credibility as a "pro-military" advocate who has vocally defended the quality of people in uniform. That should add to the power of my critique of the system.

Further, the involvement of economists in military reforms has a distinguished pedigree. The shame of the anti-entrepreneurial bent of the military personnel *management* is that it ignores the successful revolution in recruitment that has been in place since 1973. Following the protests against the draft, and the wreckage that was army morale after Vietnam, the US military adopted a radical transformation by becoming an all-volunteer force. The philosophical difference must be emphasized here: the Pentagon began using market mechanisms instead of central planning, and as a result built the highest quality military force in history.

My 2006 report, cited frequently by Pentagon officials such as Curt Gilroy, helped me forge close relationships with military officials who work to operate (and defend) the all-volunteer force structure (AVF). As a veteran, and like the vast majority of current soldiers, I support the AVF instinctively. Troops don't want anyone with them in combat who doesn't want to be there. But as an economist, I learned that the transition to the AVF was championed by Milton Friedman and other free-market advocates in the 1960s and 1970s. The talent crisis and its resolution are ultimately about the underlying economics. What's really at stake today is whether the army will complete the revolution started by the all-volunteer transformation and bring market mechanisms (and modern economics) into its 1950s-style management.

CHAPTER 1

A CAUTIONARY TALE

In universal terms, a small, free people had willingly outfought huge numbers of imperial subjects who advanced under the lash. More specifically, the Western idea that soldiers themselves decide where, how, and against whom they will fight was contrasted against the Eastern notion of despotism and monarchy—freedom proving the stronger idea as the more courageous fighting of the Greeks at Thermopylae, and their later victories at Salamis and Plataea attested.

—Victor Davis Hanson[1]

JOHN NAGL STILL HESITATES WHEN HE TALKS about his decision to leave the army. A former Rhodes scholar and tank-battalion operations officer in Iraq, Nagl helped General David Petraeus write the army's new counterinsurgency field manual with its updated doctrine that is credited with bringing Iraq's insurgency under control. But despite the considerable influence Nagl had in the army, and despite his reputation as a skilled leader, he retired in 2008 having not yet reached the rank of full colonel. Today, Nagl still has the same short haircut he had 24 years ago when we met as cadets—I an Air Force Academy doolie (or freshman), he a visiting West Pointer—but now he presides over a Washington think tank. The funny thing is, even as a civilian, he can't stop talking about the army—"our army"—as if he had never left. He won't say it outright, but it's clear to me, and to many of his former colleagues, that the army fumbled badly in letting him go. His resignation has been haunting me, and it punctuates a paradox that has been publicly ignored for too long.

Why does the American military produce the most innovative and entrepreneurial leaders in the country, then waste that talent in a risk-averse bureaucracy?

That paradox is what this book is all about. Its consequences couldn't be greater, and yet it remains unresolved despite attention from senior military and civilian Pentagon leaders. This isn't a story about whether President Barack Obama tapped the right general to lead the army, or the right commander for CENTCOM (United States Central Command). It's a story of tens of thousands of patriotic American military officers who quietly quit the ranks in frustration or "suck it up" inside a dysfunctional personnel system.

Of course, recognizing that the military has a bureaucratic problem is hardly news, nor worthy of a book, since this point was already a cliché before most of us were born. What is noteworthy is that decades of warnings and countless blue-ribbon task forces have failed to make a dent. Aggressive Pentagon commanders and secretaries of defense have put their best efforts and sometimes tyrannical zeal into changing the bureaucracy, and have changed nothing. Here I hope to address the root of the problem, which I believe is the underlying system of central planning that the Pentagon uses to manage its workforce.

Perhaps the biggest surprise one finds when digging into military personnel issues is that the same topics have been circulating for decades. For example, when General Peter Schoomaker served as army chief of staff from 2003 to 2007, he emphasized a "culture of innovation" up and down the ranks to shift the army away from its Cold War focus on big, conventional battles and toward new threats. In many respects (weapons, tactics, logistics, training), the army did transform. But the talent paradox remained unresolved for a simple reason: *the problem isn't cultural.* The military's problem is a deeply anti-entrepreneurial structure at the gritty level of personnel policy. From officer evaluations to promotions to job assignments, all branches of the military operate more like a government bureaucracy with a union-ized workforce than a cutting-edge meritocracy.

To their credit, army leaders are painfully aware of their talent paradox. Since at least 2001, the army has been emphasizing making the force more "adaptive" in its culture. A 2011 survey of general officers on active duty rated "personnel management" as one of the weakest functions in the army.[2] One general commented: "Human Capital [management] is the most important, yet the least agile system."[3]

This perception in the field is reinforced with scholarly studies. A widely circulated 2008 internal study from the Office of Economic and Manpower Analysis (OEMA) at West Point said: "Since the late 1980s...prospects for the Officer Corps' future have been darkened by...plummeting company grade officer retention rates. Significantly, this leakage includes a large share of high-performing officers."[4]

Secretary of Defense Robert Gates expressed his frustration in a farewell address to the cadets of West Point on February 25, 2011. Gates was about to step down after serving as the secretary since 2006, first appointed by President George W. Bush to help turn around the war in Iraq, then reappointed by President Obama. By almost every account, he had done well in managing two wars while continuing the transformation of the military. But the secretary hadn't made progress on every front. Although the media attention from the West Point speech focused almost exclusively on a few blunt lines about the dangerous decision to enter land war in Asia, the substance of Gates's remarks was focused very candidly on how the army and its leadership system would need to reform in order to meet the changing face of war. In his speech, Gates asked how the army in particular "can break up the institutional concrete, its bureaucratic rigidity in its assignments and promotion processes, in order to retain, challenge, and inspire its best, brightest, and most-battled tested young officers to lead the service in the future?"[5] The remarks were emotional at times, as the secretary clearly understood the sacrifices of the men and women in uniform under his command during those five years. He remarked that the Pentagon bureaucracy had in fact been reformed in almost every way except one. Gates told the assembled cadets that the "greatest challenge facing your Army, and frankly, my main worry" was the "personnel bureaucracy that awaits...often cited as [one of the] primary factors causing promising officers to leave the Army just as they are best positioned to have a positive impact on the institution."[6]

OPENING MY EYES

Like most veterans, I noticed plenty of bureaucratic silliness in the personnel system during my five years as an air force intelligence officer. But it was heavily counterbalanced by the outstanding people in uniform. Taking care of people was a priority for most commanders, and their efforts seemed to provide a common-sense balance that protected junior officers and enlistees despite the crazy system. At least I thought so. My fellow officers laughed at the meaningless and overinflated performance evaluations. And we shrugged our shoulders at the fact that pilots ruled a pecking order (some called it a caste system) that put even less-competent pilots in command of non-flying units such as logistics, maintenance, and intelligence. It's not like we didn't know it was a caste system when we signed up, and the fact was that fighter pilots lorded over the other pilots, while test pilots lorded over the lesser fighter jocks.

I fondly remember how we joked after the fall of the Union of Soviet Socialist Republics (USSR) that the Pentagon was now the last great socialist institution left in the world. Health care was free, dental visits were mandatory, and everybody got promoted on the exact same day whether they were the best or the very worst officer in their cohort. The first time I heard someone talk about the excessive paperwork at "Big Blue," I had no idea they were referring to IBM not USAF.

When I was encouraged by my mentors to pursue a PhD in economics in order to become a professor back at the Academy, the managers at Military Personnel Command (MPC) splashed cold water on the idea. They were short of intel officers, and refused to approve. So, I went anyway—as a civilian. I can still remember the last call I made to MPC when I asked the assignments officer there to "help me be a career officer" because letting me get a PhD would incur more active-duty commitment years such that I would effectively be in for a full 20-year career. He said, "I am calling your bluff." In the end, I turned in my papers and was reassured by colleagues that I could continue to serve the nation in many other ways.

For the men and women who continue in uniform, my admiration is even greater than before I joined. I am in awe of the career officers and enlistees for their capacity to serve with relatively low pay in such a vital mission. And frankly, I feel a vicarious pride for my friends who still serve. In particular, I was proud to know some of the pilots flying dangerous missions over Bosnia and Iraq, to learn that old friends were getting tapped as test pilots and commanders, to know a few of the troops sent to Somalia, and to know that my old friend John Nagl literally wrote the new army doctrine that was behind the surge in Iraq.

But then my fantasy that all was well in the military snapped, and it snapped the moment I heard the news that Nagl was leaving the army. Writing at Slate.com, Fred Kaplan reacted to Nagl's departure with this:

> Nagl, 41, has been one of the Army's most outspoken officers in recent years. (This is a huge point against him, careerwise; the brass look askance at officers, especially those without stars, who draw attention to themselves.) He played a substantial role in drafting the Army's recent field manual on counterinsurgency. His 2002 book, Learning to Eat Soup with a Knife, based on his doctoral dissertation at Oxford (another point against him in some circles), is widely hailed as a seminal book on CI [counterinsurgency] warfare. (It was after reading the book that Gen. David Petraeus asked Nagl to join the panel that produced the field manual.)
>
> ... Still, some officers who are sympathetic with Nagl's views say they find it discouraging that the Army can't find some way to hang on to a soldier of his caliber. For one reason or another, junior and midlevel officers—lieutenants, captains, and lieutenant colonels—are leaving the Army in droves.[7]

It was at this moment that I turned my gaze back to the leadership engine of the military. Something must be wrong. But now, a decade and a half wiser and armed with an advanced degree in economics, I looked at the Pentagon with very different eyes. This time, the jokes about the socialist shade of operations inside the Pentagon weren't funny, but eerily accurate.

Why wasn't anyone talking about how deeply dysfunctional the system was, wasting talent, throwing off excellent people, oblivious to matching skills with needs? What I found was that criticizing the military is hard to do. Critics within the army who spoke bluntly and/or publicly about the system's flaws risked their careers. But critics from outside the military were easily dismissed. Veterans who wrote about personnel matters could be cast as nothing more than sour grapes. This was particularly effective because Academy graduates are vulnerable to charges of elitism with expectations of grandeur, even though the exit rate of officers with four-year Reserve Officers' Training Corps (ROTC) scholarships is actually higher than for West Pointers (Wardynski et al. 2010). Other critics with no military background, like Kaplan or ForeignPolicy.com blogger Tom Ricks, can be dismissed for not really knowing about the constraints of command. The forces of the status quo have robust defenses, so for most young officers, biting the hand that nurtured them isn't worth it.

ASKING THE QUESTION

If we want to know why the military's personnel system is broken, we have to ask the question. That much seems obvious, but asking the question isn't as easy as one might think. I set my mind to conducting a study of army personnel issues, and found a partner in *The Atlantic* magazine, which agreed to publish the story.[8]

My first thought was to survey students at the war colleges, particularly the Army War College in Carlisle, Pennsylvania, or maybe some of the other professional military-training programs. The irony was that conducting a survey about the military bureaucracy ran into a military bureaucracy. I was redirected to different people for approval, and the trail seemed to be running cold when I realized this wasn't the right approach. Besides, as one friendly colonel advised me: "We get surveyed to death through formal channels." For example, the Pentagon was conducting a massive survey about letting homosexuals serve openly. One look at that monster of obtuseness, and I thought a better approach would be to conduct the survey independently.

I realized, too, that conducting a survey of active-duty officers would miss the huge segment of veterans who had retired or resigned after their four- to six-year initial commitment. Naturally, it was important to me that the survey be valid scientifically, but I had to think of a way to reach out to potential respondents that was unbiased. A biased sample, say of veterans from a single year-group who had resigned at the first opportunity, wouldn't pass muster. Likewise, a sample of only active-duty colonels would also be skewed. So in the summer of 2010, I reached out to a network I knew personally—former class presidents and secretaries of West Point. I was able to get a positive response from the classes of 1989, 1991, 1995, 2000, 2001, and 2004, and the class leaders agreed to send out an email inviting their classmates to a survey about "army leadership." We got 250 responses, and the one-third of active-duty respondents in the sample is actually a higher proportion than the surveyed population.

An astonishing 93 percent answered that half or more of "the best officers leave the military early rather than serving a full career." By

Table 1.1 West point graduates from the classes of 1989–2004 who agree that the current military personnel system…

…does a good job promoting the right officers to general.	32%
…does a good job weeding out the weakest leaders.	32%
…does a good job matching talents with jobs.	20%
…does a good job retaining the best leaders.	6%
…promotes and incentivizes entrepreneurial leaders.	4%
…should be radically reformed.	55%

Source: Tim Kane, Survey of West Point graduates, August–September 2010.

design, I left the definitions of "best" and "early" up to the respondent. Among active-duty respondents, 82 percent believed that half or more of the best are leaving. Only 32 percent of the full panel agreed that the military personnel system does a "good job promoting the right officers to general," and a mere 4 percent agreed that it "does a good job retaining the best officers." See Table 1.1 for details.

Is this so terrible? One can argue that every system has flaws and that the military should be judged on its ultimate mission: maintaining national security and winning wars. But that's exactly the point: 67 percent of the West Point graduates agreed that the current exit rate of the best officers leads to a *less competent general-officer corps*; 79 percent agreed that it *harms national security*. These are not sour grapes. This is the cream of the crop damning the farm.

One of the key distinctions I'd sensed between the military's approach to managing its workforce and the business approach was the military's emphasis on seniority at the expense of merit. A truly merit-based system would ignore seniority altogether (which is commonly confused with experience). This issue led me to develop a question in the survey that asked respondents to categorize where the military's promotion system fell on the merit–seniority spectrum.

Military officers are convinced that the military is less meritocratic than the private sector, but more pointedly that the military is not a meritocracy at all. Two-thirds of the full panel believe the military leans more toward seniority than merit, and the average score (with 10 representing a promotion system based 100 percent on seniority) is 6.8, which we can roughly interpret as a perception that 68 percent of promotion is based on seniority, and only 32 percent based on merit. For the private sector, the average score is 4.0. This view holds, albeit less strongly, when the sample is limited to active-duty officers. Further, younger cohorts tend to view the military as less of a meritocracy.

STRATEGIES AND STRATEGISTS

What is striking about the national-security conversation that plays out in the United States—in newspapers, television shows, think tanks, and so forth—is the heavy emphasis on big ideas such as strategy and weapons systems. More sophisticated commentary with smaller audiences will tangle with deeper topics such as industrial organization or long-range threat reviews, while more superficial coverage will cover budget battles over weapons systems, war casualties, and the personalities of the strategists in power. So we see lots of coverage of strategy and almost as much coverage of the strategists, but basically no attention to the system that produces those strategists. The one major exception, I believe, is a 2009 book by Mark Moyar titled *A Question of Command*. Moyar argues that strategy is overvalued, and that leader-centric warfare is what fighting an insurgency is all about (as opposed to enemy-centric or population-centric perspectives). "The tasks of finding and developing the right leaders and getting them into key command positions are far more complex and daunting than is generally realized,"[9] says Moyar, who then goes on to identify the characteristics that make for successful leaders using historical case studies from the Civil War to the Iraq War.

I couldn't agree more with Moyar's thesis, but I'd extend it one layer and ask him to think harder about the system that generates leaders. In his view, the war's commanders are the central actors such that warfare is a "contest between elites in which the elite with superiority in certain leadership attributes usually wins."[10] My query is where do these leaders come from? Is it random chance that Abraham Lincoln found Ulysses S. Grant or that Lyndon Baines Johnson stuck with William Westmoreland or that Bush chose Petraeus? More to the point, what was the system that built these generals? Moyar comments near the end of his book on the reformers who "have advocated making the U.S. Army an 'adaptive organization' by transforming the organizational culture through new policies, incentives, educational programs, and organizational cultures," which he then dismisses in favor of simply finding "senior leaders with change-oriented personalities."[11] In other words, Moyar thinks the issue boils down entirely to culture. Maybe he is correct, but logically his argument has become tautological, or what the troops call a self-licking ice-cream cone. To get successful leaders, we need to get successful leaders.

To be fair, many of the particulars Moyar goes on to discuss are insightful, such as his admonition that "senior commanders should make leadership selection and *deselection* [emphasis added] one of their top priorities."[12] He also dislikes the way the army's military promotion and command selection boards operate, and lauds the US Marine Corps' emphasis on intuitive traits. In determining who should lead, Moyar reports that in most of the nine case studies, political considerations usually trumped merit in the appointment of commanders. He then, to my surprise, remarks that "one useful method of discouraging non-merit appointments was the use of centralized selection boards," which "has generally been a success in the U.S. armed forces since it implementation after Vietnam."[13] This is an error. While the use of centralized boards may have stymied blatant favoritism, its negative effects have been devastating to exactly those leadership qualities that Moyar celebrates. Importantly, his policy recommendations are neither consistent nor, I think, meant to be authoritative. For example, one paragraph after highlighting centralization, Moyar remarks: "The other principal method of promoting merit-based command was to put command selection directly in the hands of a senior leader committed to voiding inappropriate criteria."

As noted earlier, the Pentagon has been celebrating the need for "adaptive" leaders in the future, and Moyar's analysis concurs. His ten attributes of effective counterinsurgency leaders start with "initiative, flexibility, creativity, and judgment." But is this what the army means? I believe the army sincerely values adaptive *leaders and troops*, but I'm not so confident that the need for an adaptive *institution* is understood. Can it quickly promote and deploy the right leaders when it faces unforeseen challenges? Can it even identify them?

In a nutshell, the talent paradox is made possible by an institutional hostility to Moyar's kind of leadership—by that I mean the capacity for an officer to challenge orthodoxy, think creatively, act independently. This affects each of the armed forces (army, navy, Marine Corps, air force, and even the coast guard). Despite its very real cultural emphasis on putting people first, and despite the risk-taking entrepreneurial style of the men and women in uniform, the regulations and rules that manage them— literally human capital management—are a nightmare of central planning. Unorthodox commanders or officers with unconventional careers are routinely skipped for plum assignments and higher rank.

WHEN THE PARADOX BECAME A CRISIS

The talent paradox just as certainly affects the enlisted ranks, military civilians, and even other government workers. But the spotlight falls on the army because the fighting in Iraq ripped open the problem inside the army personnel system for anyone to see. When the army didn't have a postconflict plan for day one of the occupation of Iraq, it was a warning sign of its institutional failure, which is to say a failure of its leadership system. The absence of a postwar plan to restore order, governance, and the climate for economic stability is an indictment not just of the civilian leaders at the Pentagon such as Defense Secretary Donald Rumsfeld and other political appointees, but primarily of the neglectful approach taken by the senior military commander in Iraq, US Army General Tommy Franks, and the counterproductive command of Lieutenant General Ricardo Sanchez. America in Iraq in 2003 also represented an army that had willfully forgotten how to conquer. In the immediate aftermath of Saddam Hussein's ouster in 2003, a top British official said that the American effort to institute a new order in postwar Iraq was "an unbelievable mess. No leadership, no strategy, no coordination, no structure."[14]

Subsequently, Iraq deteriorated, and heroic, and more importantly adaptive, efforts by the troops to figure out strategies and tactics of a very difficult occupation began to bear fruit. Only, amazingly, the fruit of all those sacrifices was largely neglected by the bureaucratic leadership system, which was structurally unable, intentionally unable, to highlight and promote the most talented leaders who were doing the winning. When the army neglected to promote senior officers who were the most successfully creative and unorthodox in the field, its bureaucratic paradox became obvious to younger officers. Then in 2005 and 2006 when a gusher of promising young officers quit as soon as they were free after their tours in Iraq, the media took notice.

Magazines and newspapers began writing about the alarmingly high rates of separation. Young officers were quitting in the middle of a war, which is a powerful and damaging narrative. The United States Military Academy (USMA), for better or worse, was highlighted because so many of its graduates were leaving at historically high rates—not after twenty years like John Nagl but after the bare minimum of five years. A lengthy article in the December 2007 issue of *Washington Monthly* by Andrew Tilghman told the story of an innovative junior officer named Matt Kapinos who was deployed to both Afghanistan and Iraq, but left the army in frustration for all the reasons described here. Kapinos was just the tip of the iceberg:

> In the last four years, the exodus of junior officers from the Army has accelerated. In 2003, around 8 percent of junior officers with between four and nine years of experience left for other careers. Last year, the attrition rate leapt to 13 percent. "A five percent change could potentially be a serious problem," said James Hosek, an expert in military retention at the RAND Corporation. Over the long term, this rate of attrition would halve the number of officers who reach their tenth year in uniform and intend to take senior leadership roles.
>
> But the problem isn't one of numbers alone: the Army also appears to be losing its most gifted young officers. In 2005, internal Army memos started to warn of the "disproportionate loss of high-potential, high-performance junior leaders." West Point graduates are leaving at their highest rates since the 1970s (except for a few years in the early 1990s when the Army's goal was to reduce its size). Of the nearly 1,000 cadets from the class of 2002, 58 percent are no longer on active duty.
>
> This means that there is less competition for promotions, and that less-able candidates are rising to the top. For years, Congress required the Army to promote only 70 to 80 percent of eligible officers. Under that law, the rank of major served as a useful funnel by which the Army separated out the bottom quarter of the senior officer corps. On September 14, 2001, President Bush suspended that requirement. Today, more than 98 percent of eligible captains are promoted to major. "If you breathe, you make lieutenant colonel these days," one retired colonel grumbled to me.[15]

Naturally, much of commentary had an antiwar flavor, as if the high quit rates were an indictment of President Bush and his policies to fight terrorism and promote democracy. A similar theme appeared in stories about the army's difficulty in hitting its recruiting targets, which some politicians used to scare voters about a potential return to the draft. I actually published some research on this topic that found, surprisingly, that the quality of the average enlistee actually increased in the first four years after the 9/11 attacks.[16] Rather than exploiting poor, urban areas as Michael Moore had insinuated in his pseudo-documentary film *Fahrenheit 9/11*, the data showed that wartime US military enlistees are better educated, wealthier, and more rural on average than their civilian peers. As for exploitation, the ratio of enlistees from America's wealthiest zip codes outnumbered those from the poorest zip codes (each with 20 percent of the population) by more than 3:2. The draft stories were bogus, but that didn't mean there weren't problems in Iraq.

Lieutenant General Sanchez was given command of all US forces in Iraq in June 2003. He was given this role "ahead of officers who ranked higher than him in seniority, relevant experience, and ability, apparently because top US leaders thought that he would merely oversee a short and easy occupation," according to Moyar.[17] The incoherence of Sanchez's time in command is most powerfully understood in a case study concerning a US Army colonel named H. R. McMaster. It was he who took command of the 3rd Armored Cavalry Regiment and pacified the Iraqi city of Tal Afar using tactics that were later adopted in the new counterinsurgency doctrine, but that at the time were not at all appreciated. More on that in later chapters. For now, what's important to know about McMaster are two things. First, his success in the theater was extraordinary long before 2003, notably his 1991 leadership during a battle in the Gulf War, during which nine tanks that then-Captain McMaster commanded destroyed over eighty Iraqi Republican Guard tanks and vehicles. Second, McMaster was a vocal and unorthodox intellectual when out of the theater, who took time away from the operational army to earn a PhD from the University of North Carolina and to teach at West Point. McMaster was passed over for general the first and second times he was considered by an army promotion board until Secretary Gates called Petraeus back from Iraq in early 2007 to oversee a third board.

THE RIGHT KIND OF OFFICER

The military's reliance on seniority rather than merit didn't develop suddenly in recent years. Alarms about the dangers of a mediocrity-enhancing incentive structure have been sounded for decades, long before the wars in Iraq and Afghanistan made the exit rate of good officers an acute crisis. In the mid-1980s, longtime Pentagon reporter Arthur Hadley published *The Straw Giant*, an indictment of the many failures he saw that had culminated in the disastrous April 1980 mission to rescue the US hostages in Iran on a joint mission called Desert One that left many of the rescuers dead when a massive coordination failure led to a crash of different aircraft as the mission began. Noting the constancy of reform, Hadley wrote this in the prologue:

> When one looks hard at American defense, six basic themes appear and reappear. Sometimes these six are separate, sometimes they weave together. All of them helped create the disaster at Desert One. All of them will be present at our next defeat.[18]

One theme, "Interservice/Intraservice Rivalry," has seen real progress in recent decades, but Hadley's sixth theme is what interests us because it has actually gotten worse. Hadley called it KAFKA (his acronym) for Keeping the Able from Contributing to the Action. When the Pentagon's strategic planners emphasize one form of warfare (say, heavy-armor combat against the Soviet Union), they send a powerful signal to young officers who follow what appears to be the golden career path. Officers in the right specialty not only tend to make top rank, but there is a pecking order among the different branches even among the lower ranks. An excellent officer who is branched as an engineer will never get a chance for a fourth star, and will probably be shunted aside from opportunities during his entire career. As Hadley noted, many branches naturally become "pastures for the marginally competent."[19] The irony is that the careers off the golden path are often recognized too late as critical for "new" kinds of warfare, such as, say, specialists in low-intensity conflict or economic development.

Nagl's story is instructive and ironic here. He served as a tanker, which is about as heavy/high-intensity branching as possible, but his doctoral thesis was about fighting insurgencies, which is the opposite. When Nagl was commissioned in the late 1980s, the army remained committed to heavy forces and the Cold War, not special forces. Some of the "elite" fighting troops found their careers clipped early on. While plenty of soldiers choose their branches as much for personal preference as for careerism, one wonders why the army gives careerists such an advantage. Carefully planning a career leads ambitious officers to check the right boxes, which caused Hadley to plead three decades ago: "The services themselves must end the cursed 'ticket punching' that began in the late fifties—the system that requires officers to hold a variety of jobs in order to get ahead."[20] And of course ticket punching created pressure for officers to move to new positions as often as possible, which Hadley called "an absurd game of musical chairs."

If a young officer wants to make an impact and serve at the highest levels, s/he is forced to check boxes and play the game of musical chairs. Evidence of the system's bias for "muddy boots" officers was assembled by Leonard Wong, a scholar at the Army War College:

[A] comparison of past and present career paths of general officers reflects the growing avoidance of any assignment away from Army units or staff. In 1995, 11 out of the 36 newly selected brigadier generals had attended full time graduate school earlier in their careers. Their perspectives were broadened in diverse institutions such as Duke, University of Virginia, and University of Wisconsin as these future general officers were exposed to different ways of thinking and problem solving. A decade later, the situation has changed drastically. By 2005, the number of newly selected brigadier generals who had taken time out of their careers for full time graduate study had dropped to just 3 out of 38.

Similar evidence is found in the most recent brigade command list where over 50 officers were slated for tactical command. A quick analysis of the career paths of these officers (our future general officers) shows that only about a half dozen officers ventured outside the muddy boot track for assignments such as Office of the Secretary of Defense or Joint Chiefs of Staff intern, congressional fellow, or full time graduate study. All the other officers chose to stay within traditional command and staff Army assignments focusing on the war fight.[21]

This trend toward an operational path is widely recognized as unhealthy, yet it remains because of a systemic self-reinforcement. Many blame the operations of promotions boards that make the selections, and surely that's right at the first level of analysis. But I think a deeper level of analysis will show that all kinds of personnel rules reinforce this behavior as well. A promotion board for colonels, for example, is composed of a score of senior officers who review thousands of files, one for each officer in consideration during the current cycle. The board meets for just a few days, so mathematically it has one or two minutes to scan each file. This brings us to the files themselves—the officer evaluation report (OER), which suffers from grade inflation. The board has little time to consider complex factors that would fit the skills of all the candidates with the job requirements that need to be filled, so the tendency is to default to common-denominator markers of raw leadership and potential. Layered on top are a set of regulatory requirements, such as the condition that no officer can be promoted to high rank with serving in a "joint" role. None of this is to say this system is bad or unfair, but that it cannot help but be incomplete.

As mentioned earlier, the army's official stance is that the officers of the future need to be *adaptive*. I would argue that the officers already are adaptive, but the system is squeezing them into box-checking conformity. Or as Wong says, "The crucible of Operation Iraqi Freedom (OIF) has delivered to the Army a cohort of adaptive leaders. The challenge for the Army is to encourage and leverage this priceless potential"[22]

WHAT ABOUT PETRAEUS?

My critique is not an indictment of the people who serve, nor of those who do a "five and dive," nor of those who retire after decades in service. History shows that veterans of all kinds go on to tremendous success in other arenas: academics, government, finance, and especially business. Unfortunately, when my essay on this topic was published in *The Atlantic*, the cover editor plugged it with the controversial title: "Why the Army is Getting Dumber." Ouch. Despite the fact that my air force and navy buddies loved it, the title was unfair. It implied that the troops who didn't leave were dumb. My reaction in a few speeches afterward was the troops weren't dumb, but the army as an institution was.

To be sure, there are excellent officers who stay despite the frustrations and do make high rank, just as there are weak officers who don't, but the overarching rule of the military leadership system is blind mediocrity, not recognition of merit. Nobody knows this better than the generals themselves.

However, the more common counterargument one hears is that the army may be imperfect, but it still produces great leaders. They point to Petraeus. They point to McMaster. They even point to John Nagl because John did, in fact, serve a full career. They see that he's found success in Washington as a civilian and say: "See, it all worked out for the best." Even John thinks so, but I don't. I think John should be running the Pentagon with a handful of stars on each shoulder. But that's not exactly the point, because the talent paradox is bigger than one brainy officer.

How can the army be called a failed leadership system if it produces Petraeus? Wait. Remember what the paradox says: "Why does the American military produce the most innovative and entrepreneurial leaders in the country, then waste that talent in a risk-averse bureaucracy?" I never claimed the military was bad at *producing* great leaders, but I am saying it is bad at *managing* them. Many, maybe most, of the best leaders leave, but thankfully not all of them do.

Petraeus is an extraordinary leader, a strategic genius, and a once-in-a-generation American. But I also think he succeeded in the army despite the army. And to the larger issue, we must consider the other army generals who failed in Iraq (Franks and Sanchez, to name two) or have mixed legacies (George Casey and Stanley McChrystal). Indeed, one would think that after a decade of war, America would have more than just one celebrated military commander. The fact that Petraeus was asked to take over in Afghanistan in 2009—stepping *down* from his role as CENTCOM commander—is something to interpret very positively for the man and very negatively for the institution.

One former Marine officer, Renny McPherson, sounded a similar note in a late-September 2010 essay in the *Boston Globe* that asked why Petraeus was "demoted" to replace a subordinate in Afghanistan? McPherson queried: "Why was there no other general to take the job? The short answer is that the U.S. military has failed to produce enough leaders like Petraeus—the kind of broad-minded, flexible strategic thinkers needed to lead today's most difficult missions."[23] McPherson pointed to the army's inflexible career path as the key explanation, which actively discourages young officers from taking risks. In other words, the system is wasting and stunting its talent.

The shame of this internal talent bleed is that the US military does such a good job attracting and training great leaders. The men and women who volunteer as military officers learn to remain calm and think quickly under intense pressure. They are comfortable making command decisions, working in teams, and motivating people. Such skills translate powerfully to the private sector, particularly business: although just 3 percent of the US population has served as an officer in the military, nearly 8.4 percent of chief executives of Standard and Poor's

(S&P) 500 companies are veteran officers, according to a 2006 Korn-Ferry study.[24] Examples abound of senior executives who attribute their leadership skills to their time in uniform: Ross Perot, Bill Coleman, Sam Walton, and Bob McDonald, Procter & Gamble's new CEO, to name a few. Business guru Warren Bennis reflected in his recent memoirs: "I never heard anything at MIT or Harvard that topped the best lectures I heard at [Fort] Benning."[25] Even if you limit the scope to, say, basketball coaches, Duke University's Mike Krzyzewski (West Point, 1969) and the San Antonio Spurs' Gregg Popovich (Air Force Academy, 1971) are considered the best of the best.

Why is the military so bad at retaining these people? It's convenient to believe that top officers simply have more lucrative opportunities in the private sector, and that their departures are largely inevitable. But the reason overwhelmingly cited by veterans and active-duty officers alike is that the military personnel system—every aspect of it—is nearly blind to merit. Performance evaluations emphasize a "zero-defect" mentality, meaning that risk-avoidance trickles down the chain of command. Promotions can be anticipated almost to the day—regardless of an officer's competence—so that there is essentially no difference in rank among officers the same age, even after 15 years of service. Job assignments, which cause the most heartburn among officers, are managed by a faceless, centralized bureaucracy that keeps everyone guessing about where he or she might be shipped next.

FINISHING THE REVOLUTION

There is really no escaping the conclusion that the army's leadership engine serves as both a role model for other large organizations and also as a cautionary tale. In terms of attracting and training innovative leaders, the US military is unparalleled. In terms of managing talent, the US military is doing everything wrong.

This book lays out an indictment of the current military leadership-management system, also known as its personnel structure. Pentagon leaders know they have a problem, but I've come to the conclusion that they fundamentally have no idea how to design an alternative. And so the book offers a blueprint for that alternative.

A handful of successful American corporations (with similarly large workforces) provides us with best practices on how to manage talent by promoting innovative talent and rewarding merit. It has become a science. Literally. The nascent field of *personnel economics* offers even more detailed principles for the military's entrepreneurial blueprint. But ironically, the most important role model of all for military reform in the 2010s is the military reform of the 1970s.

In the year 1973, President Richard Nixon made good on a 1968 campaign promise to end the draft. The army reinvented itself, as did the other branches, adopting an all-volunteer force (AVF) structure. It was a gamble that worked because it emphasized investing in people. Rather than using coercion to force young men into enlistments, the Pentagon was required to shift its paradigm completely and use positive incentives that would attract recruits. As an economist, I describe this transition in terms of the price the Pentagon had to pay, literally. It paid in terms of higher wages, better housing and food, and improved training and career opportunities to attract a labor supply to meet its labor demand. Once a market mechanism was utilized, a multiyear process of price discovery took place, as wages for enlistees rose to match supply and demand.

In retrospect, the all-volunteer revolution was a success, but only half a success. To be sure, it removed coercion from the accessions process, but didn't remove coercion from operations once individuals joined. The military remained and remains steeped in a culture of coercion: orders, rules, regulations. Mixing the two cultures seems to have yielded a legalistic bureaucracy unlike any other. The challenge the army faces now is whether it can complete the internal revolution of free-market forces over coercion (and in fairness, whether it should).

Some argue that using markets within a military force will destroy the selfless service value system that emphasizes duty, honor, and camaraderie, replacing it with a mercenary culture. I'll show in future chapters why that view is not only wrong but also upside down, as the existing system uses a façade of selfless values to cover up a careerist, risk-averse culture. Those who say, "this is the United States Army; it's not Apple, it's not General Electric" might be surprised by the similarities. The gist of those words, which were from Secretary Gates's West Point speech, by the way, is that what motivates the military workforce is more profound and complex than what drives profit-seeking corporate employees. That is no doubt true, but its implications are narrow to nonexistent. I'll be the first to argue that active-duty troops are more patriotic and honorable than civilians, but that doesn't mean financial factors are irrelevant. It sure doesn't mean coercion in assignments is an effective management principle.

For example, why does the Pentagon offer a retirement system that vests only after year 20? Is this pension rule not using coercion to keep employees in place longer than they otherwise would choose to remain? Retention in the military for the "second decade" is not driven by duty but calculation. This isn't hypocrisy on the part of service members, just the reality that the economic animal is and has been part of Pentagon planning already.

Let's agree that the question of whether market forces lead to a mercenary, unprofessional force has already been answered. When the AVF was proposed in the 1960s, it was called mercenary by almost the entire defense establishment. President Nixon established a fifteen-member commission to study the issue after the 1968 election. It was chaired by former secretary of defense Thomas Gates Jr. (no relation to Robert Gates). What became known as the Gates Commission was intentionally balanced at the insistence of the president with five members opposed to conscription (including economists Alan Greenspan and Milton Friedman), five neutral, and five in favor. Gates even told Nixon he was "opposed to the whole idea of a volunteer force,"[26] which is why the president wanted him. Many months later, the group formally reported that it "unanimously believes that the nation's interest will be better served by an all-volunteer force..."[27] Now, 40 years later, almost no one in uniform wants to serve with draftees, and experience has shown the men and women in uniform to be more professional than ever.

HOW THE PERSONNEL SYSTEM WORKS (OR DOESN'T)

When I described the paradox to University of Chicago labor economist Steven Davis, he was puzzled and asked: "What is the Pentagon's rationale for designing the system that way?" Which begs the question: was it designed, or is it an accident of history? Davis's attitude reminded me of what Friedman expressed at a 1966 conference concerning the draft: "[The] more puzzling question is why we have continued to use compulsion."[28] People in general tend to be conservative, meaning they do what they have traditionally done unless something forces them to change. And as many senior officers have reminded me, the army is a conservative organization.

So while Pentagon spokesmen may give rationales for the way things are currently done, I think the underlying reason is simply precedent with layer after layer of superficial reform. The system in control, what is known as Human Resources Command (HRC), emerged from a top-down tradition of administrative control.

The fact is that even if the army wanted to transform its management institutions into an adaptive structure, long-standing law inhibits reform. In particular, a 1980 law known as the Defense Officer Personnel Management Act (DOPMA) sets strict guidelines on how officers in all the services must be managed.[29] It established tenure for regular officers, making it all but impossible to fire or lay off officers short of criminality or retirement at the 20-year mark. But DOPMA's most powerful effect was defining a standard rank progression so that every officer across all the services was promoted on the same timetable. DOPMA's strict progression timetables are the origin of promotions "in the zone." The rationale was that officers should rise "up" in rank or get "out" of uniform, a principle (up or out) that clashes directly with tenure! Nevertheless, the law establishes guiding limits on the percentage of officers of each rank that should be promoted, which is reproduced in table 1.2.

Table 1.2 can be understood to guide the army to promote 100 percent of its O-1s (second lieutenants) to the rank of first lieutenant (O-2) at exactly 2 years of service. And then it should promote 95 percent of that cohort to captain (O-3) anywhere between 3.5 and 4 years. The earliest this table allows an officer to be promoted to colonel (O-6) is at 21 years of service. The "zone" for colonel is 22 years, so anyone promoted at 21 years would be "below the zone."

The Defense Science Board, a distinguished panel of civilian experts that was established in 1956 to advise the Pentagon on technical issues, was asked to study and report on the personnel system, and it made its report in the summer of 2010. Its concluded that DOPMA

Table 1.2 Official US military officer promotion rates

Officer Pay Grade/Rank	Promotion Percentage	Timing (years of service)
O-2	100	2
O-3	95	3.5–4
O-4	80	10 ± 1
O-5	70	16 ± 1
O-6	50	22 ± 1

and other restrictive regulations "have the effect today of inhibiting the Department's flexibility and adaptability."[30]

Later chapters describe the military personnel system in greater detail, but it should be clear that the frustration extends beyond the inflexible promotion opportunity defined by DOPMA. Although intertwined, it might be useful to identify five core issues with the army's personnel management: (1) personnel matters are centrally planned and managed by HRC, which is based at Fort Knox, Kentucky; (2) promotions are constrained by seniority rules and made arbitrary by box-checking; (3) compensation is almost entirely merit free; (4) assignments do not match jobs with officers very well; and (5) evaluations are ineffective in giving feedback or assessing skills.

A best-and-brightest retention crisis would seem to represent a frustration with slow promotion opportunities, but promotions can be misleading in two ways. First, the culture adapts and recognizes merit outside the rank structure, so that different job responsibilities signal more about an officer's operational power than rank alone. For example, highly competent officers might be tapped to serve as a senior officer's executive officer (XO). On the other hand, lethargic promotions can be better understood as symptomatic of the root problem, which is job matching. For example, many officers prefer not to serve in staff positions (which are vital for promotion) but to stay in specialized areas of expertise—either leading troops or studying strategy in a PhD program. But the military's governing philosophy is "up or out," which requires careful management of all personnel along the hierarchical pyramid. The time allowed for an officer to stay in each job is tightly orchestrated by central planners at HRC.

As for promotions, the DOPMA schedule locks young officers into a career of predictable steps upward. The recent retention crisis, which compressed the promotion timeline, has done so largely by removing what little variation existed among officers in the same cohort. Promotion from second to first lieutenant is universal, as it is to captain, and increasingly to major. One would have to commit a felony or two to hinder his or her chances for promotion. Only at the gateway to senior management—colonel—is merit seriously considered. Officers can be promoted to colonel no sooner than two decades in service, or maybe slightly before. Certainly no officer can make the rank of general before twenty-two years in the army, two years after which s/he can retire with a full pension. And if the army lacks qualified candidates at any step in the process, it does not allow "lateral entry" (hiring beyond entry level), even the lateral entry of former officers or highly experienced enlistees.

Compensation, likewise, follows a schedule. The Defense Finance and Accounting service (dfas.mil) makes the base-pay table publicly available on its website,[31] where one can see that an O-3 (captain) with 6–8 years in service earns $5,117.10 a month. An O-3 with 10–12 years in service earns $5,540.10. Merit pay does not exist. Performance bonuses do not exist. Critics say that distinguishing military work with pay is difficult if not impossible, since there is no way to measure profit in the same way private firms do. This is a flimsy argument, since most firms are also not able to accurately equate individual performance to specific profits. Indeed, the modern service economy utilizes labor to build up what George Mason University economics professor Garett Jones calls "organization capital" such as brand values that translate into revenue. Regardless, all sorts of organizations with and without profit do evaluate and reward performance, so why not the army?

The next line of defense is that merit pay runs afoul of traditional values of service above self in the military, and it is true that there is a strong culture of egalitarianism. In the army, officers in the field will eat only after the troops, not before. That said, is it not also true that pilots, doctors, and linguists get skill-based salary supplements? Yes, these are called "special pays."[32] Most commonly, there is pay for hazardous duty, but there are numerous skill-based special pays based on what the army and Marines call an individual's MOS, or military occupation specialty (e.g., infantry, aviation, and other specialties plus coding for rank and other skills). Naturally, each MOS has a code, called the MOSC. The air force calls this the Specialty Code (AFSC), and the navy, bless them, simply calls this "rating," not to be confused with "rates," which is their term for pay grades. There are also allowances, a form of untaxed compensation, to help service members on otherwise fixed incomes deal with different costs of living. Being stationed in Tokyo, for example, means much higher expenses for housing and dining. Ironically, the military does not allow geographic variation simply based on the desirability of different locales, meaning no bonus for living on isolated, rocky Guam or Diego Garcia, whereas jobs in Hawaii, Italy, Australia, and San Diego are given bonuses for the high costs of living there.

The inability to adjust pay on an individual basis ties directly to the heart of the personnel dilemma facing the Pentagon. Moving from a central-planning system to a market is fraught with uncertainty, as we know from the recent history of Eastern European countries. But at the center of the Gordian knot is how to match supply with demand, whether the goods in question are Soviet bread or American soldiers. Flexible prices are the only way a market can efficiently match supply with demand: allowing each element of supply (the farmer or the soldier) to name an individual price as well as allowing each element of demand (the grocer or the battalion commander) to offer an individual bid. Let us distinguish the pricing mechanism from the sorting mechanism for a moment. The true heart of any central-planning system is the matching mechanism, not the pricing. Prices are simply made up as accounting matters after the all-important plan of inputs and outputs is devised. In the modern military, the matching mechanism is called the "assignments" process.

Assignments, or job matching, is truly the heart of the matter. Even promotions are just a subset of assignments. The status quo of army assignments works like this: the G-1 (formally the Office of the Deputy Chief of Staff for Personnel, Department of the Army) is responsible for the development, management, and execution of all manpower and personnel plans, programs, and policies throughout the entire US Army. Those plans are actually executed by HRC, located as of 2011 in a vast new facility at Fort Knox, Kentucky, totaling 883,000 square feet of space and employing more than four thousand employees. HRC replaced Army Personnel Command, or PERSCOM, in 2003, which operated from the famous Hoffman Buildings in Alexandria, Virginia.

Hoffman, now HRC, is the army's name for what the officers and troops know as a stereotypical faceless bureaucracy. The staff has the thankless task of matching open jobs in the army all over the globe with thousands of available officers. To make the process as fair and manageable as humanly possible, the exercise of matchmaking is not done continuously but during a few months-long periods a year.

Since any central planner has to operate with limited information, HRC relies on performance evaluations of available officers to slate them into jobs. Evaluations in the military, unfortunately, have become formal exercises in documenting excellence across the board. The quantitative assessments are normally "firewalled" with perfect scores for even the most mediocre individuals. Even the written remarks mask degrees of performance with euphemisms and code words. During board reviews, a common practice is to simply scan the first and last line of each officer's most recent OER. According to one officer I spoke with who helped manage a recent board, an evaluator read one of the OERs aloud: "It says top one percent, which means, what, top fifty, right?"

The slating process relies on thinner and thinner information for lower ranks, but at every level officers are asked to provide their preferences. For example, one army major described how he was given 16 openings for his specialty when he came up for a new assignment, and asked to rank order them from #1 to #16, which he dutifully submitted to HRC. However, he was not told what any of the 16 positions actually involved, only their locations. Although he tells me he is a top officer (and given his current job, that can't be untrue), this major was assigned job #16.

To be fair, the staffers working assignments at HRC face an impossible task, because they are balancing multiple objectives. Needs of the army come first. Career planning is second. Addressing officer preferences and hardship considerations (e.g., this captain has a wife with cancer), filling unique slots, and predicting future trends in manpower all must be factored into every slating. And to keep things simple and under control, no trading of assignments is allowed. Almost all of the operations of the G-1 and HRC are subject to laws and requirements passed by Congress, so their room for innovation and change is essentially outlawed. In other words, even if the central planners know that the central planning is a failure, they can't change it.

To say that the members of the armed forces dislike this system is an understatement. When I surveyed 250 West Point graduates on which aspects of the military fostered innovative and entrepreneurial leadership, the various pieces described here received resounding negatives. Only 28 percent of respondents gave the job-assignment system a letter grade of A or B, with twice as many respondents giving it a D or an F. The promotion system got 27 percent, and the compensation system got 20 percent.

Of the respondents, 87 percent believe the army should expand early-promotion opportunities (77 percent of active-duty members agreed), and 90 percent believe the army should allow greater specialization (87 percent active-duty agreed). Large majorities favor lateral entry for former officers, eliminating the very idea of "year groups" after the first ten years of service. And even before I had written this book, 76 percent of respondents (including 76 percent of active-duty officers) favored a market mechanism for allocating jobs instead of the status quo.

THE TOTAL VOLUNTEER FORCE

In theory, the armed forces could reform one or more of the five core issues described earlier incrementally rather than adopting wholesale change. The army is already flirting with a market-assignments system called "Green Pages," which has real promise. The air force is redesigning its officer-performance reports. But I believe incremental reform risks backsliding in the short term and outright failure in the long term. The roots are too deep, and the bureaucracy is infinitely patient. Personnel systems cannot be half free and half planned.

In the end, experiments with market-based assignments need flexible compensation systems. Commanders need the freedom to lay off people before the plan says they can be rotated out, and they also need the freedom to promote whomever they think is best to fill jobs in their units—whether that means promoting someone ahead of schedule, hiring a former officer (even from a different service branch), or keeping the current person in place longer than normal with bonus pay. The market also can't work without better information, meaning real evaluations that distinguish not only the performance of hard, brilliant workers from drones but distinguish the complex talents of many diverse hard-charging officers.

That's why I am proposing that the military adopt a new personnel system that I call the total volunteer force. It's a corny name, I know, but I use it to emphasize the philosophical difference between the current system, which gives people freedom to choose only at the moment of volunteering (the AVF), and a system in which employees are free every day.

Every person thinking about a truly liberated military imagines exactly how it would fail. "Men," barks the lieutenant, "it's time for you to take that hill!" Who in their right mind will freely choose to charge into enemy fire? That would seem a perfect time to volunteer for the helicopter maintenance gig in Hawaii, right?

So how do I have the confidence such a system would not break down in combat? Three reasons. First, it is a despicable frame of mind to believe that American soldiers only fight because they must due to an earlier decision—lacking foresight—that put them in a position of subordination. The fact that men and women already volunteer in ample numbers for infantry positions, during wartime, and have done so for decades, should end this objection. We say that soldiers fight for values like honor and duty, but do we actually believe it? The troops do. Second reason: danger is not unique to the military. Heroes die every day policing American streets, fighting fires, and even catching fish on the high seas. Even at a moment of extreme danger, chasing and fighting armed criminals, police officers could simply walk away and apply for a safer job (writing books?), but they don't. Call it pride, or call it need, or call it noble: free people do their jobs. Third—and maybe this is hard to understand—there is a group of people who simply like to fight. Some may be amoral, but many others believe in the mission of fighting and even killing enemies of the US Constitution and citizenry. Whether flying in F-15s or aiming their M-60s, most of the veterans I know wonder why they got paid to do such awesome jobs.

The critical psychological factor in play is how different people assess risk. Some people love risk. Those sorts of people tend to be soldiers. They also tend to be inventors and entrepreneurs. That's why I think we can understand a lot about designing an effective total volunteer force by putting well-developed theories of entrepreneurship at the beginning of the design. It is that innovative and risk-loving frame of mind that has fueled not only great business careers but also great strategic geniuses such as Napoleon, Alfred Thayer Mahan, Douglas MacArthur, and Creighton Abrams.

CHAPTER 2

THE PARADOX OF MILITARY LEADERSHIP

I never heard anything at MIT or Harvard that topped the best lectures
I heard at Benning.

—Warren Bennis[1]

THIS MAY SURPRISE YOU. THE STATE OF NORTH CAROLINA
has a population of 9.38 million people, roughly 3 percent of the US
population, but 9 percent of CEOs of US companies are from North
Carolina. This fact is so statistically odd that it can't be mere coincidence. Something about the Tarheel state produces highly savvy business leaders. Maybe it's a conservative culture, or Baptist values, or the
mix of excellent universities in the fabled Research Triangle region.
The corporate boards of America have noticed, and they keep a close
eye on young executives from the state.

No? Actually, the Carolina CEOs story isn't true. I made it up
to make a point, because the truth is even more surprising. Replace
"North Carolina" with "U.S. military," and you've got the real story,
and one that's just starting to be appreciated. America's armed forces
are a leadership factory. Whether by attracting young talent predis-
posed to the right qualities or by equipping its young officers with
effective skills training and real-world experience, the net result is an
unrivaled production line of leaders.

A recent cover of *Fortune* magazine titled "The New Warrior Elite"
highlighted the renewed awareness of military experience among

business recruiters. The March 2010 story claimed that a decade of war in Afghanistan and Iraq had "created a new generation of business leaders."[2] The story also revealed that combat was giving the young officers of today altogether different, more useful, skills for the business community than the peacetime military did. Number one, officers with combat experience were less perfectionistic and more tolerant of failure, a quality often associated with Silicon Valley culture. Donovan Campbell, who went from Princeton University to lead a Marine Corps platoon in Iraq, explained that mistakes are inevitable and that he came to appreciate how much of his operating environment was beyond his control. These are the conditions that create a learning-feedback loop, and with high stakes (the lives of his troops), Campbell was grounded in the idea that "I do not have to have zero defects to be successful."[3] Lessons like this have impressed corporate leaders such as General Electric's CEO Jeff Immelt, who says that "dealing with ambiguity" is a distinct advantage of military leaders in general.[4] The wars have just amplified it.

Recall the paradox in the first chapter: *Why does the American military produce the most innovative and entrepreneurial leaders in the country, then waste that talent in a risk-averse bureaucracy?* In this chapter, we'll take a long look at the first part of that statement. Does the military really produce great leaders? How does an entrepreneurial leader differ from other kinds of leaders, and are military officers really able to be entrepreneurial?

The armed forces do more than convert random Americans into officers. And there's more than excellent training involved. The Pentagon's leadership factory starts with recruiting high-quality talent, world-class initial training, and operational experiences with serious responsibility, followed by a career-long series of personal and unit training courses.

I'll start by examining recruiting. Despite the headhunting of some soldiers by private-sector companies, a common stereotype is that soldiers are at best intellectually rigid, obedient, and uncreative. When I've described my military peers as entrepreneurial, the number-one reaction I get from civilians is disbelief. I'll revisit some earlier scholarly research of my own on this question in the first section. We will also explore the shape of the army's workforce. The heart of this chapter will walk through the training and experience of junior officers. Then I'll close by interviewing some ex-military CEOs to learn about their leadership lessons as well as the way the military's leadership engine has evolved to stress adaptive approaches.

MYTH OF THE STUPID SOLDIER

What is the quality of the typical American soldier? Compared to civilian workers, conventional wisdom holds that soldiers are generally inferior, at least in terms of charateristics such as intelligence, creativity, and independent thought. This notion that soldiers are stupid has persisted since the early 1960s when college students were able to avoid the draft, leaving less fortunate youths to bear the burden of service in Vietnam. Despite the end of the draft in 1973, military compensation remained low and so did enlistee quality, on average. Not until President Ronald Reagan and Defense Secretary Caspar Weinberger raised base pay rates significantly during the 1980s did enlistee quality improve (measured by equivalent IQ scores). Unfortunately, the cultural stereotype of "stupid soldiers" hardened and persisted. Ann Marlowe, a scholar at the Hudson Institute, calls it "the mythology that refuses to die."[5]

In a 2002 editorial in the *New York Times*, Congressman Charlie Rangel (D-NY) wrote that a "disproportionate number of the poor and members of minority groups make up the enlisted ranks of the military, while most privileged Americans are underrepresented or absent."[6] Rangel proceeded to call on the government to reinstate the draft so that all American youth would be subject to involuntary conscription into the wars in Iraq and Afghanistan. His theory was that a draft would make the sacrifices of war shared across all American communities. Few bothered to notice that his underlying assumptions were incorrect, or more charitably, out of date by at least three decades. To be fair, Rangel never explicitly called soldiers stupid, but he was definitely playing on outmoded biases, and the media followed suit.

In August 2005, another op-ed in the *New York Times*, this one by Bob Herbert, claimed that "very few" of the soldiers fighting in Iraq "are coming from the privileged economic classes." In late September, the *Los Angeles Times* misinterpreted a government study and reported: "The [GAO] report appears to support the contention that service in the military reserves is most attractive to young men living in low- or medium-income families in rural communities."[7] The myth peaked with a front-page, above-the-fold article in the *Washington Post* on November 4,

2005, which said: "[T]he military is leaning heavily for recruits on economically depressed, rural areas where youths' need for jobs may outweigh the risks of going to war."[8] A book titled *AWOL: The Unexcused Absence of America's Upper Classes from Military Service—and How It Hurts Our Country* (2006) used the myth as a starting point in order to criticize elites for abandoning military service during a time of war.

The stupid-victim-soldier stereotype had been given a boost in 2004 by what turned out to be the highest-grossing documentary ever made, Michael Moore's *Fahrenheit 9/11*:

> Where would [the military] find the new recruits? They would find them all across America in the places that had been destroyed by the economy. Places where one of the only jobs available was to join the Army.[9]

The film depicted uniformed Marine recruiters as predators in search of young dupes in the inner city. It created an image of enlistees as unwitting victims rather than volunteers. It was as if the volunteer army of 2004 was no different in effect than the conscripted army of 1964. The attitude was so pervasive that Andy Rooney commented in his eponymous *60 Minutes* television segment that "most [of the U.S. soldiers in Iraq] are victims, not heroes."[10] Were there any facts to bear this out?

No. Rather, the facts pointed in the opposite direction. In 2005, I published a comprehensive empirical study of the demographic qualities of every enlistee in the four main branches of the military during 2003. Every enlistee, not just a sample. A later study updated the coverage to include enlistees in 2004 and 2005, when the reality of the "hard slog" was becoming apparent. Both studies revealed that the average American enlistee was *more* educated—not less— than the average young civilian. The average reading level of new soldiers is roughly a full grade level higher than their civilian peers. Enlistees' high school graduation rate was 97 percent in 2003, 2004, and 2005, which was 17 points higher than the civilian graduation rate.[11] Heritage Foundation analysts Shanea Watkins and James Sherk updated this line of research in August 2008, reporting:

> More evidence of the quality of America's enlisted forces comes from the standardized Armed Forces Qualifying Test (AFQT) that the military administers to all recruits. Over two-thirds of

enlisted recruits scored above the 50th percentile on the AFQT. The military tightly restricts how many recruits it accepts with scores below the 30th percentile, and only 2.3 percent of recruits in 2007 scored between the 21st and 30th percentiles (Category IVA; see Chart 3). The military does not accept any recruits in the bottom 20 percent.[12]

Wartime recruits also came from *wealthier* neighborhoods than their civilian counterparts, on average. Most surprising, the force had been trending toward wealthier troops and smarter troops since the war in Iraq began in 2003. I was able to identify the income level of recruits by analyzing the home-of-record zip code on file with the Pentagon. For example, Montana has 67 percent more volunteers than it would if enlistees were drawn from each state by random, whereas New York is 32 percent underrepresented.

If we sort all the zip codes in America into equally populated deciles, sorted according to median income, then we can determine which income classes are over- and underrepresented. I found that the wealthiest 40 percent of neighborhoods in America are the home of 45.6 percent of 2005 enlistees. For every two US recruits from the poorest neighborhoods, three come from the richest. Another way to look at this same data is to compare recruits to civilians across income bands, which is presented in figure 2.1. The second lower half of the figure shows how overrepresented all of the higher income bands are.

There was no statistical evidence to support the claim that minorities were being targeted or exploited for military service. While some minorities, notably African Americans, were overrepresented in uniform, they were generally not serving in combat roles but in more technical fields, which if anything require higher IQs. And contrary to the mythology, the one hundred zip codes with the highest proportions of African Americans were actually *under*represented among military enlistees. To put it bluntly, the blacks in uniform were generally not from black neighborhoods.

There was some evidence that recruiting quality declined during the war years, though it was more nuanced than media stories mentioned earlier. One study by RAND scholars Beth Asch and James Hosek[13] found that "OIF [Operation Iraqi Freedom] is estimated to have reduced Army high-quality enlistments by 34 percent, with 16 percentage points attributable to the OIF effect and 18 percentage

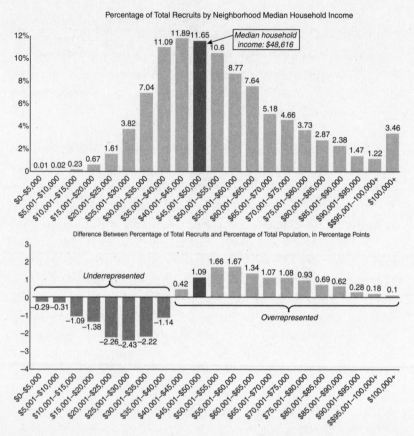

Figure 2.1 Neighborhood incomes of enlisted recruits.

Source: Heritage Foundation calculations based on data from US Department of Defense, Defense Manpower Data Center, Non-Prior Service Accessions, 2006 and 2007, US Census Bureau, United Stated Census 2000.

points due to an average fatality rate of 186 deaths per quarter." A 2007 study by the Congressional Budget Office examined the issue and confirmed the trend of higher-quality recruits under the all-volunteer force (AVF).[14] The study reported that non-prior-service (NPS) recruits with high school diplomas rose from under 70 percent in 1973 to above 90 percent in every year after 1985; and further that the percentage of enlistees in the lowest two intelligence-test categories is roughly one-tenth of the civilian population rate. More importantly, it is one-seventh of the rate of the draft-era enlisted force.

What about the officers? To play devil's advocate, just because the typical enlistee today is "higher quality" than the typical civilian does not necessarily mean that officers are above average. The appropriate comparison group may not be all civilians since the vast majority of officers have at least a bachelor's degree.

During World War II, having a college diploma was not a requirement for most commissioned officers, a situation often discussed in the context of Chuck Yeager—the famous test pilot who first broke the sound barrier—since he did not have a college degree. Is a college education necessary to become an astronaut? A fighter pilot? Perhaps this convention signals an overreliance on technical credentials rather than practical skill. Regardless, the modern military requires that all officers have at least a bachelor's degree to receive their initial commission, and in fact, consideration for senior ranks in the contemporary army all but requires an advanced degree.

When Sherk and Watkins turned their attention to the army's officer corps, they were able to gather data on those commissioned in the Army Reserve Officer Training Corps between 2004 and 2007, and cadets who were enrolled in the army Reserve Officers' Training Corps (ROTC) (source of 39 percent of officers) as of March 27, 2007, as well as information on the 2007 graduates of the US Military Academy (USMA) (25 percent), all from the Defense Manpower Data Center. Forty percent of officers come from the wealthiest 20 percent of US neighborhoods. More interesting is the fact that this percentage increased every year from 2004 to 2007, while the officers from the poorest 20 percent of neighborhoods declined from 8.7 percent in 2004 to 7.8 in 2007.[15]

According to West Point's admissions office, 70 percent of the incoming freshman (all data from the class of 2009) were ranked in the top fifth of their high school class. Of the 1,250 entering freshman, 252 were class presidents. Almost all were varsity athletes (1,138 total), and three-quarters of those were team captains. Nearly identical numbers persisted unchanged up to the most recent class of 2014. The percentages matched classes as far back as 2002 (the oldest data available online).[16]

THE SHAPE OF THE FORCE

Understanding how the military produces great leaders requires context. To put the army workforce into perspective, compare it to private-sector firms. There are 6 million firms in the United States, according to the latest data from the Census Bureau, and just 981 of those firms have a large workforce (meaning 10,000 employees or more). Those large firms employ one quarter of the 120 million paid employees in the United States, or roughly 34,000 employees on the average large company payroll.[17] In contrast, the number of people working for the Pentagon is roughly one and a half million, including civilians but not the National Guard and Reserves. The army, as one might expect, has the biggest headcount. According to the army G1, the size of the force in fiscal 2010 was 1.1 million, composed of 561,979 active-duty soldiers, 362,015 in the Army National Guard (ARNG), and 205, 281 in the US Army Reserve (USAR). Among that active-duty component, there were 78,893 officers, or about one-sixth of its overall workforce.[18]

So the average large American company with a headcount of 34,000 has about one-twentieth of the active-duty army's half million people. In other words, the total number of employees at the typical large US company is half the size of the army's *leadership*.

Google has 24,000 workers globally. General Electric has ten times as many, with 133,000 working in the United States. Just counting their American workforces, Ford Motor employs 75,000, while Procter & Gamble employs 50,000. The only company with a workforce the size of the army is Walmart (which, perhaps not coincidentally, was founded by a former army captain). The retail giant has been ranked number one on the Fortune 500 list of largest US companies for years, with annual revenues of 422 billion dollars and 1.6 million US employees.[19] While none of these companies faces mass deployment challenges similar to the army, or the need to regularly move essentially 100 percent of its workforce every few years, there are similarities. Not the least of these similarities is the need for good leadership.

Officers in the US Armed Forces are commissioned at the initial pay grade of O-1, which in the army, air force, and Marines is the rank of second lieutenant (the navy uses different titles for its equivalent ranks). After two years, the officers in that fiscal year cohort are promoted to O-2, or first lieutenant. Two years later comes the promotion to captain, followed many years later by major (O-4), then lieutenant colonel, colonel, and ultimately general. There are four pay grades for general officers, from 1-star brigadier generals (O-7) to 4-star generals (O-10). Few officers serve a 20-year career necessary to be considered for general, and even those who do are rarely selected. It is fair to say that selection to general is highly competitive, but the reality is that longevity is a bigger factor than merit in determining who makes rank. "If you breathe, you make lieutenant colonel" is a common refrain.

Table 2.1 Army officer personnel (as of August 2011)

12	General
47	Lieutenant General
114	Major General
142	Brigadier General
4492	Colonel
10,021	Lieutenant Colonel
17,094	Major
30,034	Captain
9,441	First Lieutenant
10,379	Second Lieutenant

Source: Accessed online from DMDC at http://siadapp.dmdc.osd.mil/
personnel/MILITARY/rg1108.pdf on October 10, 2011.

Even so, the shape of the officer forces is designed to look like a pyramid, with the bulk of officers in the junior ranks making up most of the officer corps, so that the numbers at each rank narrow considerably. At the top of the pyramid (see Table 2.1) is a single officer, a four-star general, with the title chief of staff of the army. Currently, that officer is General Raymond T. Odierno.

As shown in table 2.1, there are twice as many lieutenant colonels as there are colonels, which implies a roughly 50 percent promotion rate. By implication, only 5 percent of those who make the rank of lieutenant colonel are promoted to general. The dividing line between midgrade and senior officer is stark. However, once an officer becomes a general officer, promotions come easier and in a way, are less meaningful. Job assignments carry more responsibility than rank and title at that point, and some would say this is actually true at all ranks.

THE LEADERSHIP FACTORY

A 2006 study from Korn/Ferry International titled *Military Experience & CEOs: Is There a Link?* reported that among American corporate chief executives, a disproportionately high number have served in the military. "Military officers," the report said, "are almost three times as likely to serve as CEOs as are other Americans."[20] Their assessment was based on a review of the backgrounds of chief executives of Standard & Poor's (S&P) 500 companies during the second half of 2005, in which they discovered that 59 had military experience. This is roughly in line with the fact that one-fifth of adult males have been in the military at some time in their lives, according to the 2000 Census, but it was not in line when the scope was limited to officers.

To be sure, this military CEO story can be overinterpreted. Other demographic characteristics are arguably more disproportionately represented among CEOs. For example, 95 percent of chief executives hold a bachelor's degree or higher,[21] compared to 27 percent of the population at large.[22] This statistic reminds us that *ability* is likely the key variable, meaning that the correlates of ability (college education as a signal of intelligence; military officership as a signal of leadership) should be viewed skeptically as *causal* factors. Here is another correlate: while half the population is male, and 60 percent of corporate execs are male, all but a handful of CEOs are male. This reminds us that there can be hiring bias, and that if favoritism for maleness exists, it could spill over toward the qualities and characteristics inherent in military service (I can't help but think of the basic training in the use of "command voice" to officers and enlistees alike). In this light, does the threefold military officer–CEO finding become irrelevant? It might if military experience had no effect on corporate performance, but that's not what the data show.

Tim Duffy, author of the Korn/Ferry study, also discovered that the performance of military-led firms was "stellar," surpassing the S&P index in terms of shareholder return "by three to 20 percentage points per year" over one-, three-, five-, and ten-year periods, that is all periods studied. Not surprisingly, CEOs with military experience had an average tenure of 7.2 years, compared to nonveteran tenures, which averaged 4.6 years. This kind of "military" performance effect has been confirmed by other recent studies.[23]

Economists Efraim Benmelech of Harvard and Carola Frydman of MIT find in their study of ex-military CEOs that, when compared to nonmilitary CEOS, they "tend to invest less and their firms seem to perform better in times of industry distress."[24] The authors interpret the effect further, suggesting that formative experiences such as military service—even for only a few years—can have long-lasting consequences for executive performance.

The disproportionate presence of business leaders who come from the military raises two questions. One, how does the military produce such great leaders? Two, what defines great leadership? I'm not sure we can answer one question without the other, but the next section will explore some of the factors that make the military experience so influential. With that context, we can talk more about why this makes military leaders great, or rather, entrepreneurial.

WHAT MAKES SOLDIERS UNIQUE?

Those who join the US military join young, and their initiation is universally described as life altering. They are entering another world. The historian John Keegan writes in the introduction to *A History of Warfare* that warrior culture is universal, which is at its core tribalism. Keegan writes that veterans seem no different than other kinds of professional men ("They came from the same schools... they were devoted to their families... they worried about money in the same way."), but that ultimately, "soldiers are not as other men."[25] Where else can a citizen risk life and take life in defense of the highest national ideals, essentially tribal ideals? Whether it is safeguarding liberty in America or the motherland in Russia, no other work grants its members the status of protecting the tribe's core identity that soldiering does. This is why in all civilizations—feudal Japan, imperial Rome, modern America—the warrior class is usually afforded the highest status, while merchants are considered the lowest. And warriors in America, like most civilizations, can achieve this status by joining from any social class, rich or poor.

When young Americans walks onto one of the five army posts that offer basic training, they are immediately broken down and rebuilt, physically, mentally, and culturally. Men's heads are shaved, uniforms replace clothes, and even watches and clocks are taken away. All this reinforces the new overarching and singular reality: they are now in this tribe, and will soon be of this tribe. The ten-week introductory course begins with drill sergeants sternly shaping individuals into members of a group. Group identity is constantly reinforced by punishing everyone for the errors of anyone.

From these early efforts at shaping civilians into soldiers, core principles of leadership become part of one's nature. Colonel Tom Kolditz, a professor and head of the Department of Behavioral Sciences and Leadership at West Point, has thought deeply about why the military produces great leaders and has written on the topic frequently for the *Harvard Business Review*. In short, Kolditz argues: "It's nurture, not nature," and he points to three factors.[26] One, the military utilizes a carefully designed training program that is "far more time-consuming and expensive than similar training in industry or government." Basic Combat Training is a staple, an intensive ten-week program of indoctrination, but it is followed by more refined training programs that never really stop during an individual's military career. Two, the military gives its youngest leaders high levels of responsibility and authority, in terms of the number of personnel, the capital equipment, and the scope of missions under the command of the most junior officers. Three, "military leadership is based on a concept of duty, service, and self-sacrifice." This third point is what Kolditz has fleshed out as a vital difference that shapes military leaders, experiences that he calls "in extremis." In essence, the intensity of combat, with lives at stake, heightens the need for purpose-driven teams and renders transactional motivation (pay, rewards, and punishment) insufficient. Let's consider each of these three factors in more depth.

Factor 1: Early Responsibility

The army's smallest unit led by an officer is the platoon, made up of two–four squads of eight–eleven men each. A lieutenant usually leads a platoon. One level higher, a captain usually leads a company of three–five platoons. Given that an army captain is often 25–30 years old, the amount of responsibility just in terms of lives under his or her command is impressive compared to civilian managers.

"Officers get a lot of responsibility when they are really young. Real responsibility that you just don't get in college or a big business," says Bill Coleman, a 1971 graduate of the Air Force Academy.[27] After Coleman left the air force, he embarked on a career in Silicon Valley, which to date has involved starting numerous companies. Coleman makes a point to distinguish between leaders and managers, and credits his years in the air force with "shaping me to, one, understand the value of hard work and professionalism, and two, learn the values of structure, planning, and measuring."[28] What impressed me about Coleman in the years I've known him is that he had the freedom to retire as a billionaire almost a decade ago, but soon realized that what he loved more than anything was starting new companies, which is why he is seen around Palo Alto these days, mentoring young entrepreneurs.

Warren Bennis explains that his experience as a young officer during World War II was the singular leadership transformation of his life. And he credits the transformation primarily to the grave responsibility thrust upon him, not to innate or learned skills. He says: "Leaderhsip is a performance art, and most of us become leaders only when we are cast in that role."[29]

Factor 2: Training

Fighting is a primal instinct, whereas warfare is an ancient art that has evolved into a modern science. The idea of military officers as professionals was introduced by political scientist Samuel Huntington's 1957 book *The Soldier and the State*, in which he coined the term "profession of arms." Huntington's purpose was largely to define the optimal institutional arrangement for civilian control of the military in a democracy, but his definition was embraced by the US military. The shift from citizen armies to professional armies was by that time inevitable. Indeed it had been ongoing for centuries.

There is a useful distinction between warriors and soldiers, though certainly one can have both values. Warriors thrive on strength and courage, while soldiers must subordinate individuality for group efficiency. For most of human history, fighting was done by warriors, side by side an army meant little more than a mass of warriors fighting side-by-side. Soldiers, by contrast, have discipline and coordination. Roman legions were soldiers, organized as cavalry, archers, and infantry, but that type of disciplined combat was lost in the Dark Ages. The advent of gunpowder and the modern nation-state renewed the primacy of soldiering. Increasing professionalism has given advantage ever since, and modern armies take advantage of the increasing complexity of technology only through rigorous training.

A standing army is made up of soldiers who have been conditioned to the unnaturalness of constantly facing "invisible death" so that they respond with both disciplined obedience and the capacity to make decisions under stressful uncertainty. But training in the army's view is more than the initial course of indoctrination, and more than the acquisition of technical skills by specialized soldiers. Training is a constant. The day-to-day job of the modern warrior in the absence of war, which is the norm for most soldiers even in times of war, is to train for war. Adam Smith noticed this back in 1776, when he wrote: "The practice of military exercises is the sole or principal occupation of the soldiers of a standing army."[30] This discipline was noted by General Douglas MacArthur when he said: "On the fields of friendly strife are sown the seeds that on other days and other fields will bear the fruits of victory."[31]

Basic training teaches soldiers to march and salute, but it is really a breaking down of barriers so that individuals learn to trust their teammates and leaders. All soldiers are taught the difference between lawful and unlawful orders so they can use their own moral judgment. They learn about the honor code, and practice it in ways that civilians cannot. Most of all, American soldiers are forced to think for themselves. Forty years ago, draftees were generally in uniform for two years, so training emphasized obedience. But the days of cannon fodder and attrition warfare are gone. Today's soldiers serve for far longer and are expected to be "pentathletes" who are highly skilled physically and mentally in order to exercise independent judgment.

The initial regimen of army training for officers includes basic soldiering skills and technical skills, but also other skills unique to command, such as unit tactics and operations within the larger army, for one. More importantly, the young officer is given instruction in leadership. As described in *The Soldier's Guide*: "Leader Development is the deliberate, continuous, sequential and progressive process, grounded in Army values, that grows soldiers into competent and confident leaders capable of decisive action."[32] The guide also explains that leader development is more than institutional training, and will include training within the unit, operational experience, and self-development. The training process of the army is completely thought out, such that officers at all levels are expected to not only train, but to develop multiple training plans across different time frames. A variety of schools are established for officers at each stage of their careers for individual training, while a variety of training exercises and competitions are available for units. To be sure, how doctrine works in theory is infinitely smoother than in practice, especially in a time of war. But everyone who goes through even a short career as a military officer comes out drenched in leadership development.

Management expert Bennis remembers how fortunate he was, before deploying to the European theater in World War II, to attend the "same legendary Infantry Officer Basic Course that polished the military and leadership skills of Dwight D. Eisenhower, George Marshall, and later, Colin Powell" at Fort Benning, Georgia. "There I learned skills and habits that have served me well my entire life. I learned the value of organization. I learned how to work as part of a team. I learned that one of my most important jobs was to take care of my people."[33]

The enthusiasm Bennis and other veterans have for their military experience is often matched by admiration from civilians who are exposed to what can seem a rarified world. The respected futurist Bob

Johansen described visiting the Army War College in his book *Leaders Make the Future* and how he was impressed by its nickname "VUCA University," which stands for volatility, uncertainty, complexity, and ambiguity. Bob used the phrase often when we talked, and he said that the US military is way ahead of anything in the private sector in preparing its workforce through training and simulation. Live-fire training and virtual war gaming are forms of immersive experiences that Johansen credits for the army's post-Vietnam transformation as a learning organization.

A phrase I hear often in talks with today's army officers is "man, equip, train," which is the way a unit should prepare for deployment. Imagine an infantry battalion just back from overseas, planning to recuperate for a year stateside before deploying again. First, it gets its manning in place, then it prepares its equipment, and finally the troops train and learn to work together. Officially, the army describes the preparation in doctrinal terms as AFORGEN, which stands for Army Force Generation and which includes these steps: "recruit, organize, man, equip, train, sustain, mobilize, and deploy units on a cyclic basis."[34] From a unit commander's perspective, the three core functions within his domain are "man, equip, train," until ordered to deploy. Training, in a sense, is the beginning and the end of army leadership.

Factor 3: Values

"There is no limit to the good you can do if you don't care who gets the credit," said General George C. Marshall. This is one of the quotes that freshman at the service academies are required to memorize and recite on command. Service before self is a sentiment carved on the military soul, and it is fair to say it is the singular core value held by American officers. Values in general are front and center in military culture, which is why the honor codes at the service academies are strictly enforced, with dozens of honor trials held each year and multiple expulsions. Cadets and midshipmen have historically run their own honor courts, and to this day operate with minimal "adult" oversight. When a cadet, let alone an officer, violates the trust among peers by lying, cheating, or stealing, s/he is simply no longer welcome as a member of the tribe.

Values, then, are the third factor that Colonel Kolditz says distinguishes officers from managers, particularly values formed during "in extremis" experiences. He argues it is the unique perspective of extreme stress that crystallizes a leader's purpose-driven approach, principally the concern for others under one's command. With "in extremis" instincts, the military officer is able to transform soldiers into "willing, rather than merely compliant, agents." Military historian Keegan can be understood to emphasize this third factor as the core of the military identity, in contrast to self-concern. "Money, however, was not an ultimate or defining value, nor even was promotion within the military system. Officers, of course, hankered for advancement, but it was not the value by which they measured themselves."[35]

For those who have crossed the gap and served in both arenas, the similarities between military and markets are powerful. Indeed, military CEOs bring the people-centric values and missionary focus to corporations explicitly, and proudly credit their military experience with improving corporate performance. But for those without both experiences, the similarities may seem less obvious, and the contrasts greater. Civilians often scornfully characterize military subordination as a sign of blind obedience with little room for independent judgment. As ignorant as that is, one hears a similar kind of scorn among veterans for the business world. In a presidential debate in 2008, Senator John McCain asserted his distinct qualifications: "I led the largest squadron in the United States Navy. And I did it out of patriotism, not for profit."[36]

First, it is a mistake to think that values and mission have no place in the motivations of business leaders. Entrepreneurs, in particular, are deeply driven by a missionary zeal. Steve Jobs, just as an example, famously recruited a new CEO from Pepsi to Apple with the line: "Do you want to sell sugar water for the rest of your life, or do you want to come with me and change the world." Keegan is correct when he says that the "distance [between the worlds of soldiers and civilians] can never be closed," but the two worlds overlap in important ways, too.

There is a danger in the false pride that military service isn't tainted by money. More to the point, the scornful attitude toward market incentives within some Pentagon circles is simply dishonest. Dollars are used as incentives within the military constantly, in matters large and small. Retention bonuses and early-retirement bonuses are used in force shaping, as just one example. A more important example is the US military retirement package, a relatively generous monthly pension benefit of 50 percent of a retiree's final salary. This pension is only earned after nothing less than 20 years of service. Why 20 years? Why does the military pay no benefit to someone who retires at 19 years? Surely the answer isn't to compensate those who have served, because there is no serious distinction between 19 versus 20 years in uniform.

The real answer to this question is revealing. The army, navy, air force, Marines, and coast guard use a 20-year "cliff" for their retirement programs precisely as a coercive monetary tool. It all but compels officers and enlistees to stay in uniform for a full second decade. And it must be said that such a cliff is illegal in the private sector, precisely because it is coercive. Here we should remember Kolditz's argument that good leadership turns soldiers into "willing, rather than merely compliant, agents." Is a 19-year major a willing agent or a compliant agent?

Let's agree that the "market versus military" dichotomy is a false contrast. Instead, we should have in mind a model of individual motivations, such that all individuals are motivated by a mix of dimensions including money, service, risk, opportunity, and so on. I would be the first to argue that soldiers tend to put more weight, much more, on service than the typical civilian. But I will also argue that even the most patriotic soldiers cannot help but care about money, especially if they have families and value the material well-being of their families. Just as importantly, we can see how the risk dimension might be stronger among military than nonmilitary, but the risk-loving profile varies across civilians as well. The five hundred thousand or so new American entrepreneurs who start companies have a strong risk profile compared to the millions of government workers in safe careers.

If we look at the underlying theme Kolditz is really describing with his third factor, we see a contrast between motivation versus coercion. He is right that the best leaders seek to use motivation rather than mere command authority, a distinction that military officers face constantly due to the nature of their work on the knife's edge of fear and glory. Harry S. Truman, serving as an infantry officer on the battlefields of Europe during World War I, understood this lesson long before he was elected president. One of Truman's famous dictums is: "A leader is a man who had the ability to get other people to do what they don't want to do, and like it."[37]

Once we make this distinction between motivation versus coercion, we should apply it at a higher level. And this is the irony of the army, wherein its officers understand intimately the superiority of motivation (which respects the free will of subordinates), while their personal careers are controlled by a largely coercive system.

It might have been William Shakespeare who introduced the idea of leaders being born, not made, when he wrote in *Twelfth Night*: "Be not afraid of greatness: some are born great, some achieve greatness and some have greatness thrust upon them."[38] Search as one might, few Americans doubt that "leaders are made, they are not born," Green Bay Packers Coach Vince Lombardi famously quipped. Scientists and educators call this the "nature versus nurture" debate, having wrestled with it for over a century. The consensus of scholars is that both nature and nurture have a role.[39]

The US military has fair claim to excellence in both nature and nurture: recruiting talented young men and women (a parallel to nature), while also making its business the constant nurturing of leadership. The three factors described earlier—young responsibility beneath the mask of command, world-class training culture, and values steeled in the crucible of hard experience—are nurturing factors.

Most readers probably believe that these factors are not mere correlates but rather causes of improved leadership. Are we right? Economists Benmelech and Frydman explored the causality of military service on performance in their study of military CEOs. Using an econometric method that "allows us to rule out the possibility that the effect of military service is due to intrinsic characteristics of the individual,"[40] the economists found evidence that the military experience does enhance CEO performance.

ENTREPRENEURIAL LEADERSHIP

The greatest entrepreneurs of our time are interesting characters such as Jobs and Bill Gates, the founders of Apple and Microsoft, respectively. Both are college dropouts. Both were born in 1955. And both were famously intense as young entrepreneurs: brilliant, obsessive, insensitive workaholics. Although they built powerful firms and invented magical technologies, it is hard to imagine either of them in the military. If Gates had become an officer, he would have been the smartest information technology (IT) clerk in the Pentagon basement in 1982, and there he would have stayed. So the notion that the army officer is an entrepreneurial leader is discordant with our stereotypes of what an officer is and what an entrepreneur is.

The definition given by a leading textbook describes entrepreneurs as "individuals who recognize opportunities where others see chaos, or confusion.... The characteristics of seeking opportunities, taking risks beyond security, and having the tenacity to push an idea through to reality combine into a special perspective that permeates entrepreneurs."[41] This seems to square with the way in which many veteran officers define themselves. For starters, an entrepreneurial leader is not simply a person who establishes a new business. Rather, an entrepreneurial leader is comfortable with risk. VUCA comes to mind. More importantly, they see opportunities in chaotic uncertainty. Finally, they are driven by their vision, persistence, and most of all, tolerance of failure.

If the ratio of veteran CEOs is disproportionately high, the ratio of veteran *entrepreneurs* is even higher. The Small Business Administration (SBA) reports that 14.8 percent of America's entrepreneurs are veterans.[42] The SBA defines entrepreneurs as small nonfarm business owners. Many of these entrepreneurs establish new companies that grow into the largest in the world.

Consider a few of the iconic entrepreneurs who got their start in the military. Sam Walton founded Walmart after graduating from the University of Missouri as an ROTC cadet and serving as an officer in the US Army Intelligence Corps. His business fortune eventually made him the richest man in the world. *Forbes* magazine founder Malcolm Forbes received the Bronze Star for action in World War II. David Thomas, founder of Wendy's, was an army mess sergeant in Korea. Fred Smith, founder of FedEx, was a danger-loving marine pilot in Vietnam. Jim Kimsey, the founding chairman of America Online (AOL), graduated from West Point and served as an infantry officer in Vietnam. Baskin-Robbins ice cream parlor was founded by Burt Baskins, a navy enlistee in the Pacific during World War II. Wayne Huizenga enlisted in the army in 1959 and later founded Blockbuster video rentals. Finally, Craig Venter, was an enlistee in the navy before becoming famous for leading the Human Genome Project.

If we dig a little deeper into any of their biographies, we see the entrepreneurial threads emerging from their time in service. For example, Henry Bloch served as a navigator on B-17 bombers in the Army Air Corps during World War II. He founded H&R Block, the innovative and successful tax preparation service in 1955. However, that was Bloch's second startup. He started his first company in 1946, and persisted in offering accounting services to other small businesses for nearly a decade despite low sales volume. That entrepreneurial persistence is what eventually led to the discovery and pioneering development of the tax business.[43]

Brian Lamb joined the US Navy after spending his entire life, including four years of college at Purdue University, in Lafayette, Indiana. In 1979, he created the nonprofit cable channel C-SPAN, for which he received the Presidential Medal of Freedom some three decades later. Lamb calls his service in the navy "probably the most important thing I've ever done."[44] In a 2008 interview in *U.S. News and World Report*,[45] Lamb talked about his career, but gave his longest answer to a question about the risks he has taken. "I've always felt that the risks weren't very significant...if I failed, so what?" Lamb said. Then he revealed some of the mission-driven focus described earlier. "Everybody said this place couldn't work, in the beginning...but I never thought it was a risk—I never doubted it, and that's probably one asset that I have: I had a job to do, and I would do anything to succeed."[46]

Capitalism is based on competition, so it helps to recognize that the art of conflict might have useful parallels, psychologically if in no other dimension. Francis Fukuyama, in his pioneering work *The End of History and The Last Man*, defines the socioeconomic transition to modernity as a channeling of the basic human drive known by the ancient Greeks as *Thymos* away from destructive conquest and toward constructive business. That is, modern society channels spirited young men and women toward construction. Consider the term "empire building," which today has a meaning sharply different from a century ago: Fortune 500 not Ottoman. The word "dynasty" now refers to wealthy families and corporations, not ruling families and lands. This spirit of *Thymos* is arguably strong among more aggressive (military) types, but is easily translatable to market-based competition, which may explain the success of military CEOs.

"In today's Army, many junior officers—indeed a large majority— are developing adaptive capacity in the serendipitous crucible experiences of Operation Iraqi Freedom in Iraq and Operation Enduring Freedom in Afghanistan," wrote Army War College professor Lenny Wong in early 2009. "By being confronted with complexity, unpredictability, and ambiguity in a combat environment, junior officers are learning to adapt, to innovate, and to operate with minimal guidance."[47] However, Wong worries that the garrison army (i.e., the peacetime norm) is not well prepared to give satisfying careers to its entrepreneurial company-grade officers. As a retired army lieutenant colonel, Wong has been noticing the transformation of leadership realities for decades. In a heavily cited 2004 study published by the Strategic Studies Institute at the US Army War College, Wong first laid out his thesis that the two wars were enhancing innovative leadership skills within the army officer corps:

> Lieutenants and captains have conducted missions for which they never trained, executed operations that have outpaced Army doctrine, shifted constantly from adrenaline-pumping counterinsurgency to patience demanding nation-building, and received very little detailed guidance or supervision in the process. The result of this experience is a cohort of junior officers that is learning to be adaptable, creative, innovative, and confident in their abilities to handle just about any task thrown at them.[48]

What we now understand is that Iraq was an insurgency, and not until years after the invasion did army and marine strategy and tactics shift. The change toward counterinsurgency tactics, celebrated as the Petraeus "surge" by the public, is credited within the army to junior officers who pushed the lessons they learned up the chain of command. It was not a smooth learning process, but it says a great deal about the type of leaders the army had created. They may not have been trained for the kind of war in which they found themselves, but they had been trained to adapt and succeed.

Credit goes to recent army chiefs. General Peter Schoomaker used the adaptive terminology in early 2006[49] as flexible needs in the war took precedence over specialization. Soldiers who had branched to armor, artillery, and other specialties needed to think in terms of counterinsurgency as much if not more than the infantry. Wong also credits the way the army decentralized much of its training under General Eric Shinseki, who served as the army chief of staff from 1999 to 2003:

> Former Chief of Staff of the Army General Eric Shinseki set the stage for change. He chartered the Army Training and Leader Development Panel (ATLDP) in anticipation of developing adaptive leaders for the Objective Force. Under his direction, the

Army explored ways to eliminate 50 percent of nonmission related training in order to allow company commanders to be innovative in developing their own training. Additionally, he directed that all company commanders be given a week of "white space" on their training calendars to encourage junior officer creativity.[50]

The commitment to adaptive leadership has continued under General Martin Dempsey, who was the army chief until early 2011, when he was appointed by President Barack Obama as the chairman of the joint chiefs. Three months prior, in an essay in *Armed Forces Journal*, Dempsey had written: "[L]eader development is our true competitive advantage to be preserved as our first priority if we are to remain the most powerful and adaptive land force in the world."[51] And in a nod that should give confidence to reformers like Wong, Dempsey also promised that the army is "moving aggressively to adapt personnel policies."

MILITARY CIVILIAN GAP?

Much of this chapter has tried to show that the officers in our armed forces are in fact entrepreneurial leaders. This trait explains their disproportionate success in creating and leading private-sector companies.

The underlying tension throughout this discussion has been the erroneous stereotypes that exist between civilians and soldiers. This gap in our society is in some senses real and also inevitable. As Keegan says, soldiers are tribal, and the two worlds can never completely align. What concerns me is that the military-civilian gap may be growing wider in modern America.

Fewer Americans have any personal experience in uniform. Fewer politicians are veterans. Even CEOs with military experience are becoming less common (though their numbers are still disproportionately high). A 2005 story in *USA Today* by Del Jones reported that "there are fewer people in their 40s and 50s with combat experience...than at almost any time since the Industrial Revolution."[52]

One way to think about the gap is to ask what percentage of Americans have served or have a family member who served. Since 1974, the General Social Survey (GSS) has been asking: "Have you ever been on active duty for military training or service for two consecutive months or more? If yes: What was your total time on active duty?" In 1974, just under 25 percent of respondents answered yes, and 6 percent had served for more than four years. By the mid-1980s, the participation rate had dropped to 16 percent, and in 2010—after nearly a decade of war—it was just 10.4 percent, with only 3 percent serving for longer than four years.[53]

The growing gap causes at least two major problems. First, even though the military is highly respected by civilians, it is not well understood and is further removed from critical analysis. This "halo effect" makes reforming the military difficult because reform lacks a broad popular understanding. Ending the draft was easy, because it touched everyone. Reforming a broken Pentagon personnel bureaucracy simply does not touch the lives of many Americans. The second problem is that the gap makes military leaders less aware of innovations in the private sector. Generals and admirals, particularly those on active duty, are experientially limited, and don't know what they don't know.

To crack these problems, it will help to think about why the military-civilian gap developed, and what exactly it is.

The simplest economy involves some degree of complexity, which is an economist's word for the diversity of occupations stemming from the specialization of labor. The soldier fits uneasily into this network of specialized labor for a variety of reasons. The obvious discord is that the soldier, at once a destroyer rather than a creator, produces nothing tangible and is unable to establish value for his service.

Economists describe things like national defense as "public goods" precisely because they are intangible and nonrivalrous. A border twice as secure from foreign invasion cannot be "purchased" by the baker without the farmer getting it for free. Since markets cannot provide public goods efficiently, the state must do so. And here is another distinction: the soldier is a government employee, unlike those s/he protects.

Whatever gap might arise between the warrior class and the public can be avoided if the warriors come from the people. This is what justifies for some the coercion of all citizens to a year or two of conscripted military service. For example, when I interviewed Bob McDonald, CEO of Procter and Gamble and a West Point graduate who served in the 1970s, he remarked: "The all-volunteer force is a great idea, but I have one problem with it. The public isn't invested in the nation in the same way. I'm one of those for national service."[54] I personally find conscription at odds with the ideal of a free society, but I can sympathize with what motivates McDonald. Is there another way to bridge the gap?

My theory is that the gap happens because we cloister the military away from civilian society. Or rather, the military cloisters itself away. The problem is not that the military draws in members from a narrow segment of the population (e.g., the Michael Moore/*Washington Post* thesis, which has been debunked). Rather, the problem is that the path into the military is a one-way street. The only time soldiers emerge from the military communities that surround large bases around the nation is when they quit or retire. A few officers might go back to a civilian college for a couple of years of graduate school, but they aren't in uniform and they aren't working. And when veterans do retire, they often settle down in military-friendly enclaves. Florida and Texas are popular given the zero state income tax. My point is that outside of Washington, DC, the segregation of working officers and soldiers is stark. This situation would be different if the military allowed honorably discharged veterans a two-way street. Serve in the army for a few years, leave for a couple years in the private sector, apply for an opening in the army, and return. By barring this kind of lateral entry, exit, and reentry, the military widens the cultural gap.

CHAPTER 3

ENTREPRENEURS IN UNIFORM

Never tell people how to do things. Tell them what to do and they will
surprise you with their ingenuity.

        —General George S. Patton[1]

IS MILITARY LEADERSHIP SOMEHOW DIFFERENT from other styles
of leadership? Most of us probably agree that it is. Civilians, if they had
to describe military-style leadrship, would use words such as "aggressive," "brave," and "strict." But how would veterans themselves describe
it? Many, particularly American troops still on active duty, might use the
exact same terms. The one term that I guarantee wouldn't be used, but
that probably best describes military leaders, is "entrepreneurial."

I remember sitting in classes and lectures at the Air Force Academy
in which we had the history of airpower drummed into us. Hap Arnold.
Billy Mitchell. John Glenn. We learned about the Wright Brothers,
but we also learned about Napoleon's invasion of Russia and the game
theory behind mutually assured destruction. If I had paid more attention, I might have noticed that victory had far less to do with courage, strategy, and discipline, and more to do with which side was more
innovative.

This chapter will explain what entrepreneurial leadership qualities really are and then apply that lens to some surprising military
biographies. Whether we look at modern mavericks, famous five-
stars of World War II, or legends of the Civil War and the American

Revolution, the same traits emerge: innovative, risk-taking, rebellious, adaptable, persistent, opportunistic, and highly intense. Those words describe Apple cofounder and CEO Steve Jobs just as well as they describe General Robert E. Lee.

ENTREPRENEURIAL QUALITIES

The core quality that the greatest military leaders are remembered for is strategic innovation. Those who invented cannons won their wars; those who invented flanking maneuvers won theirs. Innovation is what defines the most famous entrepreneurs as well, whether it is Thomas Edison inventing the light bulb, Henry Ford inventing the automobile assembly line, or Sergey Brin and Larry Page inventing Google's search algorithm.

If the notion of entrepreneurial leadership in large organizations (especially government organizations) seems counterintuitive, it is because our definition of entrepreneurship is too narrow. The most common definition is traced to Harvard professor Joseph Schumpeter. He wrote about entrepreneurs as central actors in the very system of capitalism, a role that had been given far too little notice by economic models at the time. He wrote, "Entrepreneurship...consists in doing things that are not generally done in the ordinary course of business routine; it is essentially a phenomenon that comes under the wider aspect of leadership."[2]

New firms are routinely founded not from whole cloth but when a big company doesn't take advantage of an employee's innovation, and the employee *reluctantly* takes the risk to start a new company. The story of Steve Wozniak's departure from Hewlett-Packard (HP) in the late 1970s to create Apple is an example. Wozniak tried to give his idea for a personal computer to HP, but the company didn't see that same vision and let his golden idea slip away. The *only* option for "Woz" to see his dream product become real was to leave HP and start something new.

How can we apply this framework to organizations not perusing profit? As economist Peter Klein and his colleagues explain, "Novelty alone is an incomplete and somewhat simple characterization [of entrepreneurship in the public sphere]."[3] There is a perfect analogy in the public sector: the creation of new government agencies (e.g., the Environmental Protection Agency, NASA, the air force) or units (e.g., the Green Berets in 1952, the navy SEALS in 1961). Indeed, it is difficult to think about the air force without being struck by the fact that every aspect of it is and has always been entrepreneurial, from the Wright brothers' first flight to Chuck Yeager breaking the sound barrier.

UNDERSTANDING THE PUBLIC ENTREPRENEUR

According to one textbook,[4] one of the ten prevailing myths about entrepreneurs is that their main interest is in making money. On the contrary, their primary motivation is most often an intense focus on changing the world in some way. This missionary drive is especially relevant when we think about public servants. Government jobs may be safe and even well paying, but as the joke goes, Uncle Sam doesn't offer stock options. Other myths persist, painting entrepreneurs as misfits, gamblers, science geeks, or that they're young when in fact the number of entrepreneurs in their forties is double that of those in their twenties. The reality is that there are some common qualities, but the range of diverse entrepreneurial styles is wide. What entrepreneurs do have in common are internal motivations such as personal responsibility (hence the bias for action, misunderstood as risk-loving) and total commitment to an idea.

The key to understanding *public* entrepreneurship, according to Peter Klein and his coauthors,[5] is to view operations of human individuals in light of property rights, which in the simplest terms means how much freedom of action government employees have over resources. This is a question of authority, or more accurately, the centralization of authority. When government employees are given more freedom of action, they can exercise entrepreneurship. Alternatively, when the central bureaucracy constrains action to mere execution of checklists, there is no room for entrepreneurship or innovation of any kind.

Klein and his colleagues reveal two additional definitions of entrepreneurship we should keep in mind, aside from the Schumpeterian one (*innovation in products and processes*). The first is called "Kirzerian entrepreneurship" (named after economist Izzy Kirzner), and it stresses an individual's *alertness to opportunities*. The second is named after Frank Knight, a professor at the University of Chicago who mentored George Stigler, Milton Friedman, and James Buchanan, among others. Knight emphasized *judgmental decision making under uncertainty*. Each of these three definitions of entrepreneurship has a business context, and for our purposes, a manpower context. The military Schumpeterians constantly evolve tactics, equipment, and organization. The military

Kirznerians channel Sun Tzu, consume intel, are adaptable, and are always on alert. Military Knightians channel Carl von Clausewitz, the great Prussian operational theorist, and thrive in the fog and friction of war. No doubt the army leaders who talk of VUCA (an acronym for "volatility, uncertainty, complexity and ambiguity," which has become popular inside and outside the ranks) understand the entrepreneurial nature of what they are teaching to young officers and troops. The fact is that entrepreneurial leadership is a precious legacy of the American military, as the following examples make clear.

THE FOUNDING FOUNDING FATHER

America's founding fathers were all comfortable as entrepreneurs, from sage Benjamin Franklin (inventor of the pot-belly stove, bifocals, and the lightning rod) to polymath Thomas Jefferson. They were inventing a nation, after all. George Washington, though, seems less entrepreneurial than the rest, eulogized famously by comrade Henry "Light-Horse Harry" Lee as, "First in war—first in peace—and first in the hearts of his countrymen . . . pious, just, humane, temperate, and sincere; uniform, dignified, and commanding." But entrepreneurial? Despite the historical stereotype, Washington was arguably the most entrepreneurial of all the founding fathers and set the example of adaptability in warfare for generations of American military.

The evidence of Washington's entrepreneurial traits as an officer is straightforward. He was innovative in his use of what is known as a *Fabian* strategy, or guerrilla warfare. Rather than engage British troops in the traditional manner of the eighteenth century's pitched battles, Washington harassed his enemy during 1776 and much of 1777. "Avoid a general Action" was his guiding strategy for much of the conflict, with a commitment to never "put anything at Risque [sic]." This might seem an odd approach for a risk-loving entrepreneur, but only if our definition of risk is shallow. What it really represented was an adaptable approach to officership in the great macro risk of warfare. It is clear that Washington was not ideological, as he engaged in pitched battles when the time was right, including the Battle of Saratoga in late 1777 and Yorktown four years later.

Washington's real strength was his exceptional alertness to opportunities. Most famous is his Christmas night crossing of the Delaware River and subsequent surprise attack on the Hessians at Trenton, New

Jersey. Prior to this famous event, Washington's army had been fractured in a long retreat across the state, meaning he had to wait patiently for his subordinate officers to reunite in Pennsylvania. The American forces were in miserable condition, with nearly two thousand troops—more than one-fourth of the total under command—ill or wounded. Washington made a fateful decision to strike when an attack would be least unexpected, and won a series of victories on December 26, 1776, at Trenton and later in the British rear at Princeton. Those victories are seen as the turning point that led to American independence.

Washington showed the same kind of patience, timing, and opportunism many times during the war. The story of the overnight artillery fortification of Dorchester Heights is exemplary. The British siege of Boston began in April 1775, and it wasn't until 11 months later that Washington executed his daring maneuver, starting with a feint of artillery fire from lower batteries on the nights of March 2 and 3, which were intentionally too distant from British positions in Boston to cause or receive much damage. Then, stealthily during the night of March 4, some two thousand of Washington's forces marched up to Dorcester Heights, prepared earthworks (dirt fortifications), cleared trees, and hauled up the cannons. The reaction was described this way in David McCullough's bestselling book *1776*:

> At daybreak, the British commanders looking up at the Heights could scarcely believe their eyes. The hoped-for, all-important surprise was total. General Howe was said to have exclaimed, "My God, these fellows have done more work in one night than I could make my own army do in three months."[6]

Howe had a choice: attack the Heights and suffer severe casualties as they had at Bunker Hill or retreat. Washington couldn't know what Howe would choose, which shows that he exhibited decisiveness under uncertainty. This was clearly not a Fabian ploy, but it worked. Howe was humiliated and agreed to retreat from Boston days later.

It's worth noting that Washington had a peculiar background that likely fostered his innovative military style. He came from a business-oriented family, and his early years were spent primarily surveying, not soldiering. George's father, Augustine Washington, was a tobacco farmer who also established a business in iron mining. Biographer Harlow Giles Unger in *The Unexpected George Washington* describes the first president as "one of America's leading entrepreneurs," who expanded the two-thousand-acre Mount Vernon tobacco farm inherited from his family into a forward-looking industrial village. Unger writes that Washington "expanded a relatively small tobacco plantation into a diversified agroindustrial enterprise that stretched over thousands of acres and included, among other ventures, a fishery, meat processing facility, textile and weaving manufactory, distillery, gristmill, smithy [blacksmith shop], brick making kiln, cargo-carrying schooner, and, of course, endless fields of grain." John Berlau of the Competitive Enterprise Institute summarized the many ventures this way in a 2009 magazine article:

> During America's time as an English colony, Washington ran a fishing operation that processed 1.5 million fish per year and sold them throughout the 13 American colonies and the British West Indies. The mill he built ground 278,000 pounds of flour annually that was shipped through America and even exported to England and Portugal. In the 1790s, during the last years of his life, Washington built one of the largest whiskey distilleries in the new nation. No wonder he ended up first in the hearts of his countrymen.[7]

What should be a lesson to today's planners at the Pentagon is that Washington's active-duty service was the exception, not the rule, in his career. When first commissioned at the age of 21 as a major in the Virginia militia, Washington immediately saw action from what was literally the beginning of the French and Indian War when his small contingent ambushed a French patrol on May 28, 1754. Described in his diary as a skirmish of a "Quarter of an Hour," Washington initiated fire and coordinated an encirclement by Iroquois allies that in the end killed ten Frenchmen and helped spark the global war between Britain and France. A year later he was appointed commander-in-chief of the Virginia Regiment, the first active-duty militia in the colonies. During that war, Washington commanded the regiment during no less than 20 battles over 10 months alone. But here's the interesting thing: once the war ended in 1758, Washington retired and did not return to military life until the outbreak of the Revolutionary War in 1775, an interlude of more than 16 years. Think about that. Four years of active war/fighting command, followed by 16 years as a civilian businessman, and then he was abruptly given command of the entire American army. While famous for his wartime successes, Washington spent much more time as an entrepreneur in the private sector and brought his entrepreneurial strengths to his military leadership.

CIVIL WARRIORS

They called him the "King of Spades."

Some consider Robert E. Lee the greatest military mind in American history, while others say he was a traitor who made the grand mistake of fighting a rebellion too much like a conventional war. But no one questions General Lee's status as one of the most innovative commanders of land warfare in all history. Some historians rank him alongside Napoleon in terms of his battlefield mastery, a respect he earned with numerous victories when overmatched in terms of manpower and equipment.

Lee was so highly respected before the war broke out that newly elected President Abraham Lincoln offered him command of the Union Army. Lee refused and even proposed sitting out the conflict, which he anticipated would be a protracted "calamity." Eventually, Lee resigned his commission in the North and joined the Confederacy in the South, a decision he said was made to defend his home soil in Virginia.

Despite his status and his battlefield success against great odds, Lee's genius was not strategic. For example, he lost both major attacks into the North. More to the point, if Lee had followed the strategic model of Washington and accepted a Fabian/guerilla approach, the confederacy may well have exhausted the North's resolve. No, it is his tactical innovations for which Lee is remembered.

Put simply, Lee liked to dig, and he made his men dig trenches and bunkers whenever they stopped marching. Earthworks, as we know, were used in the Revolutionary War and had been around for centuries. But Lee combined the use of the environment with rapid decision making, tactical boldness, and excellent command of his lieutenants to give the South a real chance at victory. The result of his Confederate troops being "dug in" was an incredibly effective defensive approach to field combat. The Northern troops that attacked Lee's forces were decimated, repulsed, and forced to dig trenches of their own. Massive entrenchment was a radical innovation, one the European powers neglected to learn and were thus doomed to repeat many times until trench warfare reached its terrible climax in World War I.

The Battle of Chancellorsville in 1863 is considered Lee's masterpiece. The late Richard Holmes, a British historian, described it as "one of the most daring displays of generalship in history."[8] The attacking forces under the command of Union Army Major General Joseph Hooker outnumbered Lee's forces by 2:1. Lee flaunted doctrine by dividing his outnumbered forces not once, but twice, splitting them into three groups during the battle, which lasted several days. On May 1, Lee left one-fifth of his forces in a defensive line at Fredericksburg and marched the main group to check Hooker near the village of Chancellorsville ten miles away. On May 2, Lee split his forces when he dispatched General "Stonewall" Jackson's entire corps around Hooker's southern flank. The move was a tactical success, as was the battle, even though it resulted in the friendly-fire killing of Jackson.

Unlike inventors whose works are appreciated only posthumously, General Lee was revered as a legend in his own time. His approach to war was nuanced, balanced between the extremes of Fabian skirmishing and traditional pitched combat on wide-open plains. He enhanced the use of combat maneuver to add a new kind of dynamism, successfully adopting new capabilities in communications, transportation, and logistics that Northern generals were slower to incorporate.

What is most interesting is Lee's background that led him to be so innovative? He was not an infantryman, or an artilleryman, or a cavalryman. Lee's military training was in engineering, including his first five years of assignments in the army to places such as Cockspur Island, Georgia, and Hampton, Virginia. He spent years after that as an assistant in the chief engineer's office in Washington, which included plenty of fieldwork. In the summer of 1835, Lee helped define the state line between Ohio and Michigan, and in 1837 he supervised the engineering work for the St. Louis harbor. In 1842, the then Captain Lee was assigned to be the post engineer at Fort Hamilton in Brooklyn, New York. These decades of digging made natural for Lee what was unnatural to others: the battlefield can be shaped. And shape he did when the battles came, constantly forcing attacking armies into a battlefield of his own design.

There is some irony in Lee's greatness because of the way he achieved it. First, the fact that Lee was an engineer for most of his career allowed him to understand combat in a way other generals did not. The modern army discriminates against nonoperators when it comes to promotion. For example, in today's army, engineers are explicitly denied the opportunity to compete for four stars. Moreover, Lee was a specialist. His skill base was broadened during the Mexican-American War when Commanding General Winfield Scott brought him into his inner circle of advisers, but mostly Lee's army career was specialized in engineering, not operations. The irony is that today's army forces ambitious officers onto the merry-go-round of operational box checking, leaving little time for technical expertise or specialization of any kind.

Lee, as an entrepreneurial general, is one who learned his craft and skill set, an example of a leader who was "made, not born," and we can learn a great deal about entrepreneurial leadership by studying his military actions. Indeed, there are dozens of other officers we could examine from the Civil War alone to prove the point of this chapter, which is that all successful military officers have an innately entrepreneurial leadership style. For some, such as Lee, their entrepreneurship shows up as innovation and opportunism on a grand scale. But one officer in particular makes a very compelling case for entrepreneurship of a different kind.

Unlike many of the generals on both sides of war, this man was not educated at West Point, nor was he a soldier. He was a 32-year-old professor at Bowdoin College in Maine who didn't think much about joining the war. Then in 1862, after the Civil War had raged for more than a year, this professor was granted a two-year sabbatical trip to study and travel in Europe. Instead, he decided to volunteer to join the Union forces, against the strong protestations of friends, family, and fellow faculty. His name was Joshua Chamberlain, and he embodied the counterexample to Lee. Chamberlain was clearly not made into a great leader but rather born great, though he didn't know it until command was thrust upon him.

Chamberlain set sail with the Twentieth Regiment from Portland, Maine, a few days after volunteering as a lieutenant colonel. He and the Twentieth joined General McClellan's army just before the great Battle of Antietam, though they were kept in reserve. Later that year they saw plenty of action, but missed Chancellorsville because of an outbreak of smallpox in the unit. Two weeks later, in mid-May 1863, Chamberlain was made regimental commander after his commander was promoted. Six weeks later, Chamberlain found himself reinforcing a nearly defeated army at Gettysburg, and this is where his legendary reputation was established.

Chamberlain's Twentieth Maine was part of the Fifth Corps, which had marched some 26 miles on July 1 in order to join George Meade's main force at Gettysburg. They stopped for only three hours that night, from about 1:00 to 4:00 in the morning, then continued until reaching the battlefield early on July 2, 1863. A Union general scouting the area belatedly recognized Lee's forces flanking them on the high ground at Little Round Top and sought any available units to hold it. Colonel Strong Vincent got word from a messenger en route to his commander and ordered his own brigade to march up and hold the area before he received permission. Chamberlain's regiment was one of the four in Vincent's brigade and was tasked to hold the far edge of the line. He sent his B Company into the valley to the east of the hill in order to prevent them from being outflanked, keeping the remaining 358 men with him on high ground. The battle was fierce, and Chamberlain's actions were stunningly effective for a commander in his first year—actions that many historians credit with saving the larger army and thus winning the entire battle.

Aside from his natural calmness under fire, Chamberlain made two additional tactical decisions of note. First, as the heavy engagement began, he shifted his forces into a difficult triangular formation that essentially doubled the front and thinned his ranks to a single file. They "refused the line" for 90 minutes under heavy attack. His second decision was to order a counterattack when he recognized that his men were so short of ammunition that another wave would not be resisted. "Bayonet! Forward!" Chamberlain ordered, and the regiment swept around and pushed the Confederates down the hill and into his B Company, resulting in the capture of the attacking Fifteenth Alabama regiment. Later that evening, Chamberlain volunteered to lead his Twentieth Maine in an attempt to take Big Round Top after a fresh reserve unit commander refused. Chamberlain and his men crept up the hill in the dark, surprising and scaring off the Confederates there.

Chamberlain's entrepreneurial leadership was more Kirzerian (*alertness to opportunities*) and less innovative in the larger sense. He was also resolute, and in this is similar to Stonewall Jackson's dogged persistence in pursuit of a single goal. "What Chamberlain had done reflected not merely courage, but imagination, leadership and tactical gifts of the highest order," writes historian Max Hastings in *Warriors*, a collection of biographies, who noted "this was the achievement of a rank amateur."[9] I like to think that the military brings out the entrepreneurial traits in people that they may not realize they possess.

TWENTIETH CENTURY

Military history from an economic perspective looks different depending on what kind of economic lens one is using. Defense economics is conventionally understood to mean industrial planning and its sister subjects: procurement and appropriations. A macro economist such as Paul Krugman or an economic historian such as Paul Kennedy would see something else. Krugman sees national security as an example of a public good, that which is most efficiently provided by government, and one that serves as an intangible input to overall gross domestic product (GDP) because lower insecurity means more investment. Kennedy sees military power as a projection of a country's underlying economic power, and if allowed to overstretch, a drain on economic growth. But what would an economic forecaster see?

Forecasting is a difficult field, one that works better at identifying micro trends than macro trends. There are just too many variables and too many black swans to anticipate recessions and technology shifts in the macro picture. A forecaster would probably tell us that military history is bound to be filled with sudden, seismic shifts in the nature of war because of technological change. One thing the forecaster would see is an accelerating pace of major technological changes, volatility that now seems apparent in hindsight.

If we were to go back in time and talk to the man who was the secretary of war in 1900, it would be astounding to realize the things he couldn't anticipate in the century ahead. He couldn't know that telegraphs were a harbinger of digital communications technologies such as wireless radio, cryptography, jamming, and microprocessors. He couldn't anticipate human flight, let alone intercontinental ballistics or remotely controlled drones. He surely couldn't anticipate laser range finders or neutron bombs.

That man, interestingly, was named Elihu Root, and though he couldn't see the future, he did see a need for radical reform of the military personnel organization and oversaw major changes during his tenure from 1899 to 1904, including the rotation of staff officers to line[10] and the expansion of military education (including establishing the Army War College). It might be too much a diversion from this chapter to discuss Root's legacy here, as he was a civilian, but we will return to his reforms in later chapters. The point is that technology began shifting dramatically and noticeably at the beginning of the twentieth century. New rifles and pistols were adopted as well as new structures, yet the bigger picture, the strategic picture, remained murky.

One of the officers who did make sense of the global and technological trends of Root's time was a peculiar US Navy officer name Alfred Thayer Mahan. He is described by historian John Keegan as the "most important American strategist of the nineteenth century."[11] Ironically, if one were to have selected the one out of a hundred officers in the Naval Academy's class of 1859 least likely to change grand strategy, Mahan may well have been the man. He was born in West Point, New York, where his father was a professor and dean. According to Philip Crow, he "made more enemies than friends" at the Naval Academy and "had a lonely career as a Navy misfit,"[12] where congeniality was a key to promotion. Finally, Mahan had a lackluster record as a ship captain, marked with numerous accidental collisions, and he remarked after a quarter-century in uniform: "What a beastly thing a ship is, and what a fool a man is who frequents one."[13]

Nonetheless, Mahan impressed a mentor, Stephen Luce, who recruited him in 1885 to lecture at the Naval War College, where Mahan was suddenly appointed president in his first year when Luce was ordered back to operational command. At the college, Mahan was given the opportunity to flesh out his insight that sea power was the essential ingredient in warfare and economic growth at the time. In 1890, Mahan published his magnum opus, the immediately and profoundly influential book *The Influence of Sea Power upon History, 1660–1783*. His ideas were initially controversial, but also quickly adopted by the United States and Britain (where he was the equivalent of a nineteenth-century rock star), as well as Japan and Germany.

The notion that projecting sea power to protect global commerce and deny commercial sea lanes to rivals is commonplace today, but consider the time in which Mahan was writing. Economies were far less integrated in the late nineteenth century, as rail transportation was just then weaving together city economies across regions and continents. The dominant approach at the time is known as "cruiser strategy," or the raiding of enemy ports. Total dominance by large fleets that sought outright destruction of enemy fleets through the use of massive battleships—all of this was radical. But Mahan's insight was apparently inspired by the history of Hannibal's invasion of Roman Italy, which he surmised might have been much easier if done directly via sea, and with the dominance of the Mediterranean for communications and logistics dating back to ancient Carthage.

Although he became famous as an intellectual, there was fierce opposition to his newly invented role as an intellectual in uniform. There were efforts to close down his new college or to merge it into the Academy, but Mahan persevered and "emerged from the obscurity of an undistinguished career to achieve international renown."[14] He was not really a professional historian, more an advocate for his particular vision. In essence, Mahan applied Antoine-Henri Jomini's core principles to the sea, particularly the principle of concentration of forces at decisive points. Ultimately, actual navies validated Mahan's insights, but with some tactical modifications. The Germans, for example, held fast to Mahan's doctrine as if it were scripture, massing huge surface navies that proved less relevant than Mahan imagined with the advent of submarines in disrupting commerce. He also gave short shrift to power projection and amphibious warfare. But it's easy to forget the breakthroughs Mahan did make, even in language, coining the terms "sea power" and "Middle East."

It's fair to say that the military didn't nurture Mahan's entrepreneurial leadership, but that he exemplified this characteristic is important to note. Mahan falls into the "born-not-made" camp, and was a profoundly innovative leader. He was drawn to military service. He fought in his own way for his strategic vision when others, probably the majority of others, wanted to shut his school down. His legacy almost proves the argument of this book in one anecdote: the US military has a history of attracting and giving rise to entrepreneurial leaders despite itself.

One has to wonder if the modern navy would have ever promoted Alfred Thayer Mahan to admiral or given him command of a war college. The military today fosters an aversion to risk, not culturally, but structurally. A blemish on an officer's official record has severely negative consequences. Is it possible to imagine a young officer being promoted today after causing multiple ship collisions? Or take another famous navy officer—young Chester Nimitz—the five-star admiral who commanded the Pacific fleet against Japan in World War II. He was court-martialed for neglect of duty and formally reprimanded for running a destroyer, the USS Decatur, aground in 1907.[15] Thankfully, the navy in the early twentieth century was failure-tolerant in a way the contemporary navy is not.

THE INVENTION OF AIR POWER

The easiest case to be made for defense entrepreneurship is with the creation of the US Army Air Corps, which eventually became the US Air Force during the major post–World War II defense reorganization. The 59-second flight by the Wright brothers' flyer on December 17, 1903, set the stage for one of the most influential inventions ever. What we forget now is that, at the time, few people believed the flight was real. Newspapers refused to publish stories about the flights, and in France the Wrights were infamously libeled as bluffers. The whole array of academic and expert opinion was convinced that heavier-than-air flight was impossible. A few weeks before their Kitty Hawk success, Simon Newcomb of John Hopkins University proclaimed in an article that such a thing was "utterly impossible" unless some new force of nature was discovered.[16] Rear Admiral George Melville, chief engineer of the US Navy, wrote elsewhere that any hope of successful flight was "wholly unwarranted, if not absurd."[17] The federal government had funded manned flights of craft designed by famous scientists, which had flopped, so skepticism was high for Orville and Wilbur Wright, two Ohio bicycle mechanics without a high school education between them, let alone a college degree.

The US military showed no interest in the Wright brothers' flying machines until four years after their initial flight. Since that day, pilots and others drawn to the air services are regarded as romantic dreamers, crazy engineers, and wild blue yonder cowboys. When I interviewed Arthur Herman and asked him who America's great defense entrepreneurs were, he seized at once on a name I confess not having heard before: George Kenney.

Like so many other legendary US Air Force officers, Kenney was a pioneer in the army's Signal Corps. He distinguished himself as a brigadier general in the Pacific during World War II, particularly with his innovative tactical use of bomber aircraft for low-level raids against Japanese warships. Kenney speculated that bombs would skip across the water like skipping stones if dropped fast and low, which they did, increasing the accuracy of ship bombardment overnight.

"The whole history of the Air Force is the story of entrepreneurs, from Billy Mitchell and Hap Arnold and Jimmy Doolittle, to George Kenney and Curtis LeMay," said Herman. Each one of them merits a chapter alone. "LeMay's entire strategy for taking out Japan from the air was probably the biggest and most important strategic decision ever made by a single individual, ever."[18] Alas, in the interest of space, I'll limit my cases to two: General Billy Mitchell and fighter pilot John Boyd.

Billy Mitchell is acclaimed as the father of the air force. He was born in 1879 into a wealthy and powerful family (he was a senator's son), grew up in Wisconsin, and enlisted at age 18 to fight in the Spanish-American War. Like Kenney after him, Mitchell started his service in the Signal Corps. In 1908, he witnessed one of the early demonstration flights by Orville Wright at Fort Myer, Virginia. At age 38, when he was assigned to the Aeronautical Division of the US Army Signal Corps, Mitchell took private flying lessons because the army deemed him too old and high-ranking for its flight training. The highly regarded former general staff officer became fanatical about air power. He eventually was made a brigadier general in command of all US flying forces during World War I, in which he reported directly to General John J. Pershing.

The war made Mitchell famous, not only for his successes in supporting Pershing and his flamboyance, but because of his constant innovations. Mitchell was the first to use aircraft for mass bombardment, and the first to bomb retreating troops. Upon returning home, he began to crusade privately and publicly for an independent air force, a dream that would not be realized for another three decades. Mitchell even proclaimed that air power would eventually make other branches of the military obsolete—meaning the whole army and navy. This advocacy made many enemies (a younger Franklin Delano Roosevelt called his ideas "pernicious"), especially when later field tests proved his claims of air dominance correct.

The full story of Billy Mitchell versus the navy in 1921 is an excellent case study of a red-hot innovator clashing against an entrenched institution. In short, the navy had fudged tests of naval aircraft "bombing" an old battleship and declared the tactic a failure. Word leaked that the navy bombs were nothing more than sandbags, so Congress ordered a full, private set of tests using ex-German vessels from World

War I in early summer. In short, despite Navy efforts to hamstring the bombing effort, Mitchell's bombing tactics sunk numerous ships, most famously the battleship *Ostfriesland*, which went under 22 minutes after the first strike on July 21.

Behind the scenes, the navy maneuvered before the tests began to have Mitchell drummed out of the service, and had even secured the support of the chief of the army Air Corps. Mitchell was simply too vocal. But with so much public support on Mitchell's side, he was shielded. After the sinking of the *Ostfriesland*, Mitchell was relentless. His report was suppressed officially, but it of course leaked to the press. Eventually, Mitchell's aggression went too far when in 1925 he accused senior leaders in the army and navy of incompetence and "almost treasonable administration of the national defense" after a fatal dirigible crash.[19]

Mitchell was court-martialed for insubordination that year. Historian Rebecca Maksel recounts that his defense team emphasized the accuracy and honesty of Mitchell's criticisms. "The prosecution, on the other hand, didn't care if Mitchell's remarks were truthful or not. They were trying him for insubordination."[20] When the nearly two-month trial ended after hearing from 99 witnesses, the court (by secret ballot) declared Mitchell guilty and stripped him of his rank and command authority, as well as giving him a five-year suspension without pay. In a historical side note, a young Douglas MacArthur was one of the dozen officers who sat as a judge, which he later described "one of the most distasteful orders I ever received." MacArthur later said he voted to acquit and furthermore "that a senior officer should not be silenced for being at variance with his superiors in rank and with accepted doctrine."[21]

Today, the two-acre building at the US Air Force Academy in Colorado Springs where cadets eat three meals a day is named Mitchell Hall in honor of the famous insubordinate.

John Boyd's story is in some ways the reverse of Mitchell's. Boyd was inspired at the start by aviation, but used the ideas he learned from air-to-air combat to unlock deep, philosophical secrets in the patterns of human conflict. His influence was so widespread as a military theorist that the Marines honored him at his funeral and a loyal following of defense intellectuals likens him to Sun Tzu.

Unlike Mitchell, Boyd's father wasn't a wealthy US senator, so when he enlisted in the air force at the very end of World War II he actually failed to pass pilot training. Instead, he served in occupied Japan where, unlike Mitchell, he beat a threatened court-martial. Authorities charged him with leading a group of enlistees who tore down old hangars to use as firewood during the freezing winter (while officers lived and slept in covered housing).

When he rejoined as an officer in 1951, Boyd earned his pilot wings and immediately began truly "pushing the envelope." He became downright fanatical about the theory and practice of air combat after flying the F-86 during the Korean War. Biographer Robert Coram reports that "more than one [of his fellow pilots] said they had never seen a man before or since who was so single-minded about aviation."[22] The first decade of Boyd's career involved an obsessive love of flying fighters, maybe better than anyone in the world, but the late 1950s and early 1960s were a time of bomber-pilot dominance in the rigid promotion hierarchy. Fighters were escorts or interceptors, and the ground-support mission was (and for a long time remained) too *army* for a service insecure in its independence. Boyd was undeterred. He was asked to stay on as an instructor at Fighter Weapons School (FWS) at Nellis Air Force Base upon his graduation.

A 1956 article by "high priest" Boyd urged pilot instructors to emphasize maneuver for position rather than standardized weapon-delivery techniques. It was his first foray into formal battle theory, and its effect was as instantaneous as it was electric ("a hot property among fighter pilots,"[23] according to Coram). Boyd stunned his peers when he turned down an offer to join the Thunderbirds, the US Air Force's famous demonstration flying team that he derided as "a goddammed bunch of trained monkeys."[24]

As the FWS head of academics, Boyd rewrote fighter doctrine, pure and simple. While on the job, he taught himself calculus and suddenly saw how to turn the art of dogfighting into a science. After earning a graduate degree from Georgia Tech, he was assigned to Eglin Air Force Base and worked with a civilian mathematician, Thomas Christie, in creating energy-maneuverability (EM) theory. The importance of EM theory cannot be overstated. Coram pithily describes it as a "revolutionary, not evolutionary, way to design aircraft"[25] that isolates an aircraft's performance as the total of kinetic and potential energies and relates those to the object's thrust, weight, drag, wing area, and other characteristics. The theory was dismissed by status-quo experts, but Boyd "stole" computer time at Eglin Air Force Base with Christie to prove it, using all US and Soviet aircraft profiles. Keep in mind, Boyd was such a misfit that the air force bounced him around from job to job doing maintenance and housing assignments, so developing EM was something he did in his *spare time* during evenings and on weekends. It wasn't long after he completed his computer-generated charts that he was briefing his way up to the secretary of the air force and crushing the egos and reputations of bureaucrats and generals along the way. Because a bureaucracy is petty and hostile, there were threats of a court-martial against Boyd and an inspector general investigation of the computer time he had stolen at Eglin, but those in charge really just wanted revenge on the messenger who had discovered something that showed how inferior American fighters were.

"You gotta challenge all assumptions. If you don't, what is doctrine on day one becomes dogma forever after."[26] This is how Boyd describes his approach to saving the air force's troubled F-X fighter program mid-design in the late 1960s. He basically fought against the entrenched engineering elites at Wright-Patterson Air Force Base in Ohio to reshape the project. That aircraft became the giant winged F-15 Eagle, but Boyd was bitterly disappointed with its weight and gold-plated radar and excess gadgetry. He and his allies advocated more successfully for the lightweight F-16 Falcon, F-18 Hornet, even the A-10 Warthog, but those were successes of Boyd the civilian. His military evaluations were unbalanced (immediate commanders damning him as impolitic, higher-ups lauding his integrity and brilliance) and promotions stunted. Boyd began to understand that "while he might do big things, he would never be at the top of Air Force hierarchy."[27]

And yet Boyd's revolutionary contributions were far from complete. Today he is most famous for a massive briefing called the "Patterns of Conflict," which lays out his OODA loop theory in air conflicts. OODA stands for observe, orient, decide and act, meaning that with two adversaries of any size, whether armies or individuals, the victor almost always has a tighter OODA loop and can exploit the lag in his slower opponent.

Boyd was not much of a success in the air force if one simply measures a man by his highest rank, but one final anecdote captures the strength of his ultimate influence: Boyd is the person Secretary of Defense Dick Cheney sought out for advice on the first Iraq War, and it was Boyd who sketched what became the battle plan that started and ended Desert Storm hostilities in one hundred hours.

ARMY DOCTRINE AND WORLD WAR II

During World War II, German generals often complained that US forces were unpredictable: they didn't follow their own doctrine. Nazi leaders anticipated an invasion across the English Channel by studying British and American doctrine, but they soon learned that Americans, at least, don't care for doctrine all that much. As Mike Haynie of Syracuse University explains: "The notion of 'bootstrapping' is a way of life in the military. The military culture is 'mission first' regardless of the resource constraints. I see this mindset play out every day in the context of my work with veterans, as compared with non-veterans."[28]

Colonel Jeff Peterson, a member of the faculty at West Point, likes to illustrate this point using a story about hedgerows. After the Normandy invasion in 1944, American troops found that their movements were constrained by the thick hedgerows that dotted the countryside of Northern France; eight-foot-high walls of dirt, topped by brush, which created a quilted division of farmland. The hedges effectively channeled American units onto roads and thus directly into German ambushes. Sherman tanks were spectacularly ill-equipped to top them without exposing their unarmored bellies. Hedgerows were far too thick to cut through, and using explosives to open a hedgerow was tactically the opposite of surprise, effectively inviting a concentration of fire.

There was no piece of equipment to solve the hedgerow problem, no doctrine, no higher power. In many cultures, the attitude would be to soldier on and deal with the way things were, but not for American GIs. Peterson describes how a group of soldiers of the Second Armored Division's 102nd Cavalry Reconnaissance Squadron "invented a mechanism on the fly that they welded onto the front of a tank to cut through hedgerows."[29] Not only did the welded teeth work, they were designed and implemented by an enlisted man, Sergeant Curtis Culin. More importantly, other units quickly copied the idea, using German roadblocks as the raw material for the cutting device.

Here is a lesson that is easily forgotten in an anecdotal summary of exceptional leaders: *American military entrepreneurship is the norm* up and down the ranks. US troops are famous for the kind of individual initiative displayed by Sergeant Culin. It's a point of pride among officers that the American way of war emphasizes independent judgment in the fog and friction of battle, rather than obedience and rules.

Lieutenants, even corporals and privates, are trained to be entrepreneurial in combat.

The easiest cases to make for the US army's greatest entrepreneurs, aside from the Air Corps, are probably Matthew Ridgway or the great tank commanders George Patton and Creighton Abrams. Even though the main battle tank is named after him, few civilians today know much about Abrams, but he was arguably the best of the military entrepreneurs in World War II. Patton said during the war: "I'm supposed to be the best tank commander in the Army, but I have one peer—Abe Abrams. He's the world champion."[30]

Instead of looking at these "easy" examples, I'll showcase two seeming opposites in demeanor. The first is James Gavin, a prototype of the flamboyant and zealous personality along the lines of Stonewall Jackson and John Boyd. The second is a prototype of the organization man who has cast an undeserved cultural shadow as perhaps the least entrepreneurial of America's famous generals, Dwight D. Eisenhower.

THE PARATROOPER

Paratroopers were a new kind of fighting unit in World War II. Thanks to the development of the airplane, troops were able to parachute behind enemy lines in order to attack from the rear, take a strategic asset or chokepoint such as a bridge, or block enemy reinforcements from reaching the front lines. The soldiers of the Eighty-Second Airborne Division were nicknamed "All-Americans" when the division's first commander discovered he had men from every state in the union, hence the famous "AA" patch worn by its soldiers.

As a study in contrasts between how the army promotes talent now and how it once promoted leaders, we need look no further than the history of the Eighty-Second. Matthew Ridgway commanded the Eighty-Second during its initial combat in Italy and France, and was promoted to command the entire Airborne Division soon after the Normandy invasion. Upon his recommendation, command of the Eighty-Second was awarded to James "Jumping Jim" Gavin, who at age 37 became the youngest two-star general to command a US army division since the Civil War. His story stands in sharp relief compared to the carefully paced careers of officers in today's army.

Born on March 22, 1907, Gavin's mother gave him to an orphanage at the age of two. He enlisted in the army a few days after his seventeenth birthday, eager to escape an unhappy home. Exceedingly bright, Gavin was accepted at West Point into the class of 1929. He did well at the Academy and is described as quiet, shy, ambitious, and adventurous. Gavin chose to branch infantry after being rejected for pilot training, a result perhaps of his mediocre academic performance. In 1940, he returned to the Academy as an instructor and immersed himself in the study of airborne warfare. This was at a time when air tactics were brand new and the Air Corps was a branch within the army. He believed mobility was the key to conflict and volunteered for the new airborne infantry in May 1941, half a year before the United States was attacked at Pearl Harbor. The historian Max Hastings says that "Gavin was always an innovator," and that he "moved heaven and earth" to become part of the new parachute infantry units. In October of 1941, after completing jump school at Fort Benning, Gavin "was drafting the U.S. Army's first manual of airborne warfare."[31]

The extraordinary aspect of Gavin's rise through the ranks is its brevity. When he first volunteered for airborne, he was a senior captain. Three years later, he was a general in command of a combat division that led across Europe. The more we look into his story, the more Gavin emerges as a prototype of the kind of entrepreneur in uniform discussed in chapter 2. He seemed to languish for the first decade as an officer, but the wartime demand for quality officers fueled a dizzying series of promotions.

As for his leadership style, we know a few things for certain. One is that Gavin was entrepreneurial to the point of recklessness, leading by example to a fault in the eyes of some peers when he incessantly put himself in harm's way, even when his high rank required more strategic attention. During the invasion of Sicily in mid-July 1943, Gavin displayed both the innovative and risk-loving qualities of entrepreneurial leadership. That was his first major airborne operation, and an invaluable learning experience for the US military. The parachute drop of then Colonel Gavin's 505th Parachute Infantry Regiment resulted in chaos, with troops scattered so far afield that he later confessed some uncertainty whether he had landed in Italy or the Balkans. When his ragtag operation of roughly 250 assembled troops engaged the Germans at Biazza Ridge on July 11, Gavin attacked. His forces discovered, for the first time, that American bazookas would not penetrate the armor of German tanks. Gavin improvised, and ordered two 75-mm pack howitzers to reorient as forward-firing antitank guns. This is Kirznerian entrepreneurship at its finest (*alertness to opportunities*). The second thing we know is that he eschewed excessive managing. During early assignments with the infantry and in the Philippines, Gavin learned from mentors George C. Marshall and Joseph Stilwell to give brief orders to subordinates, allowing them latitude to execute as necessary.

General Gavin proved far less suited for the postwar army where personal heroics, spontaneous creativity, and flamboyance were irrelevant. He disliked the office politics of the Pentagon. There are clear parallels here to the private sector where some entrepreneurs establish extremely successful new companies but are less adept at managing the companies when they grow larger. Again, the story of Steve Jobs is worth remembering. When he clashed with the CEO in 1985, the board ultimately asked Jobs to leave Apple. Only later in his career did Jobs have a successful "second coming" as the chief executive of Apple.

THE ENGINE OF DESTRUCTION

By way of contrast, Dwight Eisenhower, or "Ike," became so popular as the Supreme Allied Commander in Europe during World War II that both the Republican and Democratic parties recruited him to be their nominee for president after he retired. He chose the Republicans, served two terms as president during the height of the Cold War, and is now perceived as the manifestation of the dull 1950s in contrast to the dynamic Kennedy era in the 1960s. The truth is much more interesting.

Young Eisenhower grew up with five brothers in a humble but loving home. He was a natural leader who played football and also he hit the books. His heroes were George Washington and Civil War general George Meade, and he admired how both men bore maximum responsibility with maximum calm. (Maybe that's because the young man had a problem with his temper, once beating his fists against a tree until they bled when his parents barred him from joining his siblings for Halloween trick or treat.) Accepted at West Point at 21, Cadet Eisenhower earned an outsize number of demerits for his rebelliousness and graduated with a mediocre class rank. Few recognized that his defining quality was a singular enthusiasm and commitment because, during his West Point years, the object of his attention was football. Upon graduation in 1915, Ike gave his full devotion to the US Army.

As a young officer, Ike routinely sought adventure, but was denied. He volunteered to serve under General Pershing's task force to neutralize Pancho Villa, who was terrorizing and killing Americans along the Mexican border, but was denied because his superiors recognized Ike's excellence at training. When America entered the Great War in Europe, Ike requested a transfer to an operational unit, but again his superiors assigned him to a base in Georgia to design a training program for other officers being shipped to Europe. Then in December 1917, when the base was closed, Ike was sent to Fort Leavenworth instead of the front. A formal plea months later was denied and resulted in a verbal reprimand by his commander.

Years later, Ike wrote sarcastically about the events, stating that "a man at a desk a thousand miles away knew better than I what my military capabilities and talents were..."[32] The biographer John F. Wukovits says those years made Ike "suspicious of staff officers who wielded inordinate power over others."[33] Luckily for Ike, his training had impressed a colonel who recommended him to help form a unit at Camp Meade, Maryland, responsible for training men to use the new mobile artillery invention known as the tank. Unfortunately for Ike, he never made it into battle, bouncing around numerous and increasingly important staff roles.

The turning point for Ike came when he was reassigned to Camp Meade and the Tank Corps in 1919, where he was fated to meet and befriend George Patton. Both men believed that the tank was going to be a revolutionary weapon, which "placed them at odds with army doctrine,"[34] according to Wukovits. Eisenhower penned an article for an infantry journal in late 1920 urging the army to change its doctrine and tank design. "The clumsy, awkward and snail-like progress of the old tanks must be forgotten, and in their place we must picture this speedy, reliable and efficient engine of destruction."[35] Amazingly, Eisenhower was so zealous in promoting the tank that the chief of infantry, Major General Farnsworth, threatened him with a court-martial in 1920. Patton received a similar warning, so the pair backed down. Ultimately, tank technology caught up with their vision, and the army did indeed change.

We cannot do justice here to Ike's leadership in World War II, other than to say it was as resolute in destroying the Nazi military as it was exemplary in managing a gigantic logistical, not to mention diplomatic, war effort. It would be too much to claim all of Ike's achievements as entrepreneurial achievements, but it is valuable to remember how innovative he was before, during, and even after the "Great Crusade."

To this day, the largest example of an innovation with a military pedigree is not NASA or positioning satellites but America's interstate highway system, which stretches nearly fifty thousand miles and touches every major American city. President Eisenhower promoted its development and construction after witnessing Germany's autobahn network during the war. He knew that internal mobility along superhighways would add to the army's flexibility and efficiency, particularly if the nation was ever attacked or invaded.

Though seeming polar opposites in style, both Gavin and Eisenhower were incredibly entrepreneurial in their leadership styles and innovated as much as they could within the bureaucratic constraints of the day.

PATTERNS OF INNOVATION

This chapter opened with a summary review of the characteristics of entrepreneurship, and so it is fitting to conclude with a summary review of how academics categorize two fundamental types of innovation: incremental and radical. Both are important, and both are clearly present in the US military.

The most common kind of innovation is *incremental*, and some well-known examples that we touch every day are the car, the airplane, and the ship. Every year, auto companies release new models that are incrementally better in a handful of ways (fuel efficiency, safety features, reliability). One of the great studies of technological change is Louis Hunter's history of the steamboat, because "the story is not, for the most part, one enlivened by great feats of creative genius, by startling inventions or revolutionary ideas. Rather it is one of plodding progress in which invention in the formal sense counted far less than a multitude of minor improvements, adjustments, and adaptations."[36]

The lesson here is something of an answer to the skeptics who might ask why this chapter only seems to celebrate the successful generals. Is every military success an entrepreneurial success? Or is our definition of entrepreneurship so broad that the case being made is tautological? No, the hard evidence of the high prevalence of entrepreneurial evidence was presented in the first chapters. This chapter simply makes the point that it's not just the officers who resign who are entrepreneurial; rather, it is vital that policymakers respect and recognize that the great career officers are fundamentally entrepreneurs. Some might call this the difference between leaders and managers.

The other point is that incremental innovation is constantly happening in the military. The creation of the hedgerow teeth is just one example of the entrepreneurial ecosystem in the military, an ecosystem made possible by encouragement from Pentagon as well as officers in the chain of command. To paraphrase Hillary Clinton, it takes an army to raise a weapons system.

The other kind of change is *radical* innovation. This is when a bicycle manufacturer uses his skills to make a new kind of machine altogether, namely, the Wright brothers' very first airplane. Radical innovations are almost always made by heroic individuals, whereas incremental innovations are almost always faceless and/or corporate. The heroic radicals get all the credit, but it is the incessant innovation of the corporate scientists that fuels most human progress, not to mention innovations driven by dedicated consumers or tinkering laborers.

So an innovation scholar would place Lee squarely in the heroic, radical side of the ledger, perhaps with the tag "field fortification" assigned to his name. Other radical innovations of the Civil War include the invention of the submarine, the use of balloons for reconnaissance, and the Gatling gun, but it also saw countless small innovations including rifling (and its refinement), battlefield medicine, and improvements in telegraphy and railways.

Creativity of this sort is increasingly celebrated by economists who study growth, many of whom now believe that innovation is essentially the only factor that drives long-term increases in per-capita income. "The more inventors we have, the more ideas we discover, and the richer we all are,"[37] writes Stanford professor Charles I. Jones. Since innovation relies entirely on people—or what economists call human capital—academics are showing more appreciation than ever for the early twentieth-century economist Schumpeter and his pioneering focus on entrepreneurship. Entrepreneurs take risks, experiment with new technologies and ideas, and bring about the creative destruction that enables capitalism to flourish.

The culture of rewarding initiative is an invaluable strategic advantage of the United States, and it continues today. What's amazing is how many of the great officers recounted here had to overcome adversity of the military bureaucracy to promote their innovative ideas. How many were threatened with a court-martial for advocating new ideas? There is no reason to think the army, navy, or other services have fewer entrepreneurial leaders now than during the 1940s or 1980s. What we have to ask is whether the services are nurturing those talents? We can be confident that the entrepreneurial culture runs deep in the ranks, but I think the next few chapters will show that the personnel system has become far less supportive of officers willing to color outside the lines.

CHAPTER 4

EXODUS

The increasing mechanization and complexity of defense forces make technical skills and a wide background of experience vastly more important than ever before.... But at this time when we must still maintain large forces under arms and alerted throughout the world, it is difficult to attract and retain volunteers, both enlisted and commissioned.

—President Dwight D. Eisenhower, Special Message to the Congress, January 13, 1955[1]

THE ARMY KNEW IT HAD A PROBLEM AFTER a few years of occupying Iraq, and it wasn't long before the public knew it too. On April 10, 2006, a headline in the *New York Times* announced: "Young Officers Leaving Army at a High Rate" and noted that the retention rate for West Point graduates had collapsed.[2] This was a recurrent problem that the Pentagon had struggled with since at least the end of World War II, although the shift to an all-volunteer force in the 1970s and consequent improvement in the quality of life had, it was thought, solved the problem.

Higher-than-normal attrition rates wouldn't matter so much if it weren't the young Mitchells, Nimitzes, and Eisenhowers quitting, but in the modern military the cream of the crop tend to leave fastest. A series of official army research reports published in 2010 by Major David Lyle and fellow West Point faculty members Casey Wardynski and Michael Colarusso showed higher attrition rates among the army's best junior officers: "[P]rospects for the Officer Corps future have been darkened by an ever-diminishing return on this investment, as evidenced by plummeting company-grade officer retention rates. Significantly, this leakage includes a large share of high-performing officers." They noted that the captain-retention situation had been becoming "untenable"[3] even before the 9/11 attacks in 2001.

Captains in particular were the source of anxiety for army planners, since they were choosing to resign just as their initial commitments were up, leaving behind a smaller class of midcareer officers than was needed. The numbers of officers in each cohort was essentially set in stone because army policy generally "grows its own" from lieutenant to general, and does not allow anybody to join the middle of the ranks. As for the cause of the exodus, which also included captains commissioned through the Reserve Officers' Training Corps (ROTC) at universities, the *Times* pointed to the "end of a burst of patriotic fervor" and the ongoing "burden of deployments" to both Iraq and Afghanistan.

What I'll try to show in this chapter is how severe the exodus was (and still is), but also that the larger problem of bleeding talent cuts deeper than retention of junior officers. We'll look at a number of surveys—including one I conducted for this book—to understand the motivations of departing officers as well as retained officers. These surveys also provide recommendations for a personnel system that can improve the military. I'll also explain what makes these survey results scientifically valid, which is the knee-jerk objection to studies critical of the status quo, especially surveys of active duty attitudes the generals prefer to pretend aren't representative. In the end, the exodus is a symptom of a larger problem, one that might even seem to be lessening as the wars draw down. The reality is that bad human-resource policies damage the military from the first day an officer pins on bars and long after that officer resigns.

CAPTAINS AND COLONELS

Matt Kapinos was one of half a dozen cadet regimental commanders in the class of 2001 and graduated near the top of his class at West Point. For that class in particular, the attacks of 9/11 will forever hold a special meaning. No American will ever think back on that year and forget what happened, much less anyone in the military. Like the infamous attacks on Pearl Harbor in 1941, the al Qaeda master minded suicide hijackings that destroyed the Twin Towers and a full wing of the Pentagon marked 2001 as a year of war.

Lieutenant Kapinos was assigned to the Eighty-Second Airborne, the unit led by Jack Gavin in World War II. In early 2003, he was leading a platoon of 40 men in Afghanistan. After a brief rotation home where he was reunited with his young wife, the newly promoted Captain Kapinos was commanding a company of nearly two hundred soldiers in Iraq. Andrew Tilghman described Kapinos's story in an excellent essay called the "Army's Other Crisis," which was published in the *Washington Monthly* in 2007:

> In Afghanistan, [Kapinos] had suggested that instead of merely conducting nighttime raids, his men should camp in small villages to help local leaders root out insurgents and their sympathizers. His commanders repeatedly rejected the idea. In Iraq, he was full of similarly innovative proposals, but felt his commanders disregarded his input. "After a while, you just stop asking," he said.
>
> ... Kapinos, however, is no longer in the Army. Fifteen days after his initial five-year service agreement expired, he left military life entirely. When I met him, it was near the downtown campus of the Georgetown University Law Center, where he was taking a break from classes on corporate income tax law. Tall and fit, with close-cropped sandy brown hair and a green cable-knit sweater, he resembled both the lawyer he is preparing to be and the Army captain he once was. "I was a true believer at West Point. When Afghanistan kicked off, I don't want to say I bought the propaganda, but I wanted to change the world," he said. "I thought I was going to be a four-star general."[4]

Tilghman argued that the strain of the Iraq War, visibly depreciating the military's equipment, was at the same time invisibly depreciating its human capital. Looking back on that story after five years (and a relatively successful conclusion to the Iraq War), I wonder if something may have been missed by Tilghman and others in the media. Captains are only half of the story, the superficial half; these are young warriors in harm's way with young spouses and toddlers back home. The more nuanced and more important other half of story is about the colonels.

Getting a great first assignment after commissioning is essential in climbing the ladder, especially given the nature of army promotions. When merit is all but erased from formal metrics, soldiers need to check exactly the right boxes—get the right jobs, go to the right professional schools on time, earn "distinguished graduate" from those schools—to prove themselves. And getting into the infantry, armor, or other combat-arms branches is considered important. If one is "going infantry," the ideal path is to get light but not too light. Specialized units such as the US Navy SEALs or the army's Delta Force might be too far off the beaten path (too light), whereas mechanized infantry might be a shade too heavy.

Like Kapinos, Dick Hewitt graduated near the top of the class from West Point. And also like Kapinos, his first assignment was with the legendary Eighty-Second Airborne Division at Fort Bragg, North Carolina. Hewitt, like Kapinos, also decided to leave the army a few years after the 9/11 attacks. But here's the difference: Hewitt had served a full 20-year career. He had checked all the right boxes, even getting tapped to command a battalion when he was just a major. So when Hewitt decided to leave, it was not because the army had a minor morale problem causing retention heartburn, but rather it was because of a deeper and more nuanced institutional dysfunction.

"I can still remember how he first impressed all of us during a platoon attack exercise that he commanded one night," remembers[5] Brigadier General Wayne Grigsby about the time they met at the infantry officer basic school (IOBC). "His charisma, his intellect, the way he carried himself, the way he commanded his soldiers, his physical prowess, the way he worked with his peers—I have never seen a finer leader in my 28 years of service and 50 months in combat. I thought I'd be working for Dick by now and was sure he was going to be wearing two or three stars, easy." Although the path to general is a narrow one, Hewitt did everything the army asked and more to stay out front, getting all the right jobs and impressing peers and subordinates along the way. So what happened that got him put onto the Personnel Command (PERSCOM) black list?

In the summer of 1980, Hewitt was a freshman at West Point. He graduated with the class of 1984 during the height of the Cold War, and was promoted to captain exactly four years later, just like everyone else in his year group. Hewitt's second assignment was a one-year tour of duty as the battalion maintenance officer for the 1–5 Infantry Mechanized, Second Infantry Division. A year later, Hewitt was given a company command at Fort Ord, California. Next, he was sent to the University of Chicago's Graduate School of Business, followed by a two-year assignment as a professor of economics back at West Point's famous Sosh department. At some point, he was selected a year before his peers for promotion to major. After a year of advanced military training at the Command and General Staff College (CGSC) at Fort Leavenworth, Kansas, Hewitt was sent "home" to Fort Bragg where he checked all the boxes: one year on division staff, one year as battalion ops officer, and so on. This is where his story gets interesting.

At that moment, Major Hewitt was a prime candidate to serve as a general officer someday, maybe even lead the army if he played his cards right. He had been tapped for promotion to lieutenant colonel (known as "major P" for "promotable"), and now awaited the outcome of the army's boards—formal committees of senior officers who rank-order officers in the zone for battalion command openings in the coming year. This is a cohort of lieutenant colonels and a few major Ps all across the army. In November 1999 a personnel officer visited Bragg and told Hewitt that he was a "fifty-fifty" for one of the openings, which actually meant it was a sure thing. The officer was the chief of the section that doled out jobs for PERSCOM, then located in the Hoffman building in Washington, DC. In reality, Hewitt was again at the top of the list. Of all the battalion command positions the army awards each year, the top ones are given to tactical officers. Hewitt was one of those, and he was a year younger than others in the year group. Once the list was announced in early 2000, buzz around the army and congratulations rolled in.

The next step for the selected officers—there were 16 that year for light/airborne/air-assault infantry commands—was to submit a list of their preferences to PERSCOM. The staff at the Hoffman building would sort through the preferences in order to produce an optimized match, a process known as "slating." Hewitt submitted his preferences, ranking the 16 options from first to last with a remote tour of duty in South Korea ranked last. He told the officers at Hoffman over the phone that the Korea job in particular would be hard on his family. With two preschool sons and another little one on the way, the separation required by the Korea assignment might be more than the family could bear. "It will not be well received in my house," he bluntly told the assignments officer. Now it was in the hands of the planners at PERSCOM to slate the officers and issue orders through the acquiring commanders.

As you might guess, a few weeks passed, and then Hewitt received a phone call. It was Major General Dees, calling from South Korea. "Congratulations, Dick. Welcome to the team."

Hewitt said all the right things on the phone that day and even accepted the first month of command training at Fort Benning in Georgia before realizing the outcome just wasn't acceptable. He had two conversations with senior officers after slating to see if there was any flexibility in the process to change the assignment—maybe he could trade with someone?—and was told it was a done decision.

In a move that sent tremors through the army, Hewitt called the planners at the Hoffman Building and declined command. The staffer on the other end of the phone was surprised and calmly warned: "Do you understand that this means your record will be marked 'declination with prejudice'?" He offered Hewitt 24 hours to think it over. Not necessary, Hewitt answered. In his mind, it was a choice between career suicide and tearing apart his young family.

Even though he seemed destined for high rank, that one clash with the inflexible army personnel system essentially ended his career after 15 flawless years. Hewitt committed no crime, disappointed no commander, and lost the faith of none of his troops. In fact, his career was flying high when he made the mistake of asking for a one-year reprieve from the fast track.

Today, Hewitt is a successful entrepreneur. He presides over a small, thriving financial firm in Carmel, California. "I can control my own destiny and work with partners I trust." His partner is Jerry Lidzinski, a 1995 graduate of the Air Force Academy. Hewitt made a vow after retiring from the army never to work for someone else, where he was not in control.

The story of Hewitt's departure from the army has two footnotes.

First, in early 2000 he received a phone call from the Pentagon. The chief of staff of the army, General Eric Shinseki, was having a bad year because, among other things, dozens of officers had declined battalion command. Hewitt wasn't alone. In armor, engineers, infantry, and aviation, all the branches were suffering from high rates of dissatisfaction with the command slating. So Hewitt and others like him were invited to the Pentagon to give feedback to the vice chief, General Jack Keene. Questions were asked, data collected, and the day ended. As Hewitt changed into civilian clothes for his flight home, another officer asked what assignment he had turned down.

"Korea."

"Funny," said the other officer. "My wife is from Korea. I would have loved that job."

The irony here is painful.

Second, consider what the army did with Hewitt afterward. In mid-2000, Hewitt had only one year left at Bragg, then three years before he could retire with the standard twenty-year military pension. He had an MBA from one of the top schools in the nation, so it was a no-brainer for the dean of West Point, Dan Kauffman, to bring him to campus as the director of the economics program. While at West Point, Hewitt impressed the superintendent, General William Lennox, who asked him to stay for another four or more years as permanent faculty. Hewitt agreed. Lennox sent a letter to Hoffman asking for them to "rebranch" Hewitt in strategic plans, making official what was already the unofficial end of his infantry career. The commandant of cadets Leo Brooks sent a letter of support, as did the dean.

At that time in 2004, the folks at PERSCOM understood fully that Hewitt had no further obligation to stay in uniform, and that if he was not allowed to rebranch, he could simply retire. But in their records, his file was stamped with a bright red "declination with prejudice." So the story ends this way: Hewitt's wife received a letter from PERSCOM while he was teaching classes at the Academy, so she called him during his free hour and read him the jargon-filled letter over the phone. It explained that the needs of army prevented his rebranching.

"What does that mean?" she asked.

"It means we're retiring," he said.

In May 2004, at the age of 42, Lieutenant Colonel Dick Hewitt left the army, driving out the same gates at West Point that he had entered more than two decades before. The last five years that concluded Hewitt's career are what I refer to as internal bleeding.

THE RETENTION CRISIS

All cadets who graduate from the US Military Academy commit to serve a minimum of 5 years as a military officer, after which they can resign their commissions or continue on, presumably toward the full 20-year career. Retirement is available to everyone who serves 20 years or more, which means half of one's monthly pay for the rest of one's life, plus full benefits. A few cadets agree to longer commitments (2–5 additional years) in exchange for graduate school or flight training.

When the US Military Academy (USMA) class of 1999 reached its five-year mark in 2004, 72 percent of the graduates chose to stay in uniform, and 28 percent resigned. This net retention rate sends a signal about the overall health of the junior officer corps, and 2004 was an early warning sign compared to the normal range of 75–80 percent. A year later, the retention rate dropped again to slightly less than 66 percent, the highest departure rate in 16 years. Not since the end of the Cold War had so many young officers left the service after their initial commitment. In the late 1990s, junior officers were being asked to leave, but by 2005 the military was begging them to stay.

While all branches of the military experienced challenges, only the army was in crisis. According to a March 2007 story in *USA Today*, the retention rate of West Point graduates was "as much as 30 percentage points lower than the rates for graduates of the Navy and Air Force academies."[6] A common complaint was that the elitist Academy graduates were the problem, not the army per se, since ROTC and Officer Candidates School (OCS) officers remained at high rates, but that's a myth. Retention problems afflicted ROTC *scholarship* officers even more than West Point graduates. The 2010 Strategic Studies Institute monograph by Colonel Casey Wardynski, Major David Lyle, and Michael Colarusso (the Wardynski monograph) analyzed the retention of officers in the 1996 cohort by commissioning source. While it is true that the percentage of West Pointers in the class of 1996 drops dramatically at the five-year point (from 90 to 60 percent), it must also be said that OCS officers started the year at 70 percent. And while the USMA rate declined steadily to 41 percent at the eight-year mark, this mirrored the ROTC officers who had three-year scholarships, and was higher than the 35 percent eight-year retention of four-year ROTC scholarship officers.[7]

I faced similar skepticism about West Point elitism after presenting my survey of 250 West Point grads—but the Wardynski monograph made it clear that the exodus was as real as it was widespread. But the puzzle as to why remained. As author Wardynski asked: "How did the [the Army] move from a senior captain surplus, then to shortage, then to crisis in the decade following the end of the Cold War?"[8] A report by the Government Accountability Office (GAO) in January 2007 provided even more details:

The Army, which continues to be heavily involved in combat operations in Iraq and Afghanistan, faces many retention challenges. For example, the Army is experiencing a shortfall of mid-level officers, such as majors, because it commissioned fewer officers 10 years ago due to a post–Cold War force reduction. It projects a shortage of 3,000 or more officers annually through FY 2013. While the Army is implementing and considering initiatives to improve officer retention, the initiatives are not integrated and will not affect officer retention until at least 2009 or are unfunded. As with its accession shortfalls, the Army does not have an integrated strategic plan to address its retention shortfalls.[9]

There were many reasons for the crisis, but the explanation that seems most obvious is the ongoing wars in the Middle East. As Tilghman wrote, the exodus was sending "alarming warnings about the strain that the Iraq War has placed on the military."[10] Remember that late 2006 to early 2007 was the lowest point in the war. The Bush administration was starting to admit what troops on the ground had been saying all along: the strategy in Iraq was not working. In the words of Colonel Jeff Peterson, now a permanent member of West Point's faculty: "We were losing in Baghdad in 2006. We were *losing*. The enemy was winning. It had to change."[11]

Relying on a volunteer force is challenging, especially when the economy is strong (meaning demand for talent is high), but even more so during a conflict that the public dislikes. That's all the more reason to think carefully about the intertwining issues. Peterson wasn't saying that the war or the volunteer force was the source of retention and recruiting woes. He was simply commenting on the nature of fighting an insurgency. Peterson, like almost all officers, supports the all-volunteer force and he also disagrees with characterizations of the personnel system as being in crisis. The news media, however, found the war explanation too convenient.

Here's the catch. None of the war explanations can explain why retention problems *preceded* the 9/11 attacks. In a 2002 RAND report, James Hosek and Beth Asch "identified a roughly 5 percent decline in officer annual continuation rates among those [officers] in their midcareer." The authors argued that the number is deceptively small, but "small declines in annual continuation rates can translate into dramatic declines in manpower over a several-year period. Therefore, this decline must be taken seriously."[12] Likewise, Wardynski et al. argued that declining retention has been a problem since 1983 and that "by 2001 the captain retention situation was becoming untenable."[13]

In fact, the army has been plagued with talent bleeding for decades, and its personnel practices have never been reformed to address the problem.[14,15] President Harry Truman appointed a committee to consider the problem in 1949, and the secretary of defense asked the Brookings Institution's Harold Moulton to do the same in 1950. Two more task forces were commissioned early in the Eisenhower administration, calling attention to an annual retention rate of enlistees of just 20 percent. Then in 1954, after the Korea hostilities stopped, the Senate Armed Services Committee called attention to the "critical and delicate" problem of the officer brain drain. Arthur Coumbe, a military historian, attributes the severity of the competency weaknesses in the officer corps to the centralization of command and control in the 1960s. Regardless, retention rates simply collapsed late during the Vietnam conflict, down to 34 percent for OCS officers in 1969 and 11 percent for ROTC officers in 1970. All this goes to show that the current crisis has a long precedent.[16]

RAND Corporation's Hosek produced another study in 2006 that examined the "unprecedented strains on the all volunteer force" to identify the causes behind the most recent exodus.[17] The study was comprehensive in scope, reviewing published literature and surveys of military personnel conducted by the Defense Manpower Data Center (DMDC), as well as original focus groups of active-duty service members. What Hosek found was the deployments alone were a positive, not a negative, factor in retaining soldiers. Service members valued deployments as an opportunity to participate in an activity and mission that they believed in and that also enhanced their career prospects; however, the frequency and duration of deployments were weighing negatively on soldiers. "High op tempo" is the phrase used to describe the high demands on soldiers' time—long hours of work every day with few days truly off. Wartime means there is immense stress placed on soldiers, but also on their families, with troops facing mental fatigue or worse from multiple deployments.

Now, half a decade after the crisis broke into the public's consciousness, the matter may seem resolved. Already history. The war is over, so we can forget about how hard it was, right? That would be an error.

Bleeding talent still happens every day in the army, Marines, air force, navy, and coast guard. It happens in peacetime as well as wartime. The talent that was lost and mismanaged during the Iraq War will have consequences for decades to come, and the unresolved dysfunction in the personnel system is likely to get worse if the armed forces use force-shaping techniques based on seniority instead of merit. A potential drawdown in the years ahead must draw lessons from what caused the midwar manpower malfunction.

THE WEST POINT SURVEY

In 2010, I conducted a survey of the West Point graduates from the classes of 1989, 1991, 1995, 2000, 2001, and 2004, and highlights were featured in *The Atlantic* magazine in early 2011. Before the article appeared, I was able to brief the survey's results to officers and key policymakers in Washington, DC, during the fall of 2010. I incorporated feedback from those sessions into a second part of the survey.

An email solicitation to each member of class was sent from a fellow graduate who serves as the class scribe. The initial survey (Part One) was conducted from late August through mid-September of 2010 using an online survey tool. A total of 250 individuals completed the survey. Of those respondents 78 (31 percent) were on active duty. A follow-up survey (Part Two) was created based on their comments and feedback, sent to the initial 250 respondents in mid-September, and completed by 126 of them by the October deadline.[18]

Survey—Part One

The first question asks: "Do the best officers leave the military early rather than serving a full career?" The survey did not define "best" or "early" in an effort to ensure that respondents would not bracket the question in terms of external criteria (e.g., I might have framed it as the "most entrepreneurial leaders," while other scholars might frame it in terms of effectiveness, inspiration, management excellence, and so on. I thought a neutral framing was the least biased). Only 7 percent of respondents believed that most of the best officers stay in the military. Among the active-duty respondents, only 17 percent believed that most of the best officers are staying in the military. Younger graduates were more negative than older. It must be said that the 45 percent of responses held that "about half the best leave," and another 45 percent held that "MOST of the best leave, some stay."

One respondent wrote in the optional comments box: "Good leaders, those with entrepreneurial tendencies, are crushed by the military in spirit and in deed. I think this type of leader is attracted to the military, and during their [*sic*] personal growth stage, do well. But they soon 'outsmart' the norm and become frustrated by the confines of their senior leaderships' boundaries." Another wrote, "The best junior officers have spent 8 years doing more work for the same pay as their peers who contribute only the bare minimum. There is no system to reward the best officers prior to the BZ [i.e., 'below the zone' or one year early] Major board at 8 years of service." These were comments made before the respondents saw other questions about entrepreneurial values and personnel-specific questions.

The second question asked respondents to compare military and civilian promotions systems on a one–ten scale of merit versus seniority. The results were significant by any technical metric, with a plurality giving the private sector a three and the US military an eight. This view holds, albeit less strongly, when the sample is limited to active-duty officers. Younger cohorts tend to view the military as less of a meritocracy, but all respondents give the private sector similar scores on average.

Attitudes were consistent in the comments, along the lines of: "In the civilian world, my performance is all that matters. There are no year groups. For the most part, a promotion is based on talent, not seniority. The year group system is one of the most asinine things the Army uses." Other comments pointed to the biased nature of top-down evaluations that skewed promotions, not to meritorious behavior aimed at productivity or mission, but that support the immediate rater in the chain of command. A final factor was that promotions had become less meritorious once the seniority system cracked under such low retention rates, meaning officers were pulled up to captain and major faster than the norm out of a need for warm bodies more than as a reward for their competence. In short, the top-down structure had no native capacity to handle scarcity, which is exactly what markets do.

Next, the survey asked respondents to grade, on an A–F scale, various aspects of the military in terms of fostering "innovative and entrepreneurial" leadership. As a benchmark, the raw talent (recruitment) received 55 percent As and Bs, the fourth highest. The other aspects can be understood in terms of this ratio as either improving or degrading the initial entrepreneurial talent. In general, formal training programs received average marks, including everything from service academies and war colleges to initial through senior officer training. Even doctrine received good marks. The weakest factors were all in the personnel system: evaluations (with an AB/DF ratio of 0.6), job assignments (0.5), promotions (0.4), and compensation (0.3). For example, only 8 out of 250 respondents gave the job-assignment system an A grade, compared to 39 who gave it an F. While these various personnel systems may serve other army missions, they are perceived as failing to promote entrepreneurial leadership.

An active-duty colonel recommended that I add a question to assess the culture of innovation at the unit level, in contrast to the larger organization. Brilliant idea, and he was right. More than two-thirds of respondents agreed (18 percent agreeing strongly) with the statement: "Creative thinking and new ideas are(were) valued in your military units." This is a powerful finding that army culture and army soldiers are innovative and entrepreneurial, which is exactly what the talent paradox was claiming. One respondent summarized the dilemma with some additional color: "For the most part, creative thinking is valued, but there is only so much leeway given the crushing hand of the Army regulatory system and the constant turnover of leadership at all levels."

The last question on the survey is the most direct exploration of why soldiers had left the military. Since this question speaks so directly to the subject of this chapter, I'll present the full results in table 4.1.

Table 4.1 What were the reasons you left the military? Agree or disagree if they were important reasons for your decision.

	Strongly Agree (%)	Agree (%)	Disagree (%)	Strongly Disagree (%)
Frustration with military bureaucracy	50	32	16	2
Family	57	24	15	5
Other life goals	35	45	15	5
Higher potential income	45	35	14	4
Frequent deployments	31	32	30	4
Limited opportunity in military	17	40	32	10
Pace of military promotions	22	31	39	7
Weak role models/commanders	24	22	35	19
Higher education	20	25	45	9
Better leadership opportunity	7	25	53	14
Retirement age (20 years+)	5	6	44	44
Medical discharge	2	4	25	68

Four reasons stand out as the most frequently cited by officers in explaining why they left the ranks. High op tempo during war, other life goals, and family income all play a role. But even then—during wartime—the top reason this panel cited for leaving the military is frustration with military bureaucracy, with 82 percent agreeing and 50 percent agreeing strongly.

Survey—Part Two

The nice way to introduce this section is this: Part Two of the survey was developed in response to feedback based on private presentations of the initial results. A more honest introduction would say: The initial impact of my West Point survey was tremendous, including some very high-level briefings at the Pentagon; however, there was some very aggressive pushback. Incredibly, one full colonel reacted to my presentation of the results of Part One by saying that the findings were unimportant. To paraphrase, he said: "Sure, you've described the personnel system, which has pluses and minuses like any system. But your results don't claim any harm to national security, and I think you're overinterpreting your poll results." I decided a few weeks later to extend the survey with Part Two. An email message was sent directly to the initial 250 respondents, and 126 of those individuals engaged in the follow-up.

The questions in Part Two were very direct, but I felt they had to leave no room for misinterpretation. The very first question, presented in table 1.1 presented in the first chapter, explores some of the specific potential dangers posed by bleeding talent. Only one-fifth of active-duty respondents (18 percent) think the military does a good job matching talents with jobs, and the same number thinks the army is weeding out the weakest leaders. The final option asks whether the personnel system should be radically reformed, something we asked as a contrast with common calls for incremental change, and 55 percent of respondents agree.

It was seen that 78 percent of all respondents (and 78 percent of active-duty respondents) agree that *the current exit rate of the best officers harms national security,* while 65 percent (68 percent among active duty) agree that *it leads to a less competent general officer corps.* Typical responses in conversations about military retention are that high turnover is normal in the contemporary US economy and that high attrition rates are normal in the "up or out" military rank structure. While turnover may be high, turnover of *top* talent is the issue under scrutiny in this survey.

I also asked a new question about the causes of attrition. Recall the question in Part One was directed in a very personal way ("What were the reasons *you* left the military?" rather than "What are the top reasons *some* officers leave the military?"), which runs the risk of getting feedback that dodges self-criticism. Although anonymity was promised to all respondents, I decided to ask a more general question using the language: "Many of the best officers who leave the service would stay if..." Of the respondents 90 percent agreed that the best officers would be more likely to stay if "the military was more of a meritocracy." There was overwhelming support for other core principles as well, including if "job assignments were matched with a market mechanism instead of central planning" (87 percent), if "the military had a more entrepreneurial personnel system" (88 percent), and if "pay was based on performance instead of time in service" (70 percent). A few other options had far less support, so personnel flexibility really did seem to dominate the perceived causes of high attrition, but I offered one catch-all option just to confirm the departing officers weren't simply headed for the exits no matter what. Only 30.6 percent of respondents agreed that many of the best officers would leave "regardless of reforms to the personnel system."

THE DREGS WHO REMAIN

On January 4, 2011, *The Atlantic* published the findings in the essay "Why Our Best Officers Are Leaving," a modified version of the first chapter of this book. Within hours, the essay went viral among US Army officers worldwide and then troops from all the services. It was reprinted in the influential "Early Bird" daily clippings distributed around the Pentagon. Within a few days, many military blogs had their own reactions,[19, 20] each with dozens of comments. Nothing I'd ever written had caught fire like this, and I received hundreds of letters, including a long, carefully typed letter from a World War II veteran who lamented that nothing had changed since his time. One email from Iraq stands out in my mind, as it represents the level of frustration that apparently my essay had given voice to:

> I read your article in the Atlantic Monthly and could have cried tears of joy. I am a prior enlisted 1LT and have 11 years in service. I was a Distinguished Military Graduate through the ROTC, quantified top 10% in every military course I attended

and deployed to Iraq for a total of 39 months. I have chosen to leave the Army due to [*sic*] their inability to assess talent. The only way to affect change is to publicize a need for it and circumvent the obdurate system.

Respectfully,
Name Withheld

QUESTIONING THE SURVEY'S VALIDITY

The *Defense Media Network* published a major story on the survey by Eric Tegler on February 25, 2011.[21] Tegler requested an interview with US Army Human Resources Command and with army headquarters, but those were declined; however, he was able to interview Colonel Thomas Collins, chief spokesman for Army Public Affairs. Collins, speaking for the army, questioned the survey's validity and dismissed the idea of a more flexible assignments system. "I'm not sure that a survey of only 250 people is enough to make such a sweeping judgment. Personally, I simply don't believe the best are leaving." Collins also claimed that the "battle-tested force" serving in Iraq and Afghanistan proves my underlying premise wrong.

Questioning the validity of the survey is a powerful point, and seems to be about the only serious objection I face, so let me be clear. According to the fourth edition of the textbook *Survey Research Methods* by Floyd J. Fowler Jr., the goal of a sample survey is to accurately describe the underlying population. As Fowler notes, there are a handful of ways that a survey can produce flawed results. *Margin of error* is what the lay public assumes is the big issue. *Sample quality* is another concern. But the biggest factor is *question design*.

I chose for my sample to target officers who were produced from only one commissioning source: the United States Military Academy, including classmates who were on and off active duty. Critics imply this is a biased source, but subsequent surveys that include officers from other commissioning sources have confirmed my findings.

Furthermore, I narrowed the target population to officers who served during a period of time that was generally consistent and relevant, graduating between the years 1989–2004. Why not older graduates? Mixing attitudes of officers who served in the 1970s or 1980s with those serving today would mix apples and oranges. If the sample included older officers, critics would no doubt say their experiences were irrelevant to today's military.

What about sheer size? Two hundred and fifty people may seem unrepresentative, but it's actually in the same ballpark of national surveys that use three or four hundred respondents to measure the attitudes of the entire nation. My West Point survey had a maximum *margin of error* of 6.2 percent at 95 percent confidence. So when 93 percent of army officers in my survey say that most of the best officers leave the military, statistics says the lowest the number could be for the full population is "only" 87 percent of all army officers agreeing.[22]

Let's turn now to *question design*. Solid statistical bona fides are no seal of approval. Surveys that report a small margin of error are easily corrupted with poorly designed questions or by flawed sample recruitment. For example, a widely reported Zogby poll was found to use deeply flawed question design, but not until after it garnered massive media attention questioning the US military effort in the Middle East. In early 2006, Zogby asked an anonymous sample of deployed US troops about the war in Iraq, which the media cited widely with the headline "72 Percent of Troops Say It's Time to Leave Iraq."[23] The actual survey question asked how long the United States should *stay*, not *leave*, but three of the four answers were phrased in terms of when to *withdraw*, and then those responses were summed up as a majority opinion. The only other option: stay indefinitely.

The design of my questions was intentionally neutral in the sense that each question either offered a balanced response set (with an equal number of positive and negative response options) or a mix of positive and negative statements that an individual could agree with. No one, in fact, has suggested the questions were designed poorly. What is most telling is that defenders of the status quo who objected to my survey have put forth no facts or studies claiming attitudes of the soldiers or commanders are different. There has been no counterpoint. Instead, what has emerged is a chorus of support from voices including, to my surprise, Secretary of Defense Robert Gates.

FALK-ROGERS

Other studies of service members' attitudes seem to support or echo my West Point study. In its 2011 annual survey, the Center for Army

Leadership at Fort Leavenworth reported numerous frustrations among army leaders, a group that included officers, warrant officers, and senior noncommissioned officers (NCOs).[24] Only 38 percent agreed that "the Army is headed in the right direction," which was unchanged from 2006. Of those who thought it was heading in the wrong direction, the second most-cited reason (by 58 percent of the subset) was the army's inability to retain quality leaders. About one-fourth (24 percent) of army leaders believe that honest mistakes are held against them in their unit/organization, while one-third (30 percent) believe that their unit/organization *promotes* a zero-defect mentality (emphasis added).

In March 2011, a pair of graduate students at Harvard's John F. Kennedy School published a survey that was very similar to mine. Sasha Rogers and Sayce Falk (a Marine veteran who served in Iraq) reached out to former junior military officers from the army, navy, Marines, and air force who had left the service between 2001 and 2010. They recruited their sample with the goal of including a proportional number of ROTC and OCS officers, and did so by reaching out through ROTC university alumni networks, graduate-school military organizations, and other veterans groups. While this approach assured a diversity of recently active junior officers (all respondents were O-2 through O-4), the lack of active-duty participants might have tainted the results. To counter such potential bias, Falk and Rogers also surveyed a group of 30 active-duty junior officers across the services. The executive summary states:

> Fully 80% of our respondents reported that the best officers they knew had left the military before serving a full career. Yet some factors widely portrayed as driving young officers from service were less important to our junior officer cohort than we anticipated. For instance, only 9% of respondents indicated that deployment cycles and operational tempo were their most important reason for leaving. In the same vein, nearly 75% ranked compensation and financial reasons as their least important consideration.
>
> What does matter? Two factors emerged as areas of surprising consensus among former officers: organizational inflexibility, primarily manifested in the personnel system, and a lack of commitment to innovation within the military services.[25]

Specifically, Falk and Rogers found that "the number one reported reason for separation among our respondents was limited ability to control their own careers." The active-duty component was no more forgiving of the personnel system, with a majority agreeing that the personnel system does not do a good job of "matching talent to jobs (75%) or weeding out the weakest leaders (82%)."[26]

Another surprising feature of the Falk-Rogers study was the confirmation that deployments and high op tempo were not decisive factors. As the authors put it:

[L]ess than 7% indicated that deployment strain was their most important reason for leaving. This tends to reinforce the argument that deployment, even with combat, is not a primary driver of attrition among junior officers. Nearly three-fourths of the junior officers we surveyed commissioned during or after 2001, suggesting that not only did they understand they would deploy and see combat, but in fact that was precisely *why* they joined."[27]

REACTION

The army's initial reaction to the exodus was slow. Bleeding talent had been the norm for decades, and furthermore the army was in the middle of two very difficult wars. As Falk and Rogers point out: "By 2007, the Army was predicting a total shortfall of over three thousand officers, particularly in the crucial senior captain and major range."[28]

Once it realized the problem, the Pentagon reacted like a bureaucracy typically does: It threw money at the problem using generic one-size-fits-all cash bonuses, offered to any officer who would stay, while the management system itself remained unchanged. The aforementioned studies demonstrate this bandaging of the wound rather than addressing the underlying causes of the problem. "Although it now appears as if the Army has righted its ship when it comes to retaining the right number of officers, it did so largely by filling shortages via across-the-board promotions to field-grade officer rank,"[29] wrote Falk and Rogers. "Less than 85% of available billets at those ranks were filled by officers with the requisite rank and time in service—a critical shortfall, by the Army's own definition—and today's senior lieutenants and junior captains spend less time than ever before in critical development positions such as company command."[30]

The money throwing took the form of a 2007–2008 program called CSRB, which stands for critical skills retention bonus. It offered lump-sum payments ranging from $25,000 to $35,000 in exchange for three additional years of service commitment. Wardynski and colleagues called it "counter to the sound market principles that should underpin any retention policy."[31] CSRB cost the taxpayers half a billion dollars, with scant evidence that it improved retention. The flaw with such programs is that most of the recipients were planning to stay in uniform anyway.

By addressing its quantity problem—not enough captains—the army's cure had a side effect in terms of exacerbating its quality problem. It suspended forced distribution ratings for lieutenants and captains in 2004 because by identifying its weakest young officers, it would risk losing them. But by keeping them, and in a sense hiding them from future commanders and themselves, the effect on peer officers was lower morale and thus retention of the best and brightest. Wardynski warned: "By promoting and advancing officers who previously would have been culled from the service, however, the Army only accelerated talent flight."[32] Despite the governing federal legislation known as DOPMA (Defense Officer Personnel Management Act), which in theory constrains the percentage of promotions (80 percent to major, 70 percent to lieutenant colonel, and 50 percent to colonel), all four branches were overpromoting during the last decade. The air force promoted 90 percent of its officers to major, the army promoted 94 percent, the Marines 87 percent, and the navy promoted 84 percent to its equivalent rank of lieutenant commander.[33]

Fortunately, the army instituted another program with a longer-term focus called OCSP or the Officer Career Satisfaction Program. It was designed by economists and officers at the Office of Economic and Manpower Analysis at West Point, and in short allows graduating cadets from the Academy and ROTC an opportunity to increase their branch-selection order in exchange for an additional three years of service. OCSP also gives cadets the option to add three years of service commitment in exchange for a post-of-choice or a guaranteed graduate school option. This cost the army zero dollars, and has resulted in raising the eight-year retention rate from 47 percent to 69 percent, an addition of nearly eighteen thousand motivated man-years from its application to the classes of 2006–2009. The OEMA analysts recognized that the most sensitive decision point for a junior officer is at the five-year point. If junior officers could be encouraged to stay at least eight or nine years, then the likelihood of their serving a full twenty-year career is much higher. To be sure, using economically inspired incentives was controversial, but we now know that they worked.

LOSING SECURITY

Doug Webster is a senior executive at Cisco. In the spring of 1991, he was a college senior on Yale's track team and one of the few Ivy League members of ROTC. After graduation, most of his classmates would head to Wall Street or graduate school, but Webster was waiting for his orders from the air force. And waiting. And still waiting. To the air force, Webster was at the bottom of the totem pole. The Cold War had just ended, and the air force had more people than it could use. So as graduation came and went, the US Air Force's Military Personnel Command (MPC, now renamed Air Force Personnel Command or AFPC) told Webster that his orders were to wait for a few months until they found him a job. He still owed his four years, but they wouldn't let him start.

So Webster did what any enterprising Yale track star with academic honors would do: He took a temp job selling men's clothing at a department store for the summer as he waited to be called for active duty. And then the fall. And then the winter. Eventually, 51 weeks after waiting, just one week shy of authorized limit, the air force commissioned Webster and sent him to Goodfellow Air Force Base in Texas for back-to-back programs in military intelligence. Within four years, Lieutenant Webster was lauded as the top intelligence collector of 1994 in the military by the CIA at its Langley headquarters. By then it was the spring of 1995, and Webster realized he wanted more challenges than the military was going to let him have. The Cold War drawdown and subsequent force-shaping, conducted using cash incentives for early retirement that many of the most impressive senior officers were taking, on top of a narrow career path made the air force look increasingly less interesting. It wasn't hard for Webster to decide that he wanted out, too.[34]

In the early 1990s, computer security was in its infancy. Each branch of the military was wrestling with the issue: How can we protect our secrets from foreign hackers? The new technology was beyond the expertise of senior and midlevel officers, so junior officers fresh from ROTC programs at engineering schools were tasked with developing solutions. One of Webster's friends at Yale was another air force lieutenant, named Scott Waddell, a computer programmer who was assigned to the nascent US Air Force Information Warfare Center. After building a program that worked wonders for the air force, the navy, the army, and a handful of other government agencies started adopting the technology. But Waddell and his team were constrained. They were only captains and NCOs, nonpilots besides, in a service that was a virtual caste system. It didn't take long for them to realize that they could build an even better technology and deploy it more widely in a private start-up company. And that's how Wheelgroup was born.

Wheelgroup is an exodus case study. In 1995, ten individuals cofounded the firm. All of them were recently minted veterans. They built a new technology from scratch, free of the architecture that the military regulations had imposed, and called it NetRanger, one of the first intrusion-detection software products that are now known as "firewalls."

Within two years they were on the cover of *Fortune* magazine. A year later, Cisco decided to augment its Internet security business from scratch, and it knew it needed to acquire the best young firm. Naturally, it tapped Wheelgroup. So in less than 36 months, the founders went from making $4,000 a month to making a $124 million-dollar merger with arguably the Internet's most important company. Not bad.

Some might contend that security technology is better developed in the private sector, that the Pentagon is better suited to buy its technology from the free market, just like it buys its fighter jets from Boeing and General Dynamics. But that's a dodge. The question is why the air force couldn't promote its Wheelgroup team members to lieutenant colonels to develop this technology inside the organization? For a few million dollars a year of flexible treatment, who knows what it could have achieved?

MORE QUESTIONS THAN ANSWERS

To be fair, the military is not the only organization that loses good people. Even the best private-sector firms lose good people, and the more famous they are for producing leaders—say, General Electric or Procter & Gamble—the more likely their best managers are to be headhunted away. But here's the difference: Once the military lets an officer out, it can never get him or her back in. By law. Senior officers can only be promoted from within. If IBM had been run that way, it could have never hired Lou Gerstner.

The larger question is why the army does not allow itself to promote talent early, to pay specialized talent appropriately, and to match talent with jobs effectively? Why not make Dick Hewitt a colonel at 15 years of service? Why not pay officers with cyber-warfare talents a massive skills bonus? Why not loosen the organizational reins a bit and give the "volunteers" more control of their own careers? Why not let officers take sabbaticals into the "real world" the way other professions do? In short, what is the rationale for the system?

CHAPTER 5

IT'S NOT BUSINESS, IT'S PERSONNEL

The art of war, however, as it is certainly the noblest of all arts, so in the progress of improvement it necessarily becomes one of the most complicated among them.

—Adam Smith, *The Wealth of Nations*, Book V.1.13[1]

WAR WILL CHANGE AN ARMY. AS I WRITE, the last American troops are marching out of Iraq after eight years of war, occupation, and counterinsurgency. Roughly one hundred thousand remain in Afghanistan, escalated from forty thousand to more than one hundred thousand by President Barack Obama, who is now planning a drawdown to sixty-eight thousand or fewer. The numbers of troops required has been unpredictable, but the armed forces have responded with admirable resilience and professionalism.

During this decade of war, America and her allies pushed the Taliban from power in Afghanistan, hunted down and killed most of the leadership of al Qaeda, deposed Saddam Hussein from his dictatorial rule over Iraq, and fought an ongoing, small, hot war all across the globe.

It's easy to forget how quickly the war in Afghanistan happened. *USA Today's* Rick Hampson recounts: "Three months after 9/11, every major Taliban city in Afghanistan had fallen—first Mazar-i-Sharif, then Kabul, and finally Kandahar. Osama bin Laden and Mullah Omar were on the run."[2] And it's even easier for some to forget how long America has been fighting. More than 125 months (almost 10.5 years), as of this writing, which is longer than the Civil War and World War II combined.

At the strategic level, Afghanistan and Iraq challenged the Pentagon to relearn how to fight small wars, but it also had to learn how to recruit, deploy, and supply to a theater on the other side of the world, and to do so constantly. Every aspect of war fighting was challenged, and in almost every way the army and Marine corps—the branches that bore most of the burden—adapted successfully. Make no mistake, the constant conflict strengthened and sharpened America's war fighting prowess, but in one essential way, the military hasn't been able to change at all.

The management of warriors—personnel policy—remains a mess. To understand *why* personnel policy is a mess is the only way to understand how to fix it. One cause is the unavoidable complexity of the task of managing more than a million people fairly. This is the dilemma inherent in trying to organize any market, whether that is automobiles, books, or labor, but also, like most complex systems, managing military human resources (HR) has become excessively complex because of what economists call "path dependence." In other words, the military HR is fundamentally a *legacy* system, something implemented in a previous era. Most reforms have been incremental rather than revolutionary, meaning they are based on the same legacy of laws, rules, and customs. Sure, once computers were added the system became faster and more efficient, but changing the name from PERSCOM (Personnel Command) to HRC did not involve a fundamental rethinking of the system itself.

In a nutshell, we can pin the responsibility for human resources rigidity on Robert S. McNamara, the secretary of defense from 1961 to 1968. McNamara had just been promoted to the presidency of Ford Motor Company when John F. Kennedy tapped him. The president-elect considered McNamara to be the "star" of his team, the one cabinet member who had good advice on all the issues. Today, the image of McNamara is that of the self-confident "whiz kid" from the business world who applied quantitative management techniques to an unwieldy defense establishment. That's not far off the mark, but it obscures some particulars. First, the business culture of the 1950s was much different than it is now, especially the corporate manufacturing sector where McNamara's analytical approach was so effective. On the factory floor, high productivity was the result of tighter automation and precision. McNamara preached that "systems control" forced human capital to fit the production line, not vice versa. He saw physical capital as the primary input to production and saw human capital as mere muscle, with one worker indistinguishable from another.

Second, people forget that during World War II, McNamara was commissioned as a captain in 1943 after working as a business-school statistics professor for years. We can imagine that his wartime experience shaped his ideological approach to reform. "The professor-turned-military-officer became part of a traveling statistical control group that analyzed maintenance, logistics, and operational problems in England, India, China, and the Pacific," explains H. R. McMaster, who also observes, "McNamara often met resistance from military officers who discounted his new methods."[3]

McNamara was brilliant and forceful, rejecting some reforms of the Pentagon while simultaneously centralizing decision making. A major motivation shared by President Kennedy and Secretary McNamara was to remove the authority of any military commander (of specific concern was General Curtis LeMay) to initiate the use of nuclear weapons, but the powerful side effect was to make the military bureaucracy even less personal than it had been.[4] To be fair, the cultural history has deeper roots. In the case of military personnel policy, we have a legacy system built on a legacy system built on a legacy system.

CENTRAL ROOTS

There are many threads that weave together into this story of how the modern personnel system was built. We might as well start at the Constitutional Convention at Philadelphia in 1787, when James Madison, coauthor of the *Federalist Papers* and future president of the United States, stood and warned: "A standing military force, with an overgrown Executive will not long be safe companions to liberty."[5] Skepticism of a *standing* American army was based on colonial hostility to British troops before the revolution, particularly the tradition of quartering troops in private homes involuntarily. Americans rejected the idea of a standing (i.e., permanent) army, and preferred that its federal government have essentially no army whatsoever. This is the motivation behind states being guaranteed their militias in the Second Amendment to the Constitution and the ban on quartering of troops in the Third Amendment. Consequently, for the next century, the United States essentially did not have a *professional* army. What it had was a *citizen* army, which meant a rump of officers who were professional soldiers with few enlistees under their command.

The thinking was that in times of war, a US citizen army could be raised and quickly trained by the officer corps. This explains why the United States entered World War I and even World War II very short-handed. To illustrate the point, there is a coincidence of history on September 1, 1939, which is the date when General George Marshall was sworn in as the US Army chief of staff, and also when the Nazis invaded Poland. On that day, the US Army had barely two hundred thousand troops on active duty, which Marshall would grow to over eight million by 1945.[6]

Roll back the clock to May 1917, the month John Kennedy was born. On the Italian front, a 17-year-old Austro-Hungarian soldier named Friedrich Hayek was serving in the artillery. Hayek would later become a Nobel prize–winning economist, but in those early days, the seeds of his later theories were being planted. He saw the chaos of war from on high as a reconnaissance spotter in an Austro-Hungarian biplane. He also witnessed chaos upon the empire's defeat that gave way to spontaneous order as thousands of deserted and deserting soldiers speaking a dozen languages organized themselves to return to their homes. I note this because the US decision to end the draft, discussed in later chapters, was rooted in the ideas that Hayek developed.

Returning to the Great War, the allied victory was aided in no small part by the arrival of the army from the upstart North American pow-erhouse, the United States. Although led by General Jack Pershing, the strength of the Yankee military was attributed by many to the organizational brilliance of the former US secretary of war, Elihu Root. And that's really where we see the firm foundation of the current personnel system.

Root was not a veteran but a highly respected corporate lawyer who served for six years under Presidents William McKinley and Theodore Roosevelt. The army's official history says, "Beginning in 1899, Root outlined in a series of masterful reports his proposals for fundamental reform of Army institutions and concepts to achieve that 'efficiency' of organization and function required of armies in the modern world."[7] He advocated a strong regular army as the keystone of the modern military while also integrating command authority in the War Department over the regular army, militias, and volunteers. He established a general staff and focused them on planning. It's hard to imagine an army that didn't plan. Root also changed promotion procedures, expanded West Point, established the Army War College, and consolidated the various army bureaus under the secretary's direct control. As if that weren't enough, he pushed through legislation establishing the National Guard and the Reserves. These were dramatic reforms that shaped the modern army to great effect.

Root saw the army's disorganization in 1899 as a businessman would see a mismanaged factory. Sound familiar? In testimony to Congress, Root explained his design: "The men who have combined various corporations...in what we call trusts have reduced the cost of production and have increased their efficiency by doing the very same thing we propose you shall do now, and it does seem a pity that the Government of the United States should be the only great industrial establishment that cannot profit by the lessons that the world of industry and of commerce has learned to such good effect."[8] Put simply, Root changed the army to operate more like a monopoly in order to achieve higher productivity. This is not a bad goal, and was no doubt revolutionary and positive *at the time*.

We should remember that the economy of Root's time existed during the middle of the second industrial revolution. Standardization and the interchangeability of well-machined components were pioneered in the United States, and this approach came to be known globally as the "American system of manufacturing." It was a superior approach to the European tradition of craftsmanship in terms of the price of goods, quality of goods, and most of all sheer output, but the American method also meant using unskilled labor with better equipment and highly regulated (and repetitive) industrial designs rather than skilled labor. When Root applied the paradigm to the army, he almost certainly improved army performance in just about every way measurable, but he also established a legacy, a path that future reforms would follow. Within their occupational specialty, junior officers and noncommissioned officers (NCOs) are to this day considered interchangeable parts by all of the US armed forces.

Even so, not everyone bought into Root's new system at the time. Many senior army officers pushed back for a decade, but resistance came to an end in 1912 when Root's protégé, War Secretary Henry

Stimson, fired Major General Fred C. Ainsworth, the highest-ranking officer who continued to oppose personnel and management reforms. Ainsworth, perhaps ominously, was the adjutant general at the time (i.e., the most senior officer in charge of managing personnel).

Treating labor as an interchangeable, atomized resource can be an effective organizing principle if labor is indeed interchangeable. The principle did wonders for muscle work in early twentieth-century factories; indeed, the principle is arguably the first insight of formal management theory. When troops in an industrial-era conscripted army are predominantly marching from battlefield to battlefield and doing little more than following orders to aim their rifles and affix bayonets, the principle holds, but it fits less well in a specialized, professional force. As a 2003 study by the Defense Science Board observed,

> [M]ilitary personnel systems often move people around with lit-
> tle real regard to the effect on unit performance. This might have
> been unavoidable a century ago, when Army Secretary Elihu
> Root created the current Army personnel system, but the elec-
> tronic age now permits changes.[9]

The principle of soldiers as interchangeable parts is described as a "centralized beer can personnel system" by US Marine Colonel G. I. Wilson (retired) and Army Major Donald Vandergriff (retired): "The operant idea is to reach into the stack (i.e., of human resources) of cold beer sitting in the refrigerator, grab one, slam it down, crumple up the beer can (i.e., the individual), toss it out, and reach for another."[10] This is a useful metaphor but unfair in implying that every standardized labor unit is designed to be emptied and discarded. There are advantages to standardization, one being a common culture that is established for all US officers and enlistees during basic training. Norms and standards are vital to smooth operations. What Wilson and Vandergriff are really saying is that standardization has gone too far when the governing authority treats workers as inherently interchangeable. It is also fair to say that this is exactly how the military services treat their junior officers and troops. The alternative is to respect individual skills, what the business literature calls talent. In their second monograph, Wardynski et al. explain, "This talent distribution concept is somewhat foreign to the Army's officer management culture. Standardized training and promotion gates are designed largely to create officers of one type."[11]

IT'S NOT PERSONAL

One of the most famous lines in all of film comes from *The Godfather*, a movie about a New York mob family ruled over by the supremely calm and charismatic Vito Corleone. The Corleone family runs a number of profitable activities, but at the heart of the mafia is the so-called "protection" racket. Local merchants are obliged to pay the Corleone network a regular fee in return for protection from physical violence. When it comes to the business of the crime family—thievery, bullying, bribery, even assassination—the culture within the gang is to keep personal emotions in check. At one point in the film, young Michael (the ex-Marine) volunteers to kill two men, including a crooked police chief who tried to assassinate his father. Michael until then had been the angelic son, the one who hadn't been involved in the family business, so his older, tougher, and more emotional brother, Sonny, teases him for being irrational and taking the situation "very personal." Michael responds with a line that has become a mantra: "It's not personal, Sonny. It's strictly business."

For these violent men, *business* stands for the clean calculus of profit. Business is not a mark of one's character, although it may be heartless. And this is why, when Americans talk about losing a job, whether through layoffs or firing, someone will say, "Hey, it's not personal. It's business." The sentiment is that a layoff is not a negative mark on one's character, either the employer's or the employee's. Business decisions may be cold, but at least they are logical. For the members of the armed forces doing their jobs, many triggers are pulled, bombs dropped, and missiles launched with an internal homage to that same sentiment. We do not kill for pleasure, but because the job requires it.

Yet the military culture, as we've discussed earlier, prides itself on *not* being a business. I mean to say that its management culture is confused, and possibly less open than ever to best practices from outside the Pentagon walls. Secretary of Defense Robert Gates said as much himself in his farewell speech at West Point: the military has much to learn from the business community, but the army will never be just another corporation. The value-neutral view of for-profit business is what military members like to think makes their profession different.

Action without emotion, yes, but without value, no. Values are *central* to the military culture. But are values central to military personnel management?

The values the military espouses are integrity, teamwork, and selflessness. Service above self is a constant refrain, and one in which the people in uniform believe, but if one looks closely at what then-Lieutenant Colonel Paul Yingling described as the "structural influences that produce our general officer corps,"[12] one will not see those values rewarded. A high-integrity system would not artificially inflate performance evaluations. A system that rewards selfless virtue would not punish officers for specializing in a skill that is mission critical while instead reward rigid careerism.

What's necessary is to move beyond the rhetoric of values and examine the actual rules of the personnel game. Where to start? There are thousands of pages officially devoted to the subject of military manpower, but for our purposes, let's start with Field Manual 1–0, *Human Resource Support*: This 184-page document describes the army's personnel doctrine and how it fits into the army's operational concept across the full spectrum of conflict, as well as how it supports unit commanders and soldiers. It encompasses personnel information and readiness; replacement, casualty, and postal operations; personnel accounting and strength reporting; mobilization and demobilization; and more. Another document the army publishes to help its senior leaders understand how the army runs is titled, helpfully, *How the Army Runs*, or HTAR. The document is six hundred fifty pages long and includes over one hundred tables and figures.

The currency of HTAR, now in its twenty-eighth edition for 2011–2012, shows the mixture of pressures facing senior leaders: a commitment to the US Constitution and national security, the execution of "persistent" warfare while undergoing a major transformation to a modular brigade structure, and, ironically, an explicit objective to "reduce unnecessary bureaucracy" in the very same document that tries to explain that bureaucracy. The first organizational framework presented in HTAR is the life cycle model (see Figure 5.1), which "captures the continuous cycle of developing, employing, maintaining, and eliminating organizations."[13]

All of the eight functions in the life cycle model apply to people—force management, acquisition, training, distribution, deployment, sustainment, development, and separation—use the same language

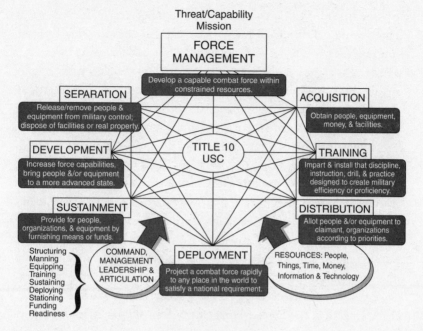

Figure 5.1 Army Organizational Life Cycle Model
Source: *How the Army Runs: A Senior Leader Reference Handbook, 2011–12.*

that is applied to materiel. This doctrine belies some fundamental assumptions of central management and control.

The heart of any leadership engine in a large organization is the way it matches talent to jobs, which is described by the army as *distribution* and by actual soldiers as assignments. In HTAR, the distribution function is described like this:

> Having produced or procured the resources necessary to form and sustain units they must be distributed according to established requirements, authorizations, and priorities. The distribution function includes the assignment of people from entry-level training to their initial unit and the delivery of new materiel from the wholesale level to the user. This activity is primarily managed and synchronized through the Army Force Generation (ARFORGEN) process that focuses equipment and personnel distribution during the reset phase.[14]

I hesitate to quote directly from *How the Army Runs*, simply because it is such tedious and jargon-laden text, but doing so shows that the thickness of bureaucracy is nearly impenetrable. If it takes this many words and this many acronyms to explain a bureaucracy, imagine how unwieldy it is to actually operate the bureaucracy—the forms, the waiting, the snafus, and the constant shifting of people within.

As an example, consider the first mention of Human Resource Command, which occurs on page 10. For some context, let's think of job matching as the intersection of supply and demand for warriors. It is impossible for the human mind to comprehend the diversity of warriors needed (e.g., pilots, commandos, drill sergeants, mechanics), so planners want and need to think of them as interchangeable pieces of different types. They turn the abstraction of a supply-and-demand curve into an actual simplified job description, which the army calls a *requirement.* Let's say the army has a requirement for 30 light infantry battalion commanders this cycle, okay? Now things get really tricky when the nature of warfare changes, because how can the planners reorient their numerous demand curves? Here's how, in the words of HTAR, section 2–4 Force Management Terms, subsection (b):

> Using the Integrated Capabilities Development Team (ICDT) management technique, TRADOC pursues timely involvement of appropriate agencies/expertise to aggressively analyze and assess future operating capabilities requirements. The Director of TRADOC's Army Capabilities Integration Center (ARCIC) charters an ICDT to conduct Capability-based Assessments (CBA) that includes functional area analysis (FAA), functional needs analysis (FNA), functional solution analysis (FSA), and the preparation of capability documents. This assessment process leads to the identification by the Commanding General (CG) TRADOC to HQDA of DOTMLPF change recommendations (nonmaterial solutions) or a materiel capability need....If the analysis results in a need for change in soldier occupational specialty structure, then the recommendation goes forward to U.S. Army Human Resources Command (HRC) for Army wide coordination and approval (See Chapter 13).[15]

Most of us reading this rub our eyes and say, "What?" As do the soldiers who are managed by this manual. This is far less personal—in word and deed—than a business transaction. Worse, the decisions made by the personnel system often defy logic, making moves that are counterproductive. Have a drink with veterans, and they will be able to list half a dozen examples. My favorite anecdote is about a young officer who was the top aeronautical engineering graduate from the Air Force Academy and who was unable to volunteer for an engineering-related position because he was deemed too valuable in his present career field, *even though he had no further obligation to serve in uniform* and thereafter left the service.

The practice of management in the modern sense is barely a century old, and businesses have been evolving quickly to figure out what works best. The legacy-bound US military has not kept up with these evolving management practices.

SNAPSHOT OF ASSIGNMENTS FROM THE ARMY OFFICER'S PERSPECTIVE

As an officer, one starts one's career first by branching, or selecting an occupational specialty. Each service has a different process, but most (though not the Marines) use a relatively straightforward merit ranking to guide the selection process. Once one has chosen a branch—infantry, artillery, logistics—one is sent to specialized training courses. At times, West Pointers have been slated with their first duty assignment before the officer basic course, but most officers across the various services are assigned to their first unit only after submitting a "dream sheet" of ranked preferences to instructors at the initial officer training course, which is then routed to the personnel system.

My experience in the air force was straightforward—I had good enough college grades to secure a coveted slot at the intelligence school at Goodfellow Air Force Base in San Angelo, Texas. After two courses and seven months of intelligence training, I was selected to specialize in HUMINT or human intelligence. Most others in my class were tasked in signal, imagery, or analysis. As the training program came to a close, we gathered for an assignment ceremony where everyone received an envelope that contained his or her first location and job description. One of the sharpest officers and a good friend, a graduate from Virginia Tech's famed ROTC program, badly wanted a tactical assignment with fighter pilots or Special Forces. His envelope revealed a placement at Offutt Air Force Base working on the staff planning nuclear warfare (basically as nontactical as possible). This officer had a distinguished career, but finally quit when the air force tried to send him for his third master's degree soon after 9/11. He gave up the 20-year retirement package in order to work for a civilian intelligence agency where he could "kill bad guys."

Oftentimes, senior officers who defend the HR system inadvertently reveal how impersonal it can be. One army general said to me, "Once our leaders get to battalion command, they're not beans anymore." That's not very reassuring for the bean counting that happens during the first 10–15 years of a career. Another senior officer explained, "[T]he officer side of the distribution system has very detailed optimization under the hood. At the company grade level *most officers are interchangeable*" (emphasis added).

In 1999, the army updated its officer professional management system (OPMS), formerly called OPMS II and now called OPMS XXI. The new system maintained the *designation* of army officers into one of 16 basic branches.[16] Unlike the old system that required all officers to broaden into functional areas (take a secondary career track) after promotion to captain, OPMS XXI allowed officers more flexibility to stay focused. After seven to ten years in their basic branch, officers choose to focus their development and job assignments in that branch or their functional area. Moreover, new functional areas were created: information systems engineering, strategic intelligence, and so on. Upon promotion to major, roughly two-thirds of officers are designated in their basic branches and one-third in functional areas. The "optimization under the hood" is the increasingly sophisticated computer algorithms used by the army to match officer preferences for career field designation (CFD), collected during the cohort's tenth year of service, with requirements, also known as the needs of the army. Alexandra Newman and then-major Dan Shrimpton wrote about the CFD optimization model they designed and the army implemented after 1999 in a 2005 journal article, highlighting the reality that the designation problem was beyond the capacity of a panel of humans to solve well. However, the Shrimpton-Newman CFD solver "optimally designates 1,5000 officers...in less than 10 seconds on a 900mHz Pentium PC with 256 MB RAM."[17] Perhaps this sounded cutting edge when it was written and implemented, but it means that for many years the army was distributing its officers using spreadsheet software on a single desktop.

The treatment changes with higher rank, but no one denies that every career starts as coldly impersonal. New lieutenants out of BOLC (basic officer leadership course) submit their "dream sheet" with a list of the locations they prefer in order, but the actual jobs at those locations are unknown, and the young officers do not meet personnel staff or talk to them. For example, one might list Fort Belvoir in Virginia as one's first choice, then Fort Carson, and so on. HRC issues assignments according to the number of officers required at each installation. Later, for captains who have attended CCC (Captain's Career Course), there is a little more interaction with the branch-assignment staffer at HRC over the phone, but preferences are still expressed in terms of locations, not specific units or jobs. The officer at this point hopes to get into a unit with a short line of peers looking for a command slot.[18]

After the officer commands his or her first company, options open up for nontactical assignments, and some branches will post a list of available jobs. When captains are coming up on the window to change stations, they can send an email to the HRC branch-assignment officer with job preferences. This time is also the chance to compete for a teaching position at USMA, fellowships, or graduate school. Following this job, the now-majors will probably be sent to their third military-development program, called Intermediate Level Education (ILE), such as the Command and General Staff College at Fort Leavenworth, Kansas. Next, officers aim for a KD, which stands for "key and developmental" assignment in the operational force. After KD, the majors will be compared relative to peers by HRC based on previous assignments and evaluations, which is a sorting process that limits distribution options. If officers are promoted to lieutenant colonel, they may be selected for battalion/brigade command select, in which case HRC sends them to what the central planners perceive to be better job assignments, and possibly to command. The rest are sent to fill the gaps. Colonels and above are managed by a separate organization for HRC that is guided by the chief of staff of the army.

By themselves, impersonal algorithms are not the enemies of flexibility nor do they stunt entrepreneurial leadership. If a centralized system is to manage interchangeable parts, this kind of optimization is necessary. The dilemma is that by relying on algorithms too much, the Pentagon has painted its officers into a corner. As US Army Major Joe Bruhl explained in a recent *Military Review* essay:

"Today's prescribed timeline for officers leaves little space for variation in a career. When an officer is selected early for promotion, this timeline compresses even more. As a result, the Army is forcing its best officers to make a binary choice too early in their career: stay in operational assignments and remain competitive for command, or pursue broadening experiences at their own professional peril."[19]

IN PURSUIT OF FAIRNESS

The modern OPMS was born in 1971 as a result of a task force initiated by US Army chief of staff William Westmoreland. The system was a reaction to a controversial 1970 study authored by Colonels Walt Ulmer and Mike Malone from the Army War College. The Ulmer-Malone study described a "disharmony between traditional, accepted ideals and the prevailing institutional pressures."[20] All the signs of failure-intolerance and careerist values were highlighted. Westmoreland was reportedly so disturbed by the report that he ordered it sealed from the public for over a decade. Amazingly, the OPMS 71 task force "ignored all of the 31 recommendations made in the 1970 study," explains Don Vandergriff in *Raising the Bar*. "Instead, OPMS 71 increased the power of the centralized personnel bureaucracy...with a new centralized Army-level personnel center."[21] This was also when promotion decisions were taken away from general officers and centralized in the board process.

We can look back now and see that the army knew it had problems with personnel even before 1971. Officers were becoming more careerist, responding to the incentives given by a system with top-down raters and inflated evaluations, but the army's solution was to fix something else. Fairness. A primary motivation of the 1971 reform was to ensure fairness for women and minorities, since it was feared that commanders in that era would favor white males. In other words, the institution did not trust its own people, so it removed their authority.

A second OPMS task force in 1985 introduced the primary and functional area career-tracking structure. This was an effort to increase the complexity of the system as a brute-force way for a centralized process to mimic the flexibility of a decentralized process. The proliferation of career "silos" ended up creating more problems than it solved.

THE DOGMA OF DOPMA

While frustrated officers might rail against bizarre decisions emanating from US Army HRC, the staffers at the command headquarters at Fort Knox are just doing their jobs with the same frustrations about bureaucracy and limited resources as everyone else. Besides, they are responsible for a lot more than *manning the force*. They also perform *essential services*, which include "awards and decorations, evaluation reports, promotions and reductions, transfers and discharges, identification documents, leaves and passes, line of duty investigations, soldier applications, coordination of military pay and entitlements, etc."[22] HR officers also oversee the mail and the sensitive but vital management of casualty operations. The other core competency is *personnel support*, issues like morale (MWR), voting support, and weight control. Last, they conduct *planning and operations*, which is essentially the careful specification of labor demanded at the unit level.

No, HRC and all of its personnel officers who conduct the feared slatings are not the villains; they simply implement the policy passed down from the army G-1, the chief administrative office of the US Army, responsible for developing policy. Are they the villains? In a sense, yes, but the G-1 is constrained by laws and regulations passed by Congress: DOPMA, which passed in 1980 and was later codified in Titles 10 and 37 of the US Code, and also the Goldwater-Nichols Act of 1986.

Although DOPMA became law in 1980, it extended HR doctrine that had been established previously by McNamara and Root, further entrenching the legacy and culture. Described as "more evolutionary than revolutionary" in a 2006 RAND Corporation report,[23] the main thing DOPMA does is enshrine the up-or-out rank hierarchy that "does not allow for much variety in the career paths of most officers."[24] DOPMA requires that if an officer is not able to be promoted to the next level of the rank pyramid then s/he must be forcibly retired. In principle, this promotes excellence in the workforce and weeds out ineffective officers, but that rarely happens when other elements of DOPMA are in effect as well. Here are some of the operating parameters:

- Competitive categories (occupations in which officers compete for promotions) are mandatory, meaning officers exist in career silos.
- Promotion zones are based entirely on seniority; this zone is narrowly defined as a single instance for each grade.
- Percentages of officers promoted at each grade are tightly constrained, unless there is a waiver.

- Involuntary retirement of officers "failed of selection" twice in a zone are mandatory.
- Tenure is established.

Essentially every one of these parameters runs afoul of best practices in the private sector. Tenure, known as "lifetime employment," has been phased out almost everywhere because of inflexibility, everywhere except in public education where bad teachers have plagued school districts for years.

"The primary result of this law is cohort management," explains Lieutenant Colonel Scott Halter, which "limits the Army's ability to flexibly manage its officers, resulting in short and rigid career timelines."[25] Artificial breadth mandates rapid turnover in assignments, which causes friction with unit manning and cohesion. Halter cites a compelling example of the negative effect of turnover when his unit, the 101st Combat Aviation Brigade, deployed "with eight of its twelve battalion executive and operations officers not completing any training with their staff or unit. It also experienced a 46 percent turnover in the course of 14 months."[26]

There are countless other examples of how the various elements of HR policy combine to yield something less than the sum of well-intentioned parts. The best planners in the world simply cannot plan for the manpower demands of two land wars in the Middle East combined with a whipsaw domestic economy. The low retention rate discussed in earlier chapters has forced the army and Marines to "overproduce" junior officers and then overpromote those willing to continue. The promise of culling weak leaders was utterly compromised for the last decade. On the other hand, the HR system routinely becomes failure intolerant during peacetime, what officers decry as the zero-defects culture that makes creativity a liability. "The 1990s were known as the era of the 'zero-defect Army,' a time when a single mistake by an officer—or even his troops—could doom his chances of advancement," explained Greg Jaffe in *The Fourth Star*.[27] "With the end of the Cold War, the Army was shrinking, and a below-average fitness report was usually enough to convince a promotion board to pass over an otherwise exemplary officer," Jaffe added.

There are few people inside or outside the HR system who defend DOPMA. In a critical 2010 report, the Defense Science

Board highlighted the law's inflexibility and blamed it for "wasting human capital." The RAND study in 2006 claimed unequivocally that DOPMA-based practices "will not meet the needs of the future operating environment" and called it a "cold war-era personnel system"[28] that was outdated. In 2004, US Army chief of staff Peter Schoomaker said, "I've thought for years the Army needed to transform its personnel system."[29] The Wardynski team published more than a half dozen monographs in their Strategic Studies Institute (SSI) series that took apart the HR system brick by brick and urged the army to transform "from an almost feudal employer-employee relationship to a talent-based model."[30] Defense Secretary Gates pushed for reform inside the Pentagon under two presidents and in the public sphere until his retirement in 2011.

Some retirees are much more colorful in their criticism, but one of the more eloquent critics is retired US Army Major Don Vandergriff, a 24-year veteran who started his career as an enlisted Marine and has published widely on the topic.[31] His essay with G. I. Wilson thundered that the armed forces today are "hobbled by an archaic and dysfunctional personnel system."[32]

Vandergriff and Wilson summarize a handful of flawed assumptions in the military HR system that can be traced back to Root's centralization of power. These are as good a summation as any for what reformers should target: (1) the *generalist assumption* that all officers should have many, broad experiences that aim them for operational command rather than specialized expertise; (2) the *up-or-out promotion* system with incessant box-checking to make rank even if officers are not interested in making rank nor on track for command; (3) a *centralized bureaucracy* that oversees evaluations, promotions, and jobs assignments and, they particularly note; (4) *standardized evaluations* based on one-size-fits-all measures for all officers, enshrined in the Officer Efficiency/Evaluation Report in 1947, which has been revised ten times.

The DOPMA legislation actually envisioned wide zones for promotion that would overlap, but regulations and norms have narrowed the zones in practice. Because of the strict timetable, promotion requires key assignment milestones to be achieved and "checked off" within each competitive occupation. Since the path to operational command is so narrow, the struggle to get assigned "key and developmental" jobs is both fierce and also very much a function of luck. Goldwater-Nichols added a requirement for *joint* assignments. To prevent officers from gaming joint tours, a minimum duration was required by regulation. Many officers have had their wings clipped (i.e., their ability to make colonel) when they were told that a certain assignment didn't actually qualify for joint. Officers are also now measured by their formal training, particularly if they attend various professional military education (PME) classes "in residence." A de facto requirement for a master's degree can be seen in the patterns of promotions of colonel, since no one seems to get to pin on a full bird unless s/he has a graduate degree of some kind, though oddly it can be a token degree.

As a consequence of the need to check career boxes, officers have traded off career depth for career breadth: fewer, shorter assignments. What is lost is the ability to focus or specialize. The officers who prefer to specialize are effectively punished and forced to retire for getting off-track. For example, language capacity is very much in demand in the field, but is not rewarded by the promotion system and so remains in critically short supply. Further, new needs of the army such as stabilization expertise in postconflict situations has been strongly endorsed by senior leaders, but junior officers know the reality of promotion boards that have not rewarded such career choices. The net effect, says Professor Lenny Wong, is an army where everyone is trying to look the same. But what else should we expect? Looking the same is exactly what the institution is asking, despite what the culture and leadership want.

ELTW (ECONOMICS LEADS THE WAY)

Edward Lazear is a professor at Stanford University who served at the pinnacle of government policymaking as the chair of the US president's Council of Economic Advisers (CEA) from 2006 to 2009. He is also the father of an academic literature known as "personnel economics" and coauthor of *Personnel Economics in Practice*. Sadly, in his time as the CEA chair, reforming military HR practices never crossed his desk. When I interviewed Lazear in the spring of 2011, he remarked that a highly regulated bureaucracy routinely leads to a surprising behavior: nepotism. An informal system will emerge spontaneously if a personnel bureaucracy is unable to sort talent efficiently. Lazear noted this would be more likely in the US military, where performance evaluations are exclusively top-down and narrow (few reviewers), measures are ambiguous because the product is nonprofit service, and probationary periods for evaluation are relatively brief. "The signal to noise ratio is likely very high," he said.[33]

Friedrich A. Hayek is the previously mentioned World War I veteran who went on to become famous as a professor at the London School of Economics. In one of the most influential books of the twentieth century, *The Road to Serfdom*, which was written during 1940–1943, Hayek warned that the rise of state central planning of the economy would lead inevitably to totalitarianism. He pointed out that Nazism was National *Socialism*, and that both communist and fascist extremes were identical in their efforts to nationalize economic control, including the use of propaganda and more direct forms of coercion. The book was an extension of Hayek's thinking into the very idea of planning any economic activity. In the 1930s he extended the idea first promulgated by Ludwig von Mises that economic planning is doomed because of what is now known as the "knowledge problem"—the only way to try to allocate resources through a central-planning solution is by using simplified data. Real knowledge of individual buyers and sellers in a market can never be fully known, and because of that no planned allocation can be superior to information conveyed by the prices in a market. A central planner sees two metal bars, each weighing half a pound, and assumes they are the same. You and I might have no better knowledge, but the market will say the gold bar is worth $14,000 and the lead bar is worth $6.

Hayek explained it most eloquently in a 1945 essay in the *American Economic Review*:

> The peculiar character of the problem of a rational economic order is determined precisely by the fact that the knowledge of the circumstances of which we must make use never exists in concentrated or integrated form but solely as the dispersed bits of incomplete and frequently contradictory knowledge which [sic] all the separate individuals possess. The economic problem of society is thus not merely a problem of how to allocate "given" resources—if "given" is taken to mean given to a single mind which [sic] deliberately solves the problem set by these "data." It is rather a problem of how to secure the best use of resources known to any of the members of society, for ends whose relative importance only these individuals know. Or, to put it briefly, it is

a problem of the utilization of knowledge which [sic] is not given to anyone in its totality.

...[T]he sort of knowledge with which I have been concerned is knowledge of the kind which [sic] by its nature cannot enter into statistics and therefore cannot be conveyed to any central authority in statistical form.[34]

What does this have to do with army personnel? Put simply, the army does not know how to value talent. All of the services use processes for designating, distributing, evaluating, and promoting their human capital that are designed *not* to value heterogenous talent. Rather than use markets to value (price) and distribute talent, they use a system to code the maximum complex information that is manageable, which isn't much. Consider, for example, the officer-evaluation report that has become so inflated in practice as to render it useless as a talent measuring device.

Finally, Hayek's final line merits real reflection. Can you imagine knowledge of your own skills and preferences that you might not wish to reveal to a central planner? Perhaps a sailor belatedly realizes that he gets seasick easily. Perhaps an airman prefers to be stationed in Asia for family reasons, but knows that emphasizing his location preference reflects poorly on his occupational commitment. We can all probably agree that a Marine in combat has the best sense when a vacation from combat is essential, but this is nearly impossible to communicate honestly.

A more immediate application of this principle is the way the Pentagon addresses time in combat. The army deployed soldiers on 12-month tours of duty in Iraq, up to 15 months when forces were surged, and eventually dropped deployments lengths down to 9 months at a time. Tours are followed by one-year or longer rotations back home. The Marines use shorter rotation cycles, with 7 months in combat per tour. Does this one-size-fits-all approach make sense? "We don't have twelve years' experience in Vietnam," remarked the famous American army officer John Paul Vann. "We have one year's experience twelve times over." Some Marines may not feel stressed by blood and death and never feel a desire to leave harm's way, while others may need a break more often than the service allows. Who are we to judge the needs and desires of individual soldiers if they are truly volunteers? If the army used a fully implemented TVF (total volunteer force), there would be no limit on the length of combat tours, nor any ability to coerce soldiers into combat duty.

WHY INCREMENTAL REFORM CAN'T WORK

I submit that there is no incremental way to fix the talent bleed in the US military. Unfortunately, this is the approach suggested by almost all critics. The problem with HR is not that the system is poorly managed, but rather that the system is based on a false premise. The premise of central planning is that enough data and enough computational resources can generate efficient allocations. That is fundamentally not true. If the system tries to enhance its specific knowledge about its inventory of people by 10 percent, then the computational problem will be much more than 10 percent harder. Furthermore, as described earlier, there is no such thing as perfect information. Incessantly trying to refine the requirements, or to better anticipate evolving requirements for skilled inventory, is a quest for fool's gold.

The philosophical impossibility of a centralized solution—a true optimization—is a key insight that most reformers have not understood, and is why so many previous reforms have led back to square one. Three iterations of OPMS have not made centralization work, and in fact have amplified the flaws of DOPMA and previous Congressional mandates. Even now, most critics think the solution is simply a matter of more competent central planning.

The 2006 RAND study is a case in point. Its centerpiece proposal is competency-based career management to replace the time-based system that exists. "We would also argue for a gradual implementation of many of these practices over a period of years, so that deal can be seen as evolving,"[35] said its closing paragraph. The authors did recommend changing some elements, such as replacing up-or-out with "perform-or-out" and decentralizing some assignment choices that would go along with wider promotion zones, but the main focus is on extending careers and deepening well-defined competencies within an expert-managed system as it largely exists now.

At least one group of reformers is calling for revolutionary change inside the army—Wardynski and his colleagues at the Strategic Studies Institute. In their first paper they called for "substantive management changes" and explained that, "the Army has relied on draft-era practices to manage an all-volunteer Army."[36] Although they make the case that reforms across all of the main HR functions are important and can be evolutionary—accessions, development, retention—assignments are the key. When SSI asked for a full series of monographs extending the initial paper, the first (volume 2) said plainly, "First, the Army needs to create an *internal* officer talent labor market."[37] A paragraph from their introduction to that volume put the need for a market in context:

> Whether it likes it or not, the Army is competing with the private sector for the best talent America has to offer. The domestic labor market is dynamic, and in the last 25 years it has increasingly demanded employees who can create information, provide service, or add knowledge. The Army cannot insulate itself from these market forces. It must change the relationship between its officers and their strength managers from one that is relatively closed, information-starved, slow-moving, and inefficient, to one that is increasingly open, rich in information, faster moving, and thus far more efficient.[38]

To understand how the TVF would be different from the current model, imagine two female graduates of Ohio State University, Jane and Lisa. Lieutenant Jane Smith submits a "dream sheet" (assignment location preferences) to HRC, but has no personal interaction with anyone outside her immediate supervisors to express preferences. The message she eventually receives from HRC is simple: gaining unit, station, and the date Jane is ordered to report. Now contrast that with the private-sector experience of her civilian roommate, Lisa Moye, who also majored in engineering, works for a midsized firm in Cleveland for two years and has just been offered a promotion to manage a team there. She also has a friend at the firm who is launching a start-up and offered to give Lisa 10 percent equity if she will join. That spurred her to scan monster.com and do some informal interviews that led to three additional job offers, one of which is in Silicon Valley.

Lisa has choices; Jane has orders.

Making change in large, conservative organizations is almost always done incrementally, and the military is a very large, very conservative organization. Lives are on the line, and the leadership culture has been refined for as long as human civilization has existed. In this case, that instinct will be a mistake, and history shows it would be repeating the same technocratic mistake for the sixth or seventh time. It is worth remembering that gradual is not how America achieved independence from the British empire, not how George Marshall raised a world war force of eight million troops, and not how the US military transitioned to the all-volunteer force in the early 1970s.

THE TOTAL VOLUNTEER FORCE

Real change requires us to sacrifice at least one sacred cow. We might begin by facing up to the fact that many of the military's espoused values are simply not those in practice with the current HR structure. Specifically, what if the mantra "the needs of the army come first" is actually wrong? That mantra is used to justify actions that displease the individual in order to serve the theoretical greater good. But if we boil it down to fundamentals, what theory says the greater good is being served when an individual is coerced to do something? The needs of the army previously justified conscription, a system we now recognize as detrimental to the army, so maybe the mantra actually encourages short-term solutions. What if we let the needs of the army come second?

The moral case for markets was argued long ago by Adam Smith in the *Wealth of Nations*. Markets look mercenary to moralizers, which is why Smith had to explain the efficiency gains as if they were from an (godly) invisible hand even when the agents in the market were acting purely in self-interest. Smith essentially argued to let the needs of the community come second. A self-interested labor market enables American companies and entrepreneurs to create the biggest, richest, most productive economy the world has ever seen. A similar market would enable an even stronger US military. Self-interested, spontaneous order is counterintuitive to some, but it happens to be that kind of liberty that the US military exists to protect.

Coercion is the key word to keep in mind when pondering what ails HR management. Coercion offends strong men and women and belittles their intelligence. And it was the coercion of young citizens to serve in uniform that defined the philosophy of conscription. When Richard Nixon promised to end the draft during the 1968 presidential campaign, he was opposed by many conservatives and even more liberals, but he was embraced by the young. He was also embraced by free-market economists who promised that a market for labor could work, that a supply of volunteer professional soldiers would come forward to replace the involuntary citizen soldiers. Economists such as Milton Friedman and Walter Oi promised that supply would meet demand. When President Nixon made good on the promise and implemented the all-volunteer force (AVF) in 1973, it was a revolutionary movement, culturally and managerially. It worked.

I'd like to think the AVF provides a model of the kind of revolutionary change that the military can take now in moving one step further in the same direction, away from coercion and toward free labor markets. Understanding what that next step will be requires that we look at the limitations of the AVF. Contrary to its name, the AVF is not exactly all volunteers, or at least not all the time. A better name is probably the "first-day volunteer force," because after men and women take their oath of office on the first day in uniform, the volunteerism ends.

If the principles in the AVF were extended past that first day, it would be an AVF+, but I think a better way to think of it would be total removal of coercion as a managerial principle, so I call it the total volunteer force, or TVF. Before trying to define the TVF, or even the basic structure of a TVF, let's first consider the recommendations of the service members themselves.

PRINCIPLES BEHIND THE TVF

When presented with ten "out-of-the-box" policy changes that might improve entrepreneurial leadership, my panel of 250 West Point graduates was strongly in favor of five, marginally in favor of three, marginally opposed to one, and dead set against one: conscription. Eighty-six percent of the respondents oppose reauthorizing the draft.

Respondents showed strongest agreement with a policy of allowing greater specialization (90 percent agree), while 83 percent of all respondents (and three-fifths of active-duty officers) agreed with expanding early promotion opportunities (87 percent), eliminating year group/cohorts (78 percent), and allowing lateral entry of former officers to rejoin.

The following is a summary of each of the ten policy changes, in order of overall support.

- *Eliminate "year groups" after ten years* (Agree or strongly agree by 67 percent of active-duty officers [AD], 83 percent of ex-military veterans [EX]). Promotions in rank are strictly controlled by consideration of the number of years an officer has served. Rare promotions are given one or two years below the "zone," but the vast majority of promotions are given to nearly every officer in the same year group at the same time, even after a decade or more in service. Minor distinctions are made in some branches for the actual date when one "pins on" lieutenant colonel versus another within the same cohort. Eliminating the notion of a year group after the first ten years in uniform would radically expand the pool of candidates to be promoted each cycle and increase competition across year groups.

• *Allow greater specialization rather than track everyone for flag officer* (87 percent AD, 92 percent EX). Ironically, the greatest call for change is not to allow merely ambitious officers to rise faster up the ranks, but rather to change the institutional assumption that all officers should proceed through the same ladder of promotions. Allowing greater specialization means letting people remain captains and majors for longer than the norm in order to become deeply competent in specific roles. A recurring theme in the comments is a desire for officers to avoid staff positions and remain in command of troops as long as possible, with the understanding that this path is not the track for promotion. Indeed, many ex-military officers left because they had no desire to pursue rank.

• *Expand early promotion opportunities* (77 percent AD, 92 percent EX). Differentiation among junior officers through early promotions is occurring in today's army, although it results largely from wartime duress through attrition rather than forward-thinking policy, that is, it is a symptom of a retention crisis at the midcareer ranks. Comments from respondents were heavily critical of the strict timetable for promotion, not only for the sake of promoting good leaders but also in order to not promote weaker leaders.

• *Allow former officers to rejoin the service (lateral entry)* (73 percent AD, 88 percent EX). Currently, once an officer resigns his or her commission in the active-duty ranks, the only option to continue serving is through the Reserves or National Guard. The recent strains from wars in the Middle East have sparked renewed respect for the skills brought back in by reservists, yet a strong bias remains among senior officers in favor of career active-duty troops. And there is a tradition dating back to the early years of the Republic against an aristocratic capacity to purchase rank, as was common in aristocratic European militaries of the eighteenth and nineteenth centuries; the concern is that no senior officer should be unfamiliar with the experiences of a junior officer. This question eliminates that objection by limiting consideration for lateral entry to former officers. Nearly three-fourths of active-duty officers agree (25 percent strongly agree) with the idea, despite the fact that it would mean greater competition for them.

- *Use a market mechanism to allocate jobs instead of central placement* (76 percent AD, 76 percent EX). Job selection is perhaps the sorest spot among officers. Interestingly, the exact same percentage of active-duty officers favors a labor-market mechanism (76 percent) as ex-military officers. A market mechanism would empower officers to apply for any open slot (at presumably any time), and also give hiring authority to commanders. HRC personnel officers would change to an advisory role for both hiring commanders and for job-seeking officers.

- *Lay off more officers involuntarily* (62 percent AD, 62 percent EX). Like most government organizations, the military very rarely lays off even its worst performers. This higher level of job security offers advantages, but there are potential pitfalls as well. *The percentage of active-duty officers who strongly disagree with this idea is just 4 percent*, compared to 25 percent who strongly favor it.

- *Force a distribution of top and bottom 10–20 percent in evaluations* (66 percent AD, 60 percent EX). A forced distribution in evaluations, especially the requirement to identify the weakest performers, is a particularly strict practice designed to weed out poor performers. For that reason, it can be unpopular among individuals within such a system. Ironically, this reform is *the only one favored by a greater percentage of active-duty officers than ex-military officers*. There are two possible reasons. First, the active-duty officers have served longer on average, and therefore become more aware of unqualified peers or commanders at higher ranks. Second, more senior active-duty officers recognize their own lack of ability to correctly evaluate poorly performing subordinates.

- *Allow former soldiers to use GI Bill money as start-up loans instead of for education* (51 percent AD, 65 percent EX). Currently, the GI Bill is geared entirely toward helping soldiers (officer and enlisted) and their family members pay for college; however, this benefit has limited use for a soldier who is uninterested in higher education or already has a degree. Why not offer the flexibility to use the GI Bill funds, in part or full, as a loan for veterans to start businesses? On the one hand, this policy might entice more (and more entrepreneurial) soldiers to leave the service. But it would also communicate the military's respect for entrepreneurship and could be coupled powerfully with skill-building for officers if they were able to come back to the service in the future.

- *Expand the academies to include graduate schools* (54 percent AD, 53 percent EX). Service academies have been subject to reform efforts on multiple dimensions in recent decades, so respondents are likely wary of this suggestion. There are various rationales for including a graduate school at West Point, but one purpose would be to eliminate the somewhat artificial tension between its graduates and officers from other commissioning sources. Undergraduates would potentially be exposed to a wide variety of graduate students, not only senior officers from other services, but also civilians with a rich variety of backgrounds and experiences.

- *Reauthorize conscription (draft)* (14 percent AD, 14 percent EX). Eliminating the all-volunteer force is highly unpopular among those who serve. While around 8 percent of ex-military respondents favor the idea strongly, *no active-duty officers agree strongly with the idea* (versus 55 percent who disagree strongly with it).

Sasha Falk and Sayce Rogers also focused on recommendations with their survey of veterans across all the services and commissioning programs. Their suggestions are in line with RAND, SSI, Vandergriff, and my own proposals, and worth summarizing given their currency. First, Falk and Rogers say "know who you have" with an evaluation process that uses 360 degrees of input and forced rankings that "focus only on identifying the top and bottom 10%, and group the remaining 80% into a middle bracket."[39] Second, echoing SSI, they recommend giving "people a say in their own careers" with a "market-based system."[40] They also recommend promoting innovation, ending the zero-defect culture, and establishing mentorships, but all of these are effects of the main structural changes regarding evaluations and assignments.

HOW THE TVF WILL WORK

The total volunteer force represents changes to the structure of officer management—the means not the ends. The final four chapters will focus on four key structures—promotions, assignments, career planning, and evaluations—while this section will overview the structural steps that a TVF represents. This is not meant to be an exhaustive list, but is an honest look at concrete steps that would provide real, revolutionary change in transforming the military's industrial personnel hierarchy into an innovative, entrepreneurial powerhouse.

Step 1. Create an internal labor market for job assignments and promotions. Creating an internal labor market sounds like a big, complicated, expensive undertaking, but it is exactly the opposite. Markets form naturally when they are allowed, so the only thing to do is to remove barriers. Right now, the barrier is a matter of hiring authority. In a market system, the demand agents have authority—a zero-step process separates the requirement (micro demand) and the job offer—whereas in a command system, there is a multistep process involving an estimate of demand (the central authority aggregates requirements from various units), an estimate of inventory, a complicated matching algorithm, and then a communication to both supply and demand agents, no doubt with a few feedback loops for back channel adjustments.

The TVF changes that by giving local commanders final, but conditional, hiring authority. Promotion boards would shift to authorization boards, meaning a new group of O-4 officers would be authorized for O-5 positions by the board. Any officer who is authorized could submit an application to the unit, and authorization would include rank and technical criteria (e.g., education, training, security clearances, and so forth). The point is that ranks would be tied to jobs, and jobs would be filled by operational commanders.

The internal labor market solves a lot more than the distribution problem. For starters, it automatically does force shaping. If the army needs to trim 5 percent of its artillery personnel and increase its sta-bilization force by 10 percent, it only needs to communicate the new allotments to operational commanders; the market actually does the force shaping. Another practical difficulty for all military services is how to effectively and efficiently draw down by retaining the best and brightest while letting go of the weaker officers. For example, one can imagine the market doing this by looking at the hypothetical story of 19-year Major Dale Dufus. Dale is a good guy, maybe once a great company commander, but he is now out of shape and uninterested in intellectual work of any kind. With the TVF, nobody has to fire Major Dufus. Rather, it is on him to apply for jobs, and if the market is tight during a drawdown, so be it. If he cannot find a job in the military, then he has a terminal period before being officially retired (perhaps he can begin drawing his 50-percent retirement pay without formally being retired).

An internal labor market would terminate the need for central planners at HRC, but it would *increase* the need for HR talent. TVF would disband personnel command centers such as HRC, reorienting personnel staffers to become counselors. Each division, brigade, and battalion would have at least one HR officer (HRO)—a peer with the XO—who would be responsible for soliciting and screening candidates for the commander to select to join the unit. The HRO would also give career guidance to officers and NCOs long before they leave the unit. Instead of being a faceless and feared voice at Fort Knox, HR profes-sionals would become flesh and blood mentors.

Step 2. End the use of year groups. By default, an internal market would seem to end year groups, but this would actually necessitate loos-ing authorization criteria for each job. If the Fourth Infantry Division commander, Major General Joseph Anderson, has an opening to fill in Third Brigade, it would be foolish to limit his choices by some nar-row cohort of available officers, say a handful of qualified O-5s who were commissioned 18–20 years prior. It would not be necessary to block a qualified officer with 17 years in, or 14 for that matter. General Anderson, the troops, and the mission deserve to select the best can-didate for the job of Third Brigade commander. Once the bureaucracy that controls assignment and promotions is removed, we can all stop being constrained according to now pointless downstream rules.

Maybe cohorts make sense for the first few probationary years in an officer's career; the O-2 promotion happens automatically at the two-year point, the O-3 promotion at the four year. After a few years of work in any career, experience is not what really matters. For example, very few résumés in the private sector list an applicant's age because that factor simply does not matter. When Google needs to hire an assistant team leader for its social networking project, the firm could not care less whether the best résumé is submitted by a 45-year-old professor or a 15-year-old prodigy. The CEO cares about work ethic, technical expertise, integrity, creativity, and personality. Ending cohorts within the military solves the specialization dilemma. The military under DOPMA/OPMS supports specialization inconsistently, and in many ways punishes it. Sure, there are four branches as well as the coast guard and merchant marines. Other forms of *unit* specialization are all around, from the 16 army branches to the specialized units such as Delta Force and the Thunderbirds. There are bomber squadrons, fighter squadrons, missile squadrons, and cyber squadrons in the USAF. Likewise, the National Guard and Reserves represent a structural specialization, but for an individual to eschew the pursuit of promotion is taboo. Nevertheless, most air force pilots reluctantly get out of the cockpit. Rather than "fly a desk," they often leave for the airlines, which is a huge loss of investment for the military. The effective ban on technical specialization will be lifted the day year groups are removed from promotion considerations, because that single change will break the up-or-out backbone of OPMS.

We can imagine a battalion commander who wants his top soldier to stay in the current job for another year, and the soldier prefers to stay, but the current culture says Captain Patton has to leave to check the next box. Wouldn't it be better if the commander could guarantee in writing a top evaluation and a financial bonus? In the private sector, this is a personal contract, and it shouldn't be outlawed in the service. The proper signal is sent to the future market that Captain Patton is very high value. This situation raises the topic a bit prematurely about evaluations, but we will get to that soon.

What about those who love their job so much they never want to leave? What does the navy do with an F-14 aviator who simply doesn't want to do anything else but fly Tomcats? Maverick never looks for a follow-on job, never applies to graduate school, and never even takes midcareer PME courses. He's just the best Top Gun there ever was, and won't make way for the next generation. Is this really a problem? If we ponder this question for a few minutes, it reveals an underlying assumption that the military needs to maintain a certain throughput rate for its officers. Maybe a metaphor here is a crowded escalator that has to keep moving everyone up, up, up at the same rate. Isn't this mindset itself a problem? If the average navy officer stayed in every job twice as long, but each career were allowed to be 50 percent longer, the result would be mathematically simple. For starters, the navy needs one-third fewer human beings in each entering cohort, so it could be much more selective in accessions. The bigger effect is that officers would be much more expert at their jobs; let's speculate twice as good. Maybe it's a leap of logic to say a person becomes twice as productive by working each position twice as long, but do not forget the training lag in each position. If it takes six months to ramp up a learning curve, then job tenures of four versus two years cut one-eighth of unproductive time from the workforce, not to mention the cost savings in half as many Permanent Change of Station (PCS) moves.

Realistically, few people want to stay in the same job for long, especially young college graduates. The fact is that job turnover is high for workers in their 20s, especially among curious, intelligent classes of workers. There may be some cases in which a person with unique expertise wants to stay "in the cockpit," and frankly commanders should have the discretion to handle them on a case-by-case basis. But the TVF would certainly not rule out some tenure caps, and we can imagine that key developmental jobs would and should have such caps. The thing to remember is that under the TVF only 10–20 percent of jobs would have rotational timetables, whereas 95+ percent have them now.

Step 3. Open the officer market. In the TVF, demand for labor comes from unit commanders. The supply of labor is the population of active-duty officers who qualify for higher jobs. The TVF market would operate more efficiently with a few old constraints in place: fixed deployment times, common wages within ranks/specialties, promotion boards, and the top-down evaluation system. But why keep all those limits?

Soon after the first two steps prove themselves, one of the more adventurous services (say the Marines) will realize that it should let the market operate more freely with more compensation discretion, fewer training mandates, and a wider labor pool.

In the real world, compensation is a powerful signal of value. It's a shame that hiring commanders cannot use it as an evaluation marker when assessing their troops today. Imagine a battalion commander assembling his/her team during a reset. Does he/she want to hire a $70,000 sniper or an $80,000 linguist? How about $110,000 for both in one package?

Here's another wrinkle: Captain X has three ACOMs (above center of mass evals) and a current salary of $130,000 as a platoon commander in Afghanistan, but hasn't been to CCC. Captain Y has three ACOMS, but a salary of $99,000 and has been to CCC. Whom do you hire? Among the other ten applications your HR officer screens, he puts one more in for your consideration, a Captain Z with 5 combat tours, only 1 ACOM, but a salary of $215,000. There is no best choice for all situations, but there is a best for the commander's local needs.

In time, the market would sort out what experiences commanders truly value within the first year. Soldiers would notice and have real incentives to respond to concerning which training to seek. No doubt a few of the superfluous PME in-residence programs would close, thanks to TVF, but the likely result is that PME overall would improve.

It would be a revolution for the army to allow a 35-year-old general to command 44-year-old colonels and majors, but such age differentials are common in the business world. Besides, somehow NCOs survive taking orders from junior officers, which makes the seniority culture of the officer corps look ridiculous. Maybe letting a 33-year-old serve as a general officer won't pan out (as it did for James Gavin), but that would actually be okay if rank were a two-way street. The military needs to get comfortable (as it once was) with officers moving down in rank, both when they have to and when they want to. A 29-year-old Marine captain should be free to apply for an O-4 slot at the Pentagon or an O-2 slot in a Special Forces unit. His choice.

A much bigger change will be allowing lateral entry of former-officers-turned-civilians into higher ranks. Barring outsiders from senior officer slots is a lost opportunity. While a 30-year-old civilian who has never been to basic training is arguably unqualified for command, using that example to deem ex-officers unfit is, bluntly, outrageous. With veterans comprising nearly 10 percent of all CEOs, why has the military declared all that talent ineligible for active duty? Truth be told, the higher ranks are sorely lacking in the kind of business experience that only veteran executives have in spades. Importantly, allowing veterans who are civilians to apply for jobs does not mean they will be hired. Some will; most won't. We can imagine that the ten-year veteran who resigned his commission to spend five years working cybersecurity in Silicon Valley would be attractive to the army. The three-year veteran who has been pumping gas for twelve years, not so much. And just because someone gets a job in the TVF does not mean s/he is guaranteed a career.

The final consideration here is retirement. The current retirement system uses a 20-year cliff for service members to qualify for a lifetime defined benefit. This approach was popularized in the mid-twentieth century, but is being phased out in the private sector. It is not long for the public sector either, one way or another. The Pentagon recognizes this, and is working on a new approach. A new pension system that drops the 20-year cliff in favor of a defined contribution (such as a 401K) will make the TVF function effectively by making lateral entry possible. The bigger benefit is fairness for those officers who leave before the 20-year career point and will now get some proportional retirement.

CHAPTER 6

WINNING BATTLES, LOSING WARS

If leadership depends purely on seniority you are defeated before you start. You give a good leader very little and he will succeed; you give mediocrity a great deal and they will fail.

—George C. Marshall, 1941, to the Truman Committee[1]

GENERALS PREPARE TO FIGHT THE LAST WAR, the saying goes, especially if that war was a victory. The proverbial case study on this is the way the military trained and structured itself after World War II, with an emphasis on Europe, big weapons systems, and mass mobilization. Instead, the army founded itself in the strange and confusing war in Vietnam starting in the late 1950s and lasting until the early 1970s. If the proverb was true, the United States would have learned its counterinsurgency lessons from Vietnam and applied them effectively in Afghanistan and Iraq.

Counterinsurgency (COIN) is a doctrine of warfare that emphasizes protection of the local population, not the search and destruction of enemy combatants. John Nagl recounts America's tortured history learning how to fight the Viet Cong insurgency in his masterful *Learning to Eat Soup with a Knife*. Based on his Oxford University dissertation, the 2002 book showed how the US Army had effectively developed COIN tactics in the latter years of Vietnam. It was known publicly then as the strategy of winning "hearts and minds," and it was successful, even though the tide of war and public sentiment were already turned by the time the tactics were widely adopted. Sadly, the hard-won lessons were neglected as soon as that war ended in 1975. The United States licked its wounds and turned its attention back to the Cold War standoff between North Atlantic Treaty Organization (NATO) and the Warsaw Pact.

Fast forward to Iraq in 2004. It became obvious to many junior officers and troops that COIN tactics were needed, but the training and operations in place paid little but lip service to those tactics. Doctrine emphasized maneuver combat and force protection, not economic development or population security (which was supposed to be a job for somebody else, maybe the State Department). After a few years, General David Petraeus tapped Nagl from his position at the Pentagon to help him update the US Counterinsurgency Field Manual. Publication of that document December 2006 was a watershed, as it became a vital building block in the new "surge" strategy that eventually helped save Iraq from descending into civil war. But there is a backstory here about personnel that inspired this book in the first place. Many senior officers in the Pentagon disliked the very idea of COIN, with its emphasis on men and deemphasis on machines. What's the need for a six-hundred-ship navy or another squadron of F-22 fighters if the focus of American combat is touchy-feely soldiers and Marines? Even in the army, there were strong opinions for and against COIN, and I have to wonder how much those attitudes shaped assignments and promotions. For Nagl, we know that he decided to retire in 2008 as a lieutenant colonel, which on its face seems like a remarkably low rank for such an important officer after such a landmark achievement.

Was the US Army biased against Nagl's new way of thinking? It's easy to jump to that conclusion, but what happened to a singular officer is not a useful metric, and Nagl himself left to spend more time with his wife and family after a full 20 years of service. Even so, it is mind-boggling to civilians to see the author of an organization's key doctrine not formally recognized as senior management material after two decades. I was shocked to learn that nobody in the army makes general before his or her third decade in uniform, and a few conversations later was disturbed to hear hints of an anti-intellectual promotion system (i.e., the muddy-boots bias).

My reading of the rather fresh history of Iraq led me to conclude that Nagl's story is just one of many revealing a Pentagon leadership system that is oblivious to entrepreneurial officers. The case study of counterinsurgency doctrine in Iraq described in this chapter shows a systematic failure of the personnel system to promote innovative leaders fast enough. *Promote* is the key term: Who gets to command?

FORGETTING HOW TO FIGHT

The younger generation can probably never understand the cloud of nuclear Armageddon that cast a shadow over the Cold War years. Doomsday felt inevitable to many, despite President Dwight Eisenhower's studied, golfing nonchalance. A common refrain was that World War I was fought by men, World War II was fought by machines, and a World War III would be fought by the push of a button. That's not how it worked out, and it took two land wars in Asia (first Korea, then Vietnam) for policymakers to understand that the future was going to be much more like the past than they had prepared for.

Of all armies, the one that should never forget the centrality of guerrilla tactics in war is the American army. George Washington, father of the Republic, exemplified the flexibility to switch from guerrilla to open-field formation tactics in his successful leadership against the British army and its mercenaries. During the American Civil War, too, "insurgent warfare composed a large proportion of the fighting," which included civilians in the South attacking supply lines, raiding positions, even assassinating Northern leaders. This harassment by irregulars is estimated to have "tied down as much as one-third of the Union army in static defense of logistical lines and bases."[2] How is it that the United States came to forget so much about war?

The army became focused on heavy warfare in Europe immediately after World War II, while the navy became focused on carrier task forces, and the air force on jet-powered nuclear bombers. In his book, *Bureaucracy,* the late political scientist James Q. Wilson explained how this kind of last-war planning happened:

> The Eurocentric focus of the army thus satisfied several organizational needs for money, political backing, the continuation of tasks and roles defined by the battles of World War II, and for minimizing conflict among the service branches. By contrast anyone who proposed changing the structure or doctrine of the

army to meet the needs of low-intensity or mid-intensity warfare in Central America, the Middle East, or Southeast Asia would threaten many of these organizational needs.[3]

The two world wars provide rich lessons, often contradictory, about the evolution of warfare, so it is understandable that the generals made the plans they did. They rightly recognized the primacy of advanced weaponry over warrior spirit: light machine guns in 1916, tanks and fighter aircraft and submarines in 1939, atomics in 1945. Charisma and courage mattered, all agreed, but were insufficient without technological weaponry. Much of strategic thinking during the latter twentieth century split the theory of conflict into two separate spheres: conventional war and nuclear war. What this mistaken worldview missed was that guerrilla warfare was not some kind of Little League or premodern evolutionary plateau of lesser states, rather it was the eternal and common denominator of conflict. Both conventional and nuclear warfare assumed that modern conflict was *national*. "A war is a war is a war," said Harry Summers, a retired US Army colonel and neo-Clausewitzean who championed the view that Vietnam was lost because of political meddling and inhibitions, not military incompetence. But a war is a war only if our field of view neglects nonstate actors: tribes, religions, and ideologues. It's fair to say that the recent *wars* in Afghanistan and Iraq have opened all of our eyes to the importance of nonstate actors.

When the United States fought in Vietnam, it escalated slowly until there were more than half a million American boots on the ground in 1968. The quantity of troops didn't matter. The surge of manpower and firepower proved unsuccessful at stopping the communist insurgency in South Vietnam. Amazingly, many policymakers did understand early on that conventional warfare was not enough, but even the highest-ranking leaders failed to change the core strategy until it was too late.

John F. Kennedy was one the visionaries. He had visited Vietnam as a senator and congressman before his election to the presidency in 1960, and it was Kennedy who pushed the chairman of the Joint Chiefs, General Lyman Lemnitzer, to expand the capacity and use of the Special Forces. Lemnitzer responded by leaking skepticism to the press in early 1961. It was also Kennedy who authorized the creation of the Green Berets during a visit to Fort Bragg in late 1961, and who said famously in his 1962 graduation address at West Point: "When there is a visible enemy to fight in open combat, the answer is not so difficult. Many serve, all applaud, and the tide of patriotism runs high. But when there is a long, slow struggle, with no immediate visible foe, your choice will seem hard indeed."[4]

While there were many adherents to Kennedy's view, the institutional inertia in favor of conventional and nuclear warfare limited the importance of COIN as a viable military career specialty. Big Army held the view that conventional soldiers could defeat insurgents using conventional tactics, and in truth, conventional war against the Soviet Union was what dominated the thinking of all the armed forces. Vietnam in the early 1960s was a very minor drama compared to the brinkmanship on display during the Cuban Missile Crisis.

Even during the late 1960s, Vietnam was considered a proxy in the larger chess match with the Soviets, a battle in the larger geopolitical war. General William Westmoreland commanded US land forces in Vietnam from 1964 to 1968, and, in hindsight, he never really understood how to win. At the time, when asked what the answer to insurgency was, Westmoreland pugnaciously answered: "Firepower."[5] He asked for more conscripts from President Lyndon Johnson and got them during four years of escalating violence. Meanwhile, the lessons of counterinsurgency were being learned very painfully and very slowly by the men on the ground.

Westmoreland was sacked in Jun 1968 after the Tet Offensive—a crushing defeat of North Vietnamese forces, but also devastating to the general's public assurances—and he was replaced by his deputy, General Creighton Abrams. This was the same Abrams, West Point class of 1936, whom George Patton had proclaimed the greatest tank commander in Europe. Mark Moyar recounts a story of the young Thirty-Seventh Battalion commander's intelligent risk-taking in World War II: "His tank was always out front, engaging the enemy with the hatch open and Abrams sticking out from the waist up...Abrams insisted that all of his tanks fight with their hatches open so that the crews could see what was going on around them."[6]

Twenty-four years later, Abrams was willing to see what Westmoreland would not: firepower was losing to people power. Abrams, along with Ambassador Ellsworth Bunker and intelligence chief William Colby, employed a new strategy focused on security of the local population, a sharp break from the "search and destroy" emphasis of Westmoreland. They immediately began emphasizing population protection, training and coordinating directly with the South Vietnamese army, nurturing the best Vietnamese commanders, and fostering local economic development. Abrams called it the "one war" approach, making political and economic progress as important as military progress.[7] The adoption of COIN had a positive effect, but the United States was too busy pulling out more than 90 percent of its troops from 1969 to 1972 for it to matter. By 1975, the Americans were gone, Saigon fell to the North Vietnamese, and the US military spent the next quarter century forgetting it had ever happened.

One cannot help but wonder what might have happened if Westmoreland had been removed faster. Why was the promotion system at the highest level so slow to recognize his four years of incompetence? Consider that the US Civil War lasted exactly four years—from April 1861 to April 1865—and President Abraham Lincoln promoted and removed numerous commanding generals before finding Ulysses S. Grant. The consensus of historians is that General George McClellan was instrumental in building the Union army, but far too hesitant to command it in battle effectively. Grant had no such problem. More importantly, Lincoln had no problem giving Grant the chance. Likewise, when the United States entered World War II, US Army chief of staff General George C. Marshall dismissed three-quarters of division and corps commanders and five hundred colonels during the course of the four-year conflict.[8] However, by the time President Johnson was the commander in chief, the careful promotion system of Secretary of Defense Robert McNamara was securely in place, so Westmoreland stayed.

FALSE SECURITY

US Army Major Andrew Krepinevich was one of the first, and certainly the loudest, of a new generation of officers who wanted the army to remember Vietnam. Greg Jaffe and David Cloud describe in their book *The Fourth Star* how thoroughly and willfully the US Army neglected its lessons from the conflict, and Krepinevich is cautionary tale number one. He was a West Point graduate recruited to teach in the Social Sciences department who published his PhD dissertation in 1986 as a book titled *The Army and Vietnam*. The book hammered at the army's doctrinal rigidity during the war and was widely acclaimed in many reviews, but the army itself saw the book as a threat, and deployed a retired general to bash it in an Army War College journal and even blacklisted its author from speaking at the Military Academy by orders of the Superintendent. Petraeus admitted later that the treatment of Krepinevich was unsettling and put a chilling effect on public dialogue about army orthodoxy.

The first Gulf War in 1990–1991 made it easier than ever to forget counterinsurgency. With the Powell doctrine firmly in place, the United States waited for months to build up a massive coalition of allied forces and a massive logistical effort getting its own troops in place before launching a veritable blitzkrieg against the Iraqi forces in occupied Kuwait. The ground campaign began on February 23, 1991, and lasted exactly one hundred hours. The Iraqi forces were crushed, and American dominance of conventional combat was established for all the world to see: better weapons, better strategy, better communications, better soldiers. Then, as if on cue for the kind of postwar action the Pentagon preferred, in early March 1991 the 540,000 US troops began to deploy out of the region.

The US effort to aid the refugees during Somalia's civil war in the early 1990s showed just as painfully that conventional strength could not do everything. An even bigger 1990s peacekeeping intervention by more than twenty-two thousand US troops in Bosnia and neighboring countries was also difficult but on-balance successful in the late 1990s. The status quo seemed to be working fine. Ironically, during the 2000 election, George W. Bush campaigned against what his advisers said was a Clinton strategy of "nation-building" and promised that if elected, he would keep the US military focused on fighting and winning wars with a direct national-security interest at stake. This is an echo of the hostility that the conventional military held for special operations and COIN.

Once he was sworn in, President Bush's new secretary of Defense, Donald Rumsfeld, got right to work transforming the military to a leaner, faster force with fewer troops and more technology. Almost by definition, COIN calls for a higher concentration of troops to technology, the better to integrate with a population, but COIN was a niche topic for intellectuals in early 2001, and the 9/11 attacks were half a year away.

There were good, albeit controversial, reasons to invade and even occupy Iraq on March 19, 2003, but these rested heavily on the competence of coalition forces to depose the brutal regime of Saddam Hussein and quickly restore order. Establishing a democracy in Iraq and nudging the Arab Spring are outcomes the war's advocates point to. But the Bush administration anticipated the invasion would be quick and the occupation would be short, costing the American taxpayer $50 to $60 billion dollars. Rumsfeld and his staff downplayed the odds of Iraq becoming a quagmire, and some joked this wouldn't be anything like Vietnam. It was a desert, not a swamp, after all. Even so, "much of the top brass wasn't persuaded by the wisdom of invading Iraq,"[9] noted Tom Ricks in his book *Fiasco*, especially senior army officers and joint staff planners, but nobody publicly voiced any concerns about the invasion.

Secretary Rumsfeld had been pushing the army pretty hard to change its force structure and mission. One success was canceling the self-propelled howitzer called the Crusader, a system that looks in hindsight like a Cold War fantasy. Rumsfeld and his transformation philosophy were right on that one and many other initiatives. The secretary also pushed to cut back the number of active-duty divisions from ten to eight, a point on which even some of his undersecretaries pushed back.

When it came to the Iraq invasion, Rumsfeld negotiated with United States Central Command (CENTCOM) commander General Tommy Franks for a smaller invasion force. As Ricks describes: "The initial plan put on the table . . . called for a tiny force, consisting of one enhanced brigade from the 3rd Infantry Division and one Marine Expeditionary Unit—all in all, fewer than ten thousand combat troops."[10] The war planning between Rumsfeld and Franks eventually seemed to wear Franks down, and though the invasion was a spectacular victory, the postwar effort proved to be nothing short of a disaster of bungled redevelopment, raging insurgency, and a civil war in all but name. With that in mind, it must be remembered that before the invasion in late 2002 and early 2003, army generals were being told by Rumsfeld's staff to "plan to have the US occupation force reduced to thirty thousand troops by August 2003."[11] In actuality, the force wasn't *reduced* to the forty-thousand level until 2011.

SENDING A SIGNAL

Eric Shinseki was born and raised in Hawaii, graduated from West Point in the class of 1965, and served two combat tours in Vietnam. He served in high-ranking roles in planning as well as commanding roles in NATO's Bosnia mission as a four-star general. Shinseki became the chief of staff of the army in June 1999. Far from being an example of a risk-averse mediocre officer produced by a broken personnel system, Shinseki was innovative and entrepreneurial throughout his career. He outlined a transformation plan in late 1999 (a year and half before the Bush administration took office) for a post–Cold War environment, specifically calling for an intermediate armored vehicle to fill the gap between the lethal, slow tank and the light Humvee. This was ultimately realized in the eight-wheeled Stryker, which has performed extremely well in the field. The point is that talented officers such as Shinseki were able to thrive despite the personnel systems.

History will remember Shinseki for a single controversial statement he made during testimony before the Senate Armed Services Committee on February 25, 2003. He was asked to give some idea of the magnitude of the force necessary for an occupation of Iraq. Deferring initially to the combatant commanders in such a scenario, the chief of staff then stated that he felt comfortable anticipating "something on the order of several hundred thousand soldiers."[12] This was on par with historical experience and the Bosnia rule of thumb: one soldier for every 50 locals. It is also a judgment that has been vindicated decisively by experience in Iraq itself, where nearly 160,000 US troops ultimately served at the peak of the surge in 2008. However, before the invasion, the Defense Department did not anticipate a long or full occupation and so it thought the number much too large, and Deputy Secretary Paul Wolfowitz reacted angrily to the testimony, countering it as "outlandish" during his own appearance before the committee days later.[13]

Shinseki wasn't fired in his last year as chief, but he was widely perceived as powerless after that testimony. The unfortunate signal sent to others in uniform was to avoid honest, public commentary about Iraq. In other ways, the military was hamstrung as it went into Iraq with false assumptions of how a post-Saddam Iraq would react to their presence. Rather than establish order on the streets, allied soldiers were instructed to let the locals run wild, more or less. Jay Garner, the retired lieutenant general tapped by Rumsfeld to oversee postwar reconstruction in mid-January, was relieved over the phone in late April as he stood amid the broken glass of Saddam's main Baghdad palace. The amount of chaos in the country cannot be overstated.

In came Paul Bremer, the presidential envoy who ran the ill-fated Coalition Provisional Authority or CPA, the transitional government in Iraq. Bremer made numerous and large mistakes. First, he instated a severe de-Baathification program, against the advice of Garner, the Central Intelligence Agency (CIA), and even contrary to what the White House had approved, which neutered civil society and fueled the meltdown of public sector operations. Second, against the strong recommendation of US Army general John Abizaid and many others, Bremer disbanded the entire Iraqi army. According to Ricks: "Together, those two orders threw out of work more than half a million people and alienated many more dependent on those lost incomes."[14] Moreover, it exacerbated ethnic fault lines. Apparently, the radical decisions surprised the White House and Defense Department, but no matter. The damage was done, Bremer kept his position, and again, American officers felt that they bore the consequences without being given responsibility to control the mess being made.

VIETNAM REDUX

Remember the proverb that America is always planning to fight the last war? Nothing could be further from the truth when it came to the invasion and occupation of Iraq in 2003. If the army had been planning to fight Vietnam all over again, it would have done so using counterinsurgency from day one, and if that had been its approach, it would have "won the peace" in Iraq much faster.

Despite the decisions of Secretary Rumsfeld to curtail long-term planning efforts for an occupation and Bremer's incompetence at CPA that fueled the multiethnic insurgency, it was fundamentally the army's broken personnel system that nearly lost Iraq because it slowed the pace of learning. Repeating the mistake of fighting an insurgency with conventional combat—precisely what the army had done in the first half of the Vietnam conflict—the US military adopted a conventional approach of finding and killing the enemy in Iraq. It was an approach that gave short shrift to political and economic development. Why did it take so long to turn around the US strategy in Iraq? For the same reason given during the Vietnam conflict. The strategy changed only when the commanding generals changed.

The eventual triumph of COIN doctrine in Iraq was covered in the media as "the surge." The general who led the effort, Petraeus, was rightfully celebrated. But why did it take so long for COIN to be implemented? The media essentially ignored the flawed personnel system that delayed the innovative COIN approach for four painful years. To be sure, there was plenty of talk was about strategy, and some about the strategists (Franks, Abizaid, Peter Pace, Ricardo Sanchez, George Casey, Peter Chiarelli, James Mattis, Richard Myers, Petraeus), but zero coverage of the *system* that produced those strategists.

True, the system promoted some supremely talented and entrepreneurial officers to high command. Most observers would name Petraeus and US Marine General Mattis at the top of the list. Abizaid and Chiarelli would be close behind. Franks, Casey, Pace, and Myers tend to get mixed marks. But almost no one would claim that US Army lieutenant general Sanchez was innovative or effective.

Sanchez, promoted from the rank of major general and commander of the First Armored Division in Baghdad, "was given command of all US forces in Iraq in June 2003, ahead of all officers who ranked higher than him in seniority, relevant experience, and ability,"[15] according to Moyar, and he held the job for exactly one year. Here is how Ricks describes his tenure:

> He was by all accounts a good man, somewhat gruff, but hard-working, dedicated, and doing what he was trained to do. But there are few people who contend that he was the man for the job, or that he succeeded in Iraq.
>
> ...The opinion of many of his peers was that he was a fine battalion commander who never should have commanded a division, let alone a corps or nationwide occupation mission.[16]

In all fairness, the system replaced the overwhelmed Sanchez relatively quickly—just one year after giving him command—but that hardly absolves the system from appointing someone so unqualified in the first place. The army is overstocked with muddy-boots generals in administrative jobs, so why was Sanchez given this prime task? Was he the absolute best candidate for the job? No. And nobody would even pretend to argue that. Sanchez was given the job because of the insane "fairness" or dumb luck dictated by the bureaucracy. He was in line.

More strategic mistakes were made, and the US civilian leadership continued to deny that an insurgency was happening in Iraq. Finally, after the 2006 elections, which saw President Bush's Republican

Party lose its majority in the House, Senate, and state governorships, Secretary Rumsfeld resigned.

The new secretary appointed by Bush was Robert M. Gates, a 26-year veteran of the CIA and a one-time USAF officer. He also served in the ten-person Iraq Study Group, which issued its influential report in December 2006 that strongly recommended a US drawdown in Iraq. There was a feeling in early 2007 that America was on the verge of losing, that Iraq was this generation's Vietnam.

US Army lieutenant colonel Paul Yingling, veteran of multiple tours in Iraq, wrote a scathing critique in 2007 setting responsibility for the failures not just on ineffective strategy but calling them a "Failure of Generalship."

> America's generals have repeated the mistakes of Vietnam in Iraq. First, throughout the 1990s our generals failed to envision the conditions of future combat and prepare their forces accordingly. Second, America's generals failed to estimate correctly both the means and the ways necessary to achieve the aims of policy prior to beginning the war in Iraq. Finally, America's generals did not provide Congress and the public with an accurate assessment of the conflict in Iraq.
>
> ...Any explanation that fixes culpability on individuals is insufficient. No one leader, civilian or military, caused failure in Vietnam or Iraq. Different military and civilian leaders in the two conflicts produced similar results. In both conflicts, the general officer corps designed to advise policymakers, prepare forces and conduct operations failed to perform its intended functions. To understand how the U.S. could face defeat at the hands of a weaker insurgent enemy for the second time in a generation, *we must look at the structural influences that produce our general officer corps.*[17]

Regardless whether readers buy into the triumph of COIN as a superior strategy, the real story here is about the leadership system's capacity to be *adaptive at a strategic level.* Lenny Wong, a senior scholar at the Army War College, thinks it is not nearly adaptive enough. Wong argues that the army has a singular focus on war-fighting— what he calls the "muddy-boots army"—that hinders career variability among top officers.

THE NUTS AND BOLTS OF PROMOTIONS

It might come as a surprise that the army keeps a very long list of every officer on active duty, ordered from the most to least senior. This active-duty list (ADL) determines who is considered for promotions and when. Although the DOPMA-authorized (Defense Officer Personnel Management Act) percentage of officers in consideration narrows with each rank from captain to colonel, the process for each rank follows three similar steps. First, a selection board meets to determine who will be promoted and in what order; second, the results are announced many months later; and third, the promoted officers are given a pin-on date set even further in the future, with the most senior officers pinning on earliest.

Once a year for each rank and competitive category (organized by functional area), a promotion-selection board is convened at Human Resources Command (HRC) headquarters at Fort Knox. The captains board meets in March, the majors board in February, and so on. For example, the group of majors in the aviation category in the 1998 year group will be considered "in the zone" for lieutenant colonel along with year group 1997 "above the zone" and 1999 "below the zone." The outcome of the board is an ordered list of selections, reviewed by HRC, which then must be approved by Congress. Army pamphlet 600–3 explains how the board participants are to evaluate the candidates:

Centralized boards, except captain, are provided minimum promotion requirements (floors) by branch, functional area or area of concentration to ensure the Army's skill and grade mix balances with its needs. Recommendations are based upon branch, MOS [military occupational specialty] and functional area competency, the potential to serve in the higher grade and the whole person concept. Factors considered include:

(1) Performance.
(2) Embodiment of Army Values.
(3) Professional attributes and ethics.
(4) Integrity and character.
(5) Assignment history and professional development.
(6) Military bearing and physical fitness.
(7) Attitude, dedication and service.

(8) Military and civilian education and training.

(9) Concern for Soldiers and Families.

...Each board receives a Memorandum of Instruction from the Secretary of the Army providing guidance for the selection process. Copies of these memorandums are released to the officer corps following approval and public release of the board results.[18]

When the dozen or so members of each board convene for the two-week promotion process, a stack of files on each candidate awaits. In each file is a photo, a series of evaluations from each previous job, and what amounts to a résumé. Given the time constraints, participating board members only have one–three minutes to consider each file. That's just enough time to maybe scan the first and last line of each written evaluation. Colonel Scott Wuestner, US Army retired, said to me something I've heard from a hundred others: promotion boards tend to self-select, tapping officers who look like them. "For example, our functional area 59 officers (strategic planners and thinkers) have the highest promotion rate to colonel, but none were selected for flag officer rank until recently," Wuestner said.[19]

"I have a pulse, of course I'll make lieutenant colonel," has been a common sentiment in the armed forces for the last decade. As Cindy Williams reported in a 2008 article,

> The active-duty Army today is short about 2,700 captains, majors and lieutenant colonels.... To compensate, the Army has increased promotion rates for every rank from captain to colonel. The usual rate of promotion from captain to major is 80 percent; in 2005, that rate climbed to 98 percent. In 2005, the chance of making lieutenant colonel shot up to 89 percent.[20]

Exceptional officers are promoted "below the zone," which is the equivalent of skipping a grade in elementary school—only the very best achieve it. A superselect few are promoted "double below the zone" (BTZ), and apparently this is being extended to colonel promotions as well. With those opportunities, promotions may seem like a meritocracy, but it is much shallower than what the total volunteer force (TVF) would allow. The bulk of officers in the zone are treated like a sea of mediocrity. Even with below-the-zone promotions, nobody makes general at the 10-year point or even the 20-year point because of time in grade constraints at each rank. In the army, if the most extraordinary officer in half a century were to appear, he would make general no sooner than 23 years on active duty, at the age of 44. By comparison, Alexander the Great died at the age of 33 after conquering the known world.

Unfortunately, the high promotion rates of recent times mean that the army will have a tough time culturally with a force drawdown. There are bigger problems, besides. One is that promotions are a one-way street. If officers are promoted to a level beyond their competence, there is no way to bring them back down to a position where they could still be effective. Instead, weak senior officers are shuffled around in "less" important jobs until they retire.

That brings us to the one board where promotion is extremely selective, and where the process is problematic in a unique way. Roughly 1,000 army officers are considered each year, and only 35–40 are selected for the rank of brigadier general. The board is composed of 15 general officers and chaired by a four-star.

THE CURIOUS CASE OF COLONEL H. R. MCMASTER

Tal Afar is an Iraqi town of a quarter million people, located in northern Iraq, containing a mix of Shiites and Sunnis. The city is ancient, thought to be mentioned twice in the Bible (under the name Telassar), with remains from cultures dating back to 7000 BCE. It served as a base for insurgents almost immediately after the US occupation, and military assaults to the area in 2004 led to complaints by the neighboring state of Turkey. In a story that is familiar to those who study Iraq, Tal Afar is seen as a turning point because of what the Third Armored Cavalry Regiment (ACR) did there in 2005. Ricks describes the transformation of the Regiment under the command of then-Colonel H. R. McMaster, practically the only glimmer of hope in the final pages of *Fiasco*.

McMaster took command of the Third ACR in June 2004 at Fort Carson, Colorado, nearly a year before it deployed to northwest Iraq, and began using counterinsurgency tactics: protecting the local population first, treating everyone respectfully, knowing the language. McMaster also relieved one of his battalion commanders who did not buy into the COIN philosophy. Once the unit arrived in Iraq, McMaster delayed attacking the entrenched insurgents in Tal Afar itself, patiently dismantling the support network outside the city and following the mantra of "clear, hold, and build." He made it a policy to treat detainees better as well, even polling them in an effort to discourage abuse of prisoners, which in the long run McMaster knew would fuel deepening resentment against his and future American troops. He met with Sunni leaders in the region early on and made an extraordinary apology for the harshness of early American efforts, but also warned that the time for legitimate resistance was over. After ringing the city with a dirt berm (barrier) to control and observe movement, he waited. "Finally, in September 2005, after four months of preparatory moves, McMaster launched his attack," says Ricks. "By that point, there were remarkably few fighters left in the city."[21]

In December of that same year, McMaster's name was one of those considered for promotion to brigadier general. What he had done in Tal Afar had already made an impression in the Pentagon, and he was singled out for praise by President Bush in 2006. Surprisingly, when the promotion board's selections were made public, McMaster was not listed. When the next board met in late 2006 and the results were made public in 2007, McMaster was passed over a second time.[22]

Even while McMaster's tactics were being turned into doctrine, the old guard that ran the promotion process was effectively punishing him. Fred Kaplan wrote a highly influential op-ed in the *New York Times* about the situation in August of 2007, for which he provided this update a year later on SLATE.com:

When I was reporting a story last summer about growing tensions between the Army's junior and senior officer corps, more than a dozen lieutenants and captains complained bitterly (with no prompting from me) about McMaster's rejection, seeing it as a sign that the top brass had no interest in rewarding excellent performance. The more creative captains took it as a cue to contemplate leaving the Army.[23]

Recall also Andrew Tilghman's essay warning about the retention crisis in the December 2007 issue of *Washington Monthly*. He wrote about the negative reverberations the nonpromotion was sending as well:

Like many young officers I met, Kapinos and Morin were particularly disturbed by the experience of a colonel named H. R. McMaster. McMaster earned a Sliver Star in Operation Desert

Storm.... As the rest of Iraq deteriorated in 2006, Tal Afar was relatively calm, and President Bush touted it as a success. Despite these achievements, McMaster has been passed over twice for promotion to brigadier general. Kapinos concluded, "The junior officers see a guy who they worship—he's smart and successful—and they see him get the short end of the stick. If he doesn't make one star, if he doesn't go on to great things, if the cream stops rising at some point—then the good guys are going to say, 'What's the point?'"[24]

In the summer of 2008, Kaplan celebrated the fact that McMaster's name was announced on the one-star list along with a slew of other innovative, unconventional colonels such as Sean McFarland, who used COIN to pacify Ramadi and spark the Anbar Awakening. "This was why many Army officers were excited when Petraeus was appointed to chair this year's promotion board. Rarely, if ever, had a combat commander been called back from an ongoing war to assume that role,"[25] noted Kaplan. And it was true, Petraeus was instrumental in overseeing the promotion board that year, as were other members such as General Chiarelli and General Stanley McChrystal, to name a few.

What Kaplan didn't know was that McMaster actually had been passed over a third time. The initial board had been chaired by the vice chief of staff of the army, but when the results were submitted to the new chief of staff, General Casey, he disapproved and made the extraordinary decision to reseat a new board. That's when Petraeus was called back from Iraq to chair the new board.

Some wondered if there was something seriously wrong with a military promotion system that pulled the top field commander from a hot war to conduct paperwork half a world away, but on the contrary, the move signaled something seriously right. Nagl explained to me: "The importance of resetting the promotion board that ultimately selected McMaster and McFarlane is hard to overstate. It was extraordinarily unusual."[26] It meant that the usual order was no longer functioning well.

Was the selection of the 40 unorthodox officers for brigadier general a watershed moment? I don't think so. An important moment, yes, but the core system remains firmly in place and it is more likely than not to lapse into habits set by the unreformed rules of the game.

Besides, we shouldn't forget that McMaster's trajectory was delayed by two years and his subsequent assignments have not checked the traditional command boxes on the golden path.[27]

PROMOTIONS IN THE TOTAL VOLUNTEER FORCE

I'm sympathetic to the view that the military's promotion process is optimized within its constraints, a view held quite strongly by officers who have spent their whole careers trying to make the boards function as efficiently as possible. It is not the optimization at fault, but the constraints. Why year groups? Why inflated and neutered performance evaluations? Why no lateral entry? Those inside simply don't know anything else. In the world outside of the vast military autarky, promotions and assignments are not cleaved in two. When a person is hired to a senior-level position at Citigroup or even at the US Labor Department, as two examples, they are promoted and assigned *simultaneously*.

What the army (and air force, navy, Marine Corps, and coast guard) promotion process really serves is a qualifying function. Officers who make the rank of colonel are qualified to fill certain colonel jobs, but the dominoes tumble back a few more steps because active-duty officers also have to qualify for promotions with specific training requirements and key jobs along the golden path. In other words, they have to be qualified to be qualified. They need joint service jobs. They need professional military education (PME) in residence. They need command experience. So the question is: why bother with all this?

Consider the total volunteer force alternative, outlined in chapter 5. Commanders would have sole authority in hiring the officers who directly report to them. There would be a reduction, but not elimination, of HRC and promotion boards in the promotion process. The TVF would recast them as promotion *qualifying* boards as opposed to promotion *selection* boards. Necessary credentials for consideration by a board would still include things like PME, joint service, and so forth, but commanders would have much more latitude in selecting whomever they identify as the top candidate. As for the officer candidates, being qualified under TVF as a battalion commander will not immediately translate into a command job. The candidate would need to apply for such a position, and in many cases may not be tapped for many years, if ever.

For example, the 2005 board that initially passed over McMaster in favor of 40 of his peers could instead have tapped McMaster and perhaps 130 other candidates as brigadier-qualified. It would be up to the assignment process, which we will talk about in the next chapter, to actually put the rank on his shoulders on the day he moved to the new job. No more line numbers or pin-on dates. As it is in the real world, one becomes CEO the day one moves into the CEO's office.

Demotions would be even easier. If a brigadier general performs poorly in the TVF, we can imagine him or her being removed after a few months. As a rule, poorly performing officers could be moved sideways for a transition time of two months to let them seek a new job. If none are available at their current rank, they would need to find an opening at a lower rank or retire. Again, this is how the real world works. A vice president for a financial firm may not be able to find a similar job and will take something with less seniority (actually, that means power, not age in the private sector). It happens all the time.

I would like to believe that a TVF military wouldn't have suffered the strategic sluggishness of the United States in Iraq in 2004–2006. Bright junior officers would be promoted faster and dullards would either never make the rank or be pushed aside faster in the flexible TVF. But it is impossible to judge hypothetical histories fairly. We can't even be sure, at this point, if my long example of counterinsurgency is the right war lesson for the future. The one thing we can say is that ideological bias in a bureaucracy harms innovation. A TVF promotion-qualification function would replace the potential bureaucratic bias of the strict promotion chokehold that HRC now has.

CHAPTER 7

COERCION

It was understood that the military was a planned society. Like the family, the university and the church, it was almost entirely free of market logic.[1]

—David Warsh, *Economic Principals*

DUTY. HONOR. COUNTRY. MEN AND WOMEN who wear the uniform of their country's military share a set of values that set them apart. What those values are is a matter of deep importance, but we know that they represent more than physical courage and teamwork, which are just means to an end. Rather, it is the devotion to higher ends that inspires, captured by the mantra "Service above self."

Cadets at all of the service academies are required to memorize a score of quotations by famous officers and statesmen to initiate their values education. One quote attributed to General Robert E. Lee is: "Duty then is the sublimest word in the English language. You should do your duty in all things. You can never do more, you should never wish to do less." The words hint at an obligation one has, which raises the question of individual liberty. Not to oversimplify, but once a person has taken the oath of office, his or her obligation to submit to the orders of the military chain of command becomes law. The system of values undergirds an operational structure that emphasizes creativity, to be sure, but commands obedience in the end.

In this chapter, we will examine the tensions in the values of the US military. I submit that the traditional values are mostly but not entirely compatible with a *profession* of arms, and definitely at odds with the creation of a more entrepreneurial personnel system. Sorting out the priority of different values is inevitable when a personnel system is reformed, and one of the models for the coming reforms in the total volunteer force (TVF) that I propose is the experience of the 1973 transition to the all-volunteer force (AVF).

Critics now have used much the same logic against my market-based reforms that the critics in the 1960s used against advocates who called for an end to the draft. We'll explore those debates in detail because it is vital to understand what values are at stake. What's not at stake is a choice between *service* values and *self-interested* markets. A better way to think about the embedded values is to ask what role coercion should play in our design of personnel rules for the twenty-first century.

PHILOSOPHY AND VALUES

Coercion is defined as the practice of forcing another person to behave involuntarily, a violation of the individual's free will. According to the law, coercion is a crime defined as duress in which a person only acts under the threat of violence. The philosophical idea of coercion has been at the heart of the writings of Thomas Aquinas, Thomas Hobbes, John Locke, John Stuart Mill, and the late-1960s writings of modern philosophers, including Robert Nozick. In its most extreme form, coercion is slavery. However, most political philosophers believe coercion is necessary for a legitimate state to exercise its authority in the enforcement of law.[2]

Ancient military service coerced all young men to fight for their village or city, and nineteenth-century armies and navies in the "civilized" world still pressed slaves and citizens alike into service. Modern respect for individual rights, especially in the American cultural tradition, recoils at such coercion, but there is no denying that the military's legacy of strict discipline runs deep here. For our purposes, we can understand a spectrum of state necessity to use coercion for just causes, particularly war, which loses legitimacy as it moves along the spectrum from less to more coercive intensity. For example, requiring new soldiers in basic training to salute officers, to run the obstacle course, and to cut their hair a certain way is the essential coercion of creating a well-ordered unit. When a senior officer *orders* a soldier to do something, the soldier must *obey*. We recognize these requirements are based on an underlying premise of voluntary action, however, despite the roots.

There are some coercive acts that cross a line into illegitimacy. We are taught to understand "unlawful orders" to kill innocents or torture prisoners have no authority, and a senior officer's effort to coerce subordinates to follow such orders is a punishable violation of their authority. More to the point, our moral tradition and training require soldiers to disobey such unlawful orders, placing our rich system of values supreme over interpersonal authority.

Despite the values the military proclaims and tries to live by, what concerns me is the coercive cultural tradition that remains manifest in the personnel system. Remember, it is called an *all-volunteer force*, but is it 100 percent voluntary in practice? As Aquinas wrote centuries ago, it is impossible for a thing to be coerced and at the same time voluntary. Unless every action a soldier takes in today's army is fully voluntary, then coercion remains a central thread. Let us ask whether these coercive pieces are useful.

When we explore the personnel system, we see that most elements have threads of voluntary autonomy and coercion woven together. Assignments and promotions are given as orders, with a severely limited right of refusal. Career plans and training follow strictly defined checkpoints with little variation. And so on. The coercive thread is inevitable once the centralized design is set. Political scientist James Q. Wilson described the general principles at stake in any public employment design:

> The central dilemma of any public personnel system involves the choice between a bureaucratized and a professionalized service. The former consists of a set of rules that specify who are to be hired, how they are to be managed, and what they are to do; the latter consists of rules that specify who are to be hired but that leave great discretion to the members of the occupation, or to their immediate supervisor, to decide what they are to do and how they are to be managed.... The biggest struggles in the federal personnel system have been over autonomy—allowing local managers to make decisions and allowing actual or quasi-professionals to do their jobs.[3]

VANGUARDS OF CAPITALISM

The great irony of the Cold War military was that statist communism, posing the constant threat of nuclear Armageddon was opposed by a US military force that was and remains in some fundamental ways a socialist organization. Health care in the military is not only universal and free, but it is also *mandatory and enforced*. Soldiers are ordered to visit the dentist, and they face punishment for being tardy. Troops are paid in large blocks called "pay grades" that are defined by time in service, not individual merit. Soldiers learn to follow orders and respect obedience to strict chains of command. Yet they defend a society based on individual liberty and free-market capitalism. Ironic, no?

There remains a deeply mistaken belief that military culture is incompatible with market mechanisms that grant freedom of choice to soldiers. The Pentagon seems to believe that order is not something that emerges spontaneously from choices made freely; it is imposed by central command. After all, marching in formation is not something that happens without careful training and command. That sense of imposed order makes veterans culturally suspicious of material incentives, a feeling that was epitomized in the 2008 presidential campaign when Senator John McCain contrasted his service as a young man to the business experience of Mitt Romney. He said he had been motivated by "patriotism, not profit"—an attitude shared by many retired veterans.

While the culture—especially the American military culture—emphasizes individual choices and even trains for individual initiatives far down the chain of command, ultimately decisions are made and orders are given that are not flexible about the core mission and who must "take that hill." So, in a sense, the "command and control" DNA remains strong in the military. When a soldier changes units, she is given "orders." When she reports to work, she is "on duty," and when not, it's called "liberty." When she salutes her superior officer, she is signaling her deference.

Is military culture irreconcilable with a market system where both sides of a transaction have the freedom of choice to say yes or no? Let me explain why it is not, with three arguments. One, the two cultures are already fused. Two, markets enhance values. And three, the military shifted away from coercion in daily operations long ago.

First, markets are already deeply ingrained throughout military life. If soldiers in today's army went back in time to the army of the 1940s, they would be shocked to see how far the service has come in jettisoning central planning. There are the obvious external market-provided goods and services such as the use of contractors for sanitation (remember scrubbing toilets, Gomer Pyle?), food preparation, and even some combat operations. All of the equipment is market provided, from F-14s and handguns to meals ready to eat (MREs) and leather shoes. It should also not go unsaid that base pay is a market incentive, not to mention bonuses and allowances. In fact, there have been a hundred little market revolutions over the decades. Soldiers and sailors today pay out of their own pockets for many things that were once handed out equally. Food in the chow hall comes to mind, but also bedding and clothing, not to mention housing.

Second, it is a fallacy to think that markets are value eroding. A deeper examination of the "values versus market" framing shows it to be a false dichotomy. While officers and enlistees are undoubtedly driven by a sense of service, they also have material needs and motivations that factor into their career choices. It's long been understood by scholars and troops that many young men and women select a technical specialty when volunteering for the armed forces in order to enhance their careers while serving their country. And think about this: every year, each of the armed forces spends millions of dollars *advertising* about its values in order to attract volunteers with the best qualities. Indeed, advocates of conscription argued that it was a system that embedded higher values than the AVF could. Nobody believes that now. There are other arguments in favor of conscription that we will address later in this chapter, but values are no longer on the table.

Third, a culture of obedience, or coercion, is not really what the military relies on now, even in the most dangerous combat situations. A battalion commander cannot order his soldiers to reenlist. This is not what George Washington did in the winter of 1776, and it is not what the Pentagon did in 2006. An officer can issue orders, but talk to those who served as officers before 1973, and they will tell you that today's soldier is managed infinitely more by motivation than by decree.

BACKWARD OR FORWARD?

When we think of coercion in today's military, we imagine the reluctant soldier being ordered into combat. The need for this kind of coercion is rooted in the historical nature of warfare. As the historian John Keegan observed: "Bondage, in a stronger or weaker form, is a common condition of military service."[4] He recounts the convention of Mamelukes—slave soldiers in many Muslim states—who often rose up to become rulers of those states for generations but were "adamant" in preserving the institution. Think of them as the logical extreme of the conservative nature of warriors, resisting gunpowder and even crossbows as cowardly threats to their superior system of values. This is the legacy of coercion that still thrives in all militaries.

Let's suppose a young marine refuses to join his unit on a combat mission, refuses to "take that hill." What then? The answer is that he can (and should) be dishonorably discharged. The analogous situation at a private sector firm is autonomous employees who refuse to do their jobs. What happens to them? They get fired and have a black mark on their job history. In sum, coercion and duty are not intertwined. Employees can maintain autonomy and duty.

Where coercion remains very much in play is in the military assignments mechanism. This was illuminated when journalist Eric Tegler interviewed army spokesman, Colonel Thomas Collins:

TIEGLER: Given the Army's growing personnel cost issues, could an internal job market assist the service in cutting or better managing its personnel costs?

COLLINS: The Army has Congressionally-mandated requirements. The "internal job market" concept would not work for an organization whose number one mission is to fight and win our nation's wars. I mean, can you imagine trying to implement such a concept in our units in Afghanistan that are waging daily combat? It would be very difficult, to say the least.[5]

Actually, yes, we can imagine it. The implication of this spokesman's statement is that our soldiers don't want to fight, that they would avoid combat if allowed. Does the army really believe that? Men and women continue to enlist today as they have for years, eyes open, knowing they will go to war. American troops are not coerced into accessions, so why would anyone think they have to be coerced into assignments?

If instead Collins is suggesting that soldiers would prefer an assignment to Hawaii over an assignment to Afghanistan, that too is unclear. Most fireman want to fight fires, and most soldiers want to fight in wars if national security is at stake. To the extent that labor supply for combat jobs in Afghanistan is weak, economics has only one explanation: we are not paying a fair wage to clear that market. Offer the right incentive, and there will be ample labor supply.

Unfortunately, the case is never closed against coercion. There are always those who believe that citizen and nation are intertwined, yielding an involuntary duty in all of us. Rather than move the military forward toward more autonomy for professional soldiers, they would have America move backward toward the draft. US Army colonel Paul Yingling is one of the more eloquent of these voices, and though I think he is wrong, his arguments deserve full consideration. After witnessing the heavy burden the United States carried during the long war in Iraq, Yingling penned this 2010 essay in the *Armed Forces Journal* calling for a return to a citizen army:

> The dangers of military service are born solely by volunteers, a disproportionate number of whom come from working- and middle-class families. The wealthiest and most privileged members of American society are all but absent from the ranks of the U.S. military.
>
> …The U.S. should therefore abandon the all-volunteer military and return to our historic reliance on citizen soldiers and conscription to wage protracted war. This approach proved successful in both world wars and offers several advantages over the all-volunteer military. First and most important, this approach demands popular participation in national security decisions and provides Congress with powerful incentives to reassert its war powers. Unlike the all-volunteer force, a conscripted force of citizen soldiers would ensure that the burdens of war are felt equally in every community in America. Second, this approach provides the means to expand the Army to a sufficient size to meet its commitments. Unlike the all-volunteer force, a conscripted force would not rely on stop-loss policies or an endless cycle of year-on, year-off deployments of overstressed and exhausted forces. Third, conscription enables the military to be more discriminating in selecting those with the skills and attributes most required to fight today's wars.[6]

If we break this argument down to particulars, Yingling is calling for fairness and equality, and his preferred mechanism is to guarantee equality in sharing the war fighting burden through coercion. Oddly, though, his argument that stop-loss (denying soldiers the freedom to leave the ranks when their enlistment term is complete) is unfair, in particular, is a call for less coercion, not more. Yingling wants current volunteers to have the power to disengage. I couldn't agree more.

Now consider Yingling's first observation that justifies coercion: "The dangers of military service are born solely by volunteers." So? This is hardly unique to soldiering. The dangers of coal mining are born solely by volunteers. Policing as well. Caretaking of the elderly. Deep sea fishing. Trash collecting. Dangerous work is no justification for slavery if that slavery is spread thin enough.

Every year, about 170,000 men and women volunteer to join the military, and many reenlist. In contrast, before the AVF, only 10 percent of enlistees were willing to stay longer than the minimum of two years. Such turnover drives recruitment and training costs sky-high and decimates productive service time. A Government Accountability Office (GAO) study in 1998 concluded that an equivalent draft force would cost $2.5 billion more annually than the AVF in budgetary terms alone.

Perhaps this matter would make more sense if we took a long look at the way the AVF came to supplant conscription. We already know it happened largely as a consequence of Vietnam. Could the drawdown of another bitterly fought counterinsurgency spur the next step in personnel evolution?

AMERICAN CONSCRIPTION

On December 7, 1966, Milton Friedman walked through the freezing rain across the University of Chicago's campus, through what had been an inch of snow just days before. Friedman was already a famous economist, and would go on in the next half century to become an iconic one. Earlier in the year, he had published what would come to be recognized as the first major salvo against the ruling orthodoxy of monetary economics, which was fueling inflation through excess stimulation. But on that day, he was part of a four-day conference that was nothing less than a revolt against what he considered modern slavery: the conscription of young men into involuntary military service.

Exactly a quarter century after the surprise attack on Pearl Harbor, an anthropologist named Sol Tax organized the conference of economists at the University of Chicago where Friedman was a professor. Seventy-four invited participants included "essentially everyone who had written or spoken at all extensively on either side of the controversy about the draft"[7] and was open to the public as well. Campuses around the country were protesting the Selective Service system, and protests would only intensify as the Vietnam conflict forced hundreds of thousands of young men into boot camp against their will. Lyndon Johnson was in the White House, and the conflict in Vietnam was escalating quickly.

Inside the conference, Friedman was impressed by one professor in particular, a blind economist named Walter Oi. "I have attended many conferences," Friedman later wrote, but "I have never attended any other that had so dramatic an effect on the participants. A straw poll taken at the outset of the conference recorded two-thirds of the participants in favor of the draft; a similar poll at the end, two-thirds opposed." He credited Oi's speech, which made the novel distinction between budgetary and economic costs, as the key. In a paper published the next year, Oi estimated the economic loss to draftees to be nearly $1 billion (which would be more than $7 billion in 2012 dollars). Friedman became the face of economists arguing against the draft. He was an eloquent libertarian who was famous by then, and about to become more famous in the decades ahead, because of his insights about monetary and macro economics. But he may be best remembered by the 1960s generation as the outspoken conservative who took on their case against forced service.

Conscription has been a part of human existence for a long time, perhaps as long as humans have existed. It was understood as an integral duty of young men in any community, from feudal manors to modern democracies. As Bernard Rostker and K. C. Yeh describe in the invaluable documentary book *I Want You!: The Evolution of the All-Volunteer Force*, the history of conscription in America is a story of competing philosophies of duty, obligated and autonomous. George Washington thought a draft was "disagreeable" but necessary during the Revolutionary War. As he wrote to the Continental Congress in early 1778: "Voluntary inlistments [*sic*] seem to be totally out of the question; all the allurements of the most exorbitant bounties and every other inducement, that could be thought of, have been tried in vain."[8] So Yingling is right, the founding father did come around to the idea after the war that universal, compulsory service was an obligation.

Certainly that idea was enshrined in the Constitution (Article 1, Section 8) with its hostility toward a professional army in favor of a citizen militia, but the idea did not fit well with the American people, nor did it ever prove practical. As French political scientist Alexis de Tocqueville noted during his travels in the 1830s:

> In America conscription is unknown and men are induced to enlist by bounties. The notions and habits of the people of the United States are so opposed to compulsory recruiting that I do not think it can ever be sanctioned by the laws.[9]

And so for 80 years after the Revolutionary War, there was no national draft in America. The first was initiated by the Confederacy during the Civil War, though it was highly unpopular and not universally enforced by all the rebelling states. The draft in the North signed into law by Abraham Lincoln in March of 1863 was the first in US history, though it proved calamitous, leading to vicious riots in Boston, New York, and elsewhere. Wealthy draftees were allowed to buy a deferment, which explained some of the fury. In the end, the draft law added precious few soldiers to the Union army, though the rioting did persuade elected officials to increase bounties and troop pay.

The major shift in American attitudes toward compulsory service came in 1917 when the United States entered World War I. President Woodrow Wilson, like George Washington, was reluctant to use conscription, but felt it was necessary. On the day a formal declaration of war against Germany was made by Congress, Wilson asked for a draft, which was passed into law on May 18 as *The Selective Service Act of 1917* and lasted through the end of the war in 1918. The idea, like the war, was very popular. The act itself had an ingenious design to provide impartiality, requiring all able-bodied males to register (23.9 million did so) but selecting only a portion (2.8 million during the course of the war). Deferments were common for men in college or with children.

The draft was reauthorized in September 1940 in anticipation of World War II, and again the emphasis was on the need for a system of equal sacrifice. The impartiality of who was to be drafted was an integral component, which was instituted through the use of a national lottery. Although the war lasted only four years, the draft became increasingly unpopular. President Harry Truman, a veteran of World

War I, advocated for a half-draft—universal military training, but not service—but his idea got no traction with Congress or the public. In 1947, Truman ended the draft, but military pay was insufficient to attract much of an all-volunteer force. Rising tensions with the Soviets and the outbreak of war on the Korean peninsula brought the draft back permanently in 1948.

Even though selective service continued for the next decade, deferments became so common by the early 1960s that draftees needed the barest rationale to exempt themselves from service. No doubt there was racial and class discrimination at the local draft boards, which fueled a low-burning resentment. The Pentagon actually began to study a transformation to an all-volunteer force under the guidance of Defense Secretary Robert McNamara in 1964. The head of economic analysis for the study was AVF advocate Walter Oi. Unfortunately, the pay increase necessary to attract sufficient volunteers could not be justified by the Department of Defense (DOD), so the study was buried.

Student protests were growing in 1966 against the pending reauthorization of the draft act by Congress. In July, President Johnson appointed an advisory commission by executive order to reform selective service. Later that December, Congress appointed its own advisory panel. Both commissions rejected the idea of an AVF, but agreed on little else. President Johnson instructed McNamara to establish a bigger and more formal task force to propose reforms to selective service. All the while, the spirit of reform among economists was catching fire.

UNLIKELY HEROES

During the middle of the twentieth century, military attitudes were strongly pro-draft, and skepticism surrounding the idea of an all-volunteer force was deep. When the AVF was being seriously studied during the height of the conflict in Vietnam, the Associated Press reported that "key defense officials consider [that] a presidential commission's proposals for an all-volunteer military force will be unrealistic."[10] That attitude delayed the implementation of the AVF for years and led to some efforts at sabotage even after it became law. However, not everyone in uniform thought conscription was justified, and some surprising advocates for reform were instrumental. One of those was a young congressman from Illinois named Donald Rumsfeld. Another was the Republican candidate for president, Richard Milhous Nixon.

Congressman Rumsfeld had attended the Chicago conference in late 1966, which changed his opinion regarding the draft on the spot. Even though he was a junior member and not part of the Armed Services Committee, Rumsfeld made public his desire to transform the military in short order. He publicly asked Congress in 1967 to vote on a plan to extend selective service for two years and "declare its intention to establish a voluntary military force,"[11] and then sponsored legislation to that effect with Thomas B. Curtis, a Republican congressman from Missouri.

As fate would have it, candidate Nixon appointed an associate professor at Columbia University named Martin Anderson to be his campaign's research director. Almost immediately, Anderson championed the all-volunteer military, starting with a memo to Nixon in April 1967. Over the summer, Nixon bounced the idea off of dozens of his advisers, and by the fall felt comfortable enough to go public. In November, at a University of Wisconsin event, he announced: "What is needed is not a broad-based draft, but a professional military corps. The nation must move toward a volunteer army…"[12]

Once Nixon was elected president in 1969, he immediately authorized a change in direction in Vietnam and in manpower policy. His policy of Vietnamization meant drawing down US troops and increasing support for local forces, and, by 1973, the conflict was officially over (though Saigon wouldn't fall for another two years). Oddly enough, the exact same timeline mapped the conversion of the US draft/citizen armed forces to the AVF/professional armed forces.

Nixon encouraged the new defense secretary, Melvin Laird, to move on an all-volunteer plan posthaste, but Laird dragged his feet. Although supportive of an eventual end to the draft, Laird recognized that the political class needed to be persuaded, which would take time. Laird was somewhat vindicated when the US Senate defeated AVF legislation in August 1970 by a vote of 52–36. That bill, sponsored by Republican Senators Barry Goldwater of Arizona and Mark Hatfield of Oregon, would have "provided pay increases of up to 50 percent for first-term enlistees and sharply boosted pay scales in most other enlisted and officer categories."[13] Opponents cited the cost as prohibitive and also made a fantastic claim that a force of volunteers might become a political threat to democracy.

Meanwhile, less than three months into office, Nixon had appointed a fifteen-member commission to seriously study and plan an all-volunteer force. This commission came to be known as the Gates Commission, in reference to its chairman, former Secretary of Defense Thomas S. Gates Jr. The fifteen members were not stacked to favor a transformation by design: five members favored a voluntary force, five favored the draft, and five were neutral. Milton Friedman was one of the fifteen members, and he recounted that one of the most dramatic moments was when General Westmoreland testified before it:

> In the course of his [Westmoreland's] testimony, he made the statement that he did not want to command an army of mercenaries. I stopped him and said, "General, would you rather command an army of slaves?" He drew himself up and said, "I don't like to hear our patriotic draftees referred to as slaves." I replied, "I don't like to hear our patriotic volunteers referred to as mercenaries." But I went on to say, "If they are mercenaries, then I, sir, am a mercenary professor, and you, sir, are a mercenary general; we are served by mercenary physicians, we use a mercenary lawyer, and we get our meat from a mercenary butcher." That was the last that we heard from the general about mercenaries.[14]

After 10 months of serious analysis, which economist David Henderson noted[15] is of the highest quality he has seen in his 30 years of policy work, the Gates Commission reported back to Nixon with a recommendation. All 15 members unanimously supported a transformation away from the draft and quick adoption of an all-volunteer force. The commission was partially swayed by the analysis of conscription as a hidden tax on the labor of draftees, but the more persuasive argument it endorsed was that drafted labor encouraged waste of vital labor resources, or in other words, a free-market price for labor might seem more costly, but would yield higher productivity per dollar spent.

After another year of political wrangling, President Nixon was able to overcome Pentagon objections and forge a bipartisan consensus. On August 4, 1971, the House passed the conference bill ending the draft, followed by the Senate in late September, with votes roughly 2:1 in both chambers. On September 28, 1971, Nixon signed the bill and made it law. The draft was to continue for two more years and then terminate in 1973.

Almost immediately, the military had a hard time getting enough recruits. It dropped its quality standards after 1973, shifting from a

70:30 ratio of high school graduates to nongraduates to a ratio of 50:50. On the other hand, reenlistments were higher than predicted, so force strength increased. All through the years of the Carter presidency, a battle raged within the Democratic Party (which controlled the executive and legislative branches) to bring back the draft. President Nixon wrote that the AVF experiment had failed. Not until 1981 did the tide of quality change, when a major pay increase in the *Defense Appropriation Act* finally made the AVF a more competitive option for high-quality recruits. An across-the-board base pay increase of 11.7 percent was authorized in fiscal year 1981, and an additional 14.3 percent in fiscal year 1982. President Ronald Reagan's defense team also enhanced the fringe benefits of service, everything from base facilities across the services to educational support for advanced degrees.

Today, the voluntary nature of military service is taken for granted. While quality standards vary slightly from year to year, troop quality today is significantly higher than in previous decades. More than 90 percent of enlistees today are high school graduates, and more than a few are college graduates. The educational and IQ level of the typical enlistee is significantly higher than the average civilian, a fact that would have been truly unthinkable when the draft was in place. Contemporary attitudes toward the draft in the United States are decisively negative. One group's attitude toward conscription is of particular interest: soldiers themselves. While a very small group in my West Point survey support a return to conscription (14 percent), the majority are *strongly* opposed (57 percent), which is double the strength of opinion toward any other reform I polled.

A MARKET FOR OFFICERS?

I hope the lessons of the AVF transformation are clear. Although controversial at the time, the shift to job market for troop accessions proved to be a much stronger foundation for national security than the coercive draft. Is that an appropriate model for a transformation of military assignments? Let's be honest: The revolution in assignment markets is well underway. The navy experimented with markets for its enlistees years ago with a program called Project Sail, and the army's new test market called Green Pages worked well for engineering officers. However, Green Pages is not a central program and seems to be starved of funds. The incremental revolution may be already happening, but the central process is still stuck in concrete.

Now is as a good a time as ever to force a complete overhaul, but because of the military's conservative nature, there remains a resistance to embrace an assignments market in all fullness and simplicity. For example, consider the typical reaction to my *Atlantic* magazine essay, "Why Our Best Officers Are Leaving,"[16] that looked at the results from my survey of West Point graduates and offered some solutions to the problem of officer attrition. On March 23, 2011, Tom Ricks posted on his *foreignpolicy.com* blog an open letter from four senior officers constituting the 2010–2011 class of military fellows at the Atlantic Council in Washington, DC.[17] The officers—Colonel James Miller, army; Captain Anthony Calandra, navy; Lieutenant Colonel Gabriel Vann Green, air force; and Marine Lieutenant Colonel R. G. Bracknell—expressed numerous objections to the reforms I had originally proposed in the *Atlantic* magazine article:

> But in the military, labor requirements frequently exist in places the market cannot satisfy. Kane's system works fine for the Army unit in Texas, Air Force units in Nevada, Navy units in Florida, and Marine units in California; ostensibly, enough people will want or find it acceptable to live and serve in these places that most units would be able to select suitable service members to fill their requirements. This model does not necessarily work when the posting becomes Diego Garcia (Indian Ocean), Kandahar (Afghanistan), Camp Butler (Okinawa), Manas Air Base (Kyrgyzstan), or Thule Air Base (Greenland). This is why orders are more useful than job applications to meet those requirements. Kane's model would cluster talent in a few of the most popular units and duty locations—the competition for assignment to bases in Southern California and Europe has the potential to choke out the labor markets in less desirable locations such as Korea, Bahrain, and Alaska, risking mission failure.[18]

Let's take this argument seriously for a moment. The underlying point is that once one loses the ability to coerce officers to take hazardous jobs, they will all move to Schofield Barracks, the 17,725-acre army post in central Oahu, Hawaii, that is home to the Twenty-Fifth Infantry Division (ID). Once we think about this objection seriously, it falls apart. First, there are only so many positions available in the Twenty-Fifth ID. Second, the units will presumably have to deploy to combat zones. Now even if the critics counter by suggesting how coveted noncombat assignments would be—say, Pentagon jobs or headquarters jobs—it's still a fact that the labor demand for all of those positions is finite.

Consider a mental experiment. There are 30,000 active-duty captains in the army and roughly 5,700 in the Marine Corps. So let's imagine that in any given month there are 400 job openings for Marine captains worldwide. A few are pilots, a few are recon, and so on. Let's just suppose that there are 12 job openings for Marine intelligence officers this very month. Two are sweetheart gigs, working for an awesome commanding general at whatever is the nicest base the Marines have. I'd say Okinawa, but everyone has a different preference. Wait, isn't that the point? Everyone has a different preference. Imagine that two of the Marine intel captain job openings seem unappealing to anyone. In the current AVF world, Marines would fill those slots using orders to match the available captains as best they could, then ship off the people, nice and simple. What if too many or too few qualified personnel are available? What if their talents and preferences aren't well known (the Hayekian knowledge problem)? What if one captain is burned out and ready to commit a war crime, but can't confess his mental condition for fear of ruining his career? Now consider the TVF approach. The 12 job openings would be posted at *marines.monster.com* (or *marines.craigslist.com*, etc.). Applicants could send in their packages, and I grant that the two worst options would most likely get zero applicants initially. But after the "best" jobs clear—and I don't believe the linear ranking is an accurate description, but we're playing by the skeptics' rules for this thought experiment—what happens? Half a dozen officers are left, and half a dozen openings are left as well. Maybe Captain Jones didn't get selected for his first three slots, so he sends off his package to three more. The point is that eventually the market clears.

In this thought experiment, there is no need to modify pay and no need to thicken the market with extra supply, but a fully functioning TVF would allow both. Supply thickens by increasing flexibility across occupational specialties and even branches. Why not let army intel officers apply for the Marine jobs? So long as a candidate meets the qualification for a specific job, who could object to more

interservice experience? In fact, if a coast guard O-4 meets the qualifications for a Marine job, he would be free to apply. That does not mean
he gets the job, only that the hiring commander sees his package. Or
take it one step further and allow ex-military officers to apply. How
about the ex-Marine captain who spent four years out of uniform, two
getting a master's in electrical engineering and two working for the
Central Intelligence Agency (CIA)? Why can't the navy commander
hire a logistics expert who spent seven years in the army and five at
Walmart? In the TVF world, you get 50 job applicants for every dozen
jobs available.

As it stands, the military has a hermetically sealed labor pool with
literally thousands of labor silos that severely diminish productivity on
the organizational side and morale on the individual side. When the
army's spokesman, Colonel Collins, was asked to comment on a proposed "internal job market for officers" that mirrors the private-sector
job market in terms of its supply-and-demand logic, he said:

> You have to remember that in the Army, our jobs aren't about
> business models and the bottom line. Our job is about protecting
> the lives of our soldiers and taking it to the enemy. We rely on
> officers to be highly proficient in technical, tactical and leader-
> ship skills. It would be hard to attain the levels of proficiency that
> are required to be effective in combat if we had officers moving
> around in various branches or skills every couple of years. I don't
> think that would engender the same level of confidence from our
> soldiers either. At it stands now, officers at about the 8- or 9-year
> mark of their career can apply to another branch of the Army,
> and many do move on to do something different from what they
> originally came into the Army to do.[19]

This is a nonanswer. First, the mission of the army may be different
from the mission of Google. But that is irrelevant. Google is different
from Dairy Queen. What matters is whether any mission is optimized
better by coercing workers or by using market incentives and choice.
Second, nothing says an internal market would lead to more job turnover, as Collins implies. Using a market, bad leaders would be retasked
more quickly rather than staying in place for three painful years, while
talented officers could stay focused on a job for longer durations than
the army now allows. The internal job market respects workers' rights

to make their own decisions at the optimal time, not some social planner's cookie-cutter timeline.

COMPENSATION

Currently, compensation in the armed forces operates without incentives for merit or entrepreneurial leadership. My survey of 250 West Point grads rated it the worst component of the personnel system, with 79 percent of respondents giving it a grade of D or F. Let's consider three components of military compensation that would change under a TVF. First, pay and allowances are not merit-based, and have no flexibility to provide performance bonuses. Second, pay cannot be adjusted by hiring commanders to make the assignment process less coercive and more like a market. Third, the retirement system is an industrial-age defined-benefit program that is inefficient, unsustainable, and anti-entrepreneurial.

Military pay scales are strictly stratified by rank and time in service. Since rank is closely correlated with time in service, pay is doubly so. Base pay is supplemented by "allowances"—extra compensation for such things as the geographic cost of living, hazardous duty, and various specialties (pilots, doctors, judge advocates). There are no performance bonuses, but there are some bonuses given for recommitting after a term of service is completed. The overriding factor is that pay is not linked to performance. The most dynamic, hard-working lieutenant in the navy is paid exactly the same as the least inspiring, laziest lieutenant. This dilemma may sound familiar, as it's also a hotly debated topic with US teachers in the education system—does it really make sense to pay a great teacher and a lousy teacher the same salary?

Another major problem with pay is that bonuses seem heavily skewed toward technical expertise, but not hazardous duty. On one level, it makes sense that an E-4 working with computer hardware makes more than an E-4 with a rifle, but the demands of combat duty for the rifleman are greater than ever. As Philip Carter and Owen West argued in a 2005 SLATE.com essay: "For years, the infantryman was underpaid because he had no civilian proxy; computer technicians and aircraft-maintenance chiefs were paid bigger bonuses because of direct civilian competition for their services. Today, the infantryman has an option. It's called private military contracting [and] it pays six-figure salaries."[20]

Private contractors are a complex issue, but the key fact here is that they are paid up to five times what uniformed soldiers are. The rise of contractors suggests that the economics of military pay are out of line. This harkens directly back to the AVF transformation, when volunteers were underpaid for almost a decade, and it indicates that combat pay has fallen woefully behind during the last decade. A flexible TVF compensation system would give hiring commanders extra pay flexibility to fill their ranks. Skeptics should not make the naïve claim that soldiers would game this market and ask for million-dollar combat bonuses. A market with any thickness of supply will settle on a fair wage. It is highly doubtful ground troops are being paid a fair wage today.

Already, the assignments process uses market incentives—hazardous duty pay, other allowances, heightened advancement potential, and first choice of duty station for follow-on assignments—but when those don't work, the military falls back on coercion. The TVF could guarantee that no job would go unfilled, unless there are officers who would prefer to retire rather than accept a position. The more common situation will be numerous soldiers who don't want to retire but cannot find a commander to hire them for any job. For the military, this is a good problem to have, but for the unwanted major with four years to go until retirement, this would be a very tough dilemma. The loss of retirement after investing 16 or more years is without question a raw deal, but that means we cannot fix the assignments process without also changing the existing military pension.

Nate Fick, author of *One Bullet Away* and now the CEO of the Center for a New American Security, recently wrote that the existing "cliff retirement at 20 years of service" was a relic of an earlier era.[21] Payment "cliffs" are techniques that give full compensation after some set period of time. As it stands now, all of the armed services offer a generous pension to veterans who serve for 20 full years. The pension is a lifetime monthly payment equal to 50 percent of base pay, and also includes medical benefits for life.

There is nothing wrong with caring for lifetime soldiers, but the cliff system is full of coercive unfairness and bad incentives. Essentially, a 20-year vesting cliff forces employees into indenture. Professor Ed Lazear notes such a vesting system would be illegal in the private sector, where, by law, vesting cannot exceed 7.5 years. Seriously, how many soldiers voluntarily leave the military with 14 or 15 years of service, thereby giving up their retirement? The cliff pension is a financial coercion.

The easy fix, which would be a starting point for TVF reform, is to offer terminal retirement packages that equal the pro-rata portion of years served. For example, the pension after ten years would yield a monthly payment equal to 25 percent of base pay. This is the first step toward a defined contribution plan, which would mirror what is common in the private sector: things such as 401K and 403B plans. Whether or not the TVF is adopted, the current retirement plan is becoming unsustainably expensive. In 2010, the Defense Business Board, tasked by Defense Secretary Gates, reported that the military retirement system's annual cost would rise from $47.7 billion to $59.3 billion by 2020.

The next five years are a critical time for personnel reform. Just as the wartime experiences of Vietnam guided the military branches and policymakers in Washington to consider radical reforms, so the wartime stresses of Iraq and Afghanistan have illuminated flaws in the AVF. The danger is that reformers will try to manage the complexity of the vast existing labor market with an even more complex centralized planning mechanism, huge human resources (HR) staffs, and computerized matching algorithms. As Professor Mike Haynie, an Air Force veteran and entrepreneurship expert, explained to me, this would be a mistake: "The role that this centralized HR system should play in the assignments process is information sharing and counseling."[22] The TVF system would create a virtual marketplace where matchmaking is not done by a third party but by "mutual agreement between hiring managers and employees."[23] Remember that in my survey, this market mechanism proposal was supported by 76 percent of active-duty officers and veterans alike, and only 2 percent strongly disagreed.

There's another advantage of an officer market that puts autonomy first and ends coercion forever, and that has to do with career planning. You can already imagine that a market system would free up individuals to specialize in ways unimaginable now. As it stands, the military takes career management of every individual soldier as its centralized responsibility. In this, it tries to do right by the soldiers, but individuals' careers are always secondary to the needs of the service.

So here's a riddle: each branch thinks it knows what its needs are today, but what are its needs 10 years from now? It takes 14 years to "make a major," as one HR officer explained to me, "but do we know what kinds of majors will be most important in the combat environment of 2027?"

CHAPTER 8

WAR MACHINES

The world is very different now. For man holds in his mortal hands the power to abolish all forms of human poverty, and all forms of human life.[1]

—President John F. Kennedy

SPLITTING THE ATOM DID BRING AN END to World War II, but it did not, as some prophesized, bring an end to war itself. Scientists and strategists were sure that nuclear arms would change the nature of war, but they didn't know how. Albert Einstein, the German-born American physicist, famously warned President Franklin D. Roosevelt about the possibility of weaponized fission and urged the allies to make a nuclear bomb before the Nazis could. Soon after, President Roosevelt and British Prime Minister Winston Churchill pooled their nations' top physicists to produce "the bomb." Although the work of the Manhattan Project was not complete until 1946, after the Nazis had been conquered, testing in July, 1945, led to President Harry Truman's decision to drop the first atomic bomb on Hiroshima on August 6 and then, still waiting for surrender from Tokyo, a second bomb on Nagasaki on August 9. In the decades after, the threat of nuclear Armageddon cooled passions among European and East Asian states that would otherwise probably have touched off a third conventional "total" war. Instead, many believe the Cold War led directly to a scaling back of most conventional armies and navies, aside from the United States and the Soviet Union.

Unlike the sword-favoring Samurai and Mamelukes of the world who eschewed gunpowder, the soldiers and statesmen of 1945 embraced nuclear weapons as a brutal savior of lives that would otherwise surely be lost in conventional combat. When the news of the nuclear tests in New Mexico reached Churchill, he remarked: "What was gunpowder? Trivial. What was electricity? Meaningless. This Atomic Bomb is the Second Coming in Wrath!"[2]

Still, we would be too quick to conclude that atomics alone altered military structure and strategy. German advances in ballistic and cruise rocketry during the 1940s were without peer. The United States continued to develop those technologies, marrying them with new electronics and larger atomics in an arms race to make more and better intercontinental and submarine-launched ballistic missiles first, then later air-breathing cruise missiles. What was really happening throughout the entire twentieth century was a wave of technologies that changed warfare. The sudden appearance of atomic weaponry in 1945 only seemed sudden because, as with other technologies, human mastery of the underlying science incrementally improved. Technological revolutions are not singular events, and, more importantly, they never really end. A young Churchill in 1890 never imagined the fast-moving armored tanks of George Patton or the buzz bombs that rained on London, and the elder Churchill of 1945 never imagined ex-fighter pilots walking on the moon or nonfighter pilots remotely controlling unmanned Predator drones while sitting in air-conditioned trailers in Nevada.

As military analyst P. W. Singer summarized in 2009 in his eye-opening book, *Wired For War*: "In the blink of an eye, things that were just fodder for science fiction are creeping, crawling, flying, swimming, and shooting on today's battlefields. And these machines are just the first generation of these new [unmanned] technologies, some of which may already be antiquated as you read these lines."[3] As Singer explained, this isn't just an issue of remote-controlled aircraft. Robotics are revolutionizing air, land, and sea warfare right now. I'll focus on the unique challenge these new war machines are having on the US Air Force, particularly its pilot culture, but an even bigger culture shock is coming to the army, navy, and Marines soon.

The story of robotics is really just a convenient example of the principle of technological change and the adaptive flexibility of the armed forces. Is the Pentagon's personnel system able to keep pace with the rapid pace of advances in technology? Sadly, it is not. Not only is human resources (HR) failing to manage change fast enough, its static approach to career management makes it unable to do so. All of the military services use some kind of military occupational specialty (MOS) or specialty code (AFSC) to pigeonhole their people. A fixed wing pilot has one code; an imagery intelligence officer has another. This helps organize people when they are thought of as interchangeable parts, matching round pegs to round holes, but it is woefully slow at adapting when the technology of warfare shifts.

AN OFFICER IS AN OFFICER IS AN OFFICER?

Nobody seems to know how to categorize the United States as a country, so they call it an empire.[4] For most of us, this is a tired theme, but it is driven by the unprecedented dominance of American military power relative to all other nations. Add up the military budgets of all other nations, and they barely surpass the $500 billion annual US defense budget. The $70 billion spent on military research and development alone is higher than the entire defense budget of any other nation, yet the secret to America's military prowess is not quantity or weaponry, but the elite troops in uniform. As Max Boot explains, the difference is "not manpower"; rather, it is the *quality* of manpower in the all-volunteer force (AVF). The Pentagon's 1.4 million active-duty troops are overshadowed by European North Atlantic Treaty Organization's (NATO's) 2.2 million and China's 2.2 million. "Operating high-tech military equipment requires long-service professionals, not short-term conscripts,"[5] says Boot.

The American experience with a high-quality all-volunteer force wasn't a singular event either, but rather the result of slow and constant progress in the design and operation of an ever-more sophisticated workforce over the decades since 1973. Smarter soldiers are a force multiplier even when operating the same weapons systems, but economists recognize that higher levels of human capital make possible the use of labor-saving physical capital. Political scientist James Q. Wilson opens chapter eight of his book *Bureaucracy*, entitled "People," with an anecdote about a US Navy personnel specialist. It was in 1977 that the specialist visited an electronics engineer, announcing, "I'm here to classify your job." After an unproductive interview, she decided that the civilian engineer's job did not justify a GS-15 pay grade (i.e., government service level 15) and recommended a two-level downgrade to GS-13. What she didn't know was that the engineer was the world's leading expert on torpedo guidance logic. The unit supervisor erupted at her suggestion and made sure the recommendation was never acted upon. In other words, the necessity of classifying people using a top-down central planning model involves a constant use of management time. This scene illustrates the unnatural tension between local commanders and central personnel administrators, particularly the knowledge problem faced by central bureaucracies. Both the local manager and the central administrator invested time in classifying the role of a third person, the actual worker, with a net value-added of zero for all of their efforts, which was actually nearly a net negative. How should a large organization classify its people? Or maybe the right question to ask is: should a large organization classify its people at all?

If the world were constant, any given company would have a well-defined menu of talent requirements, meaning it could in theory specify every aspect of its labor demand. Friedrick Hayek tells us that this approach will fail in practice due to the knowledge problem. Even in a static world, it is impossible to centrally understand the nuances of one's own company and its employees. The failure is even worse when the environment is dynamic. Put it this way: How many archers does the army need? How many radiomen? How many Farsi speakers? How do our answers change between 1979 and 2009?

The fundamental problem facing the armed forces HR manager is that the combat environment is radically dynamic. Most obviously, the strategic-threat landscape shifts constantly in unpredictable ways. Nonstate actors are fundamentally different from rising Pacific naval challengers. More importantly, the technological landscape is evolving even faster, meaning that nonstate actors of 2020 will be different from those of 2010, which we know were upgrades from 1990. Consider a handful of words that were barely on the strategic horizon when this generation of generals started their careers: unmanned aerial vehicles (UAVs—more on these later), nanotechnology, stealth, gigabyte, and Internet.

How does centralized HR manage officer careers in an evolving, dynamic strategic environment? It doesn't. It just pretends to. My thesis is that when technological change reshapes warfare, a flexible personnel system will respond to shifting talent demands in a way that a rigid system cannot imagine, and, regardless of the HR system, the most important quality of the officers in a dynamic environment won't be their hard skills, but their adaptability. This means promoting entrepreneurial leaders should be an even higher consideration.

WHY AN "AIR" FORCE?

During my first assignment as an air force intelligence officer, I shared living quarters with five junior army officers and got to know them well. As one might guess, I got no end of friendly hazing from the "grunts," but liked to tease them about their one hundred hours in Desert Storm following many months of missions there by my fellow airmen. It was all in fun, but painted a picture of how the different branches see each other and each other's jobs. General David Petraeus told a joke during some remarks at the US Marine Corps Association Foundation dinner on July 30, 2009, that made the whole room laugh, but also spoke to the larger perception:

> Come to think of it, in fact another bedrock element of the Marine Corps is unquestionably having the best recruiting ads on television. [laughter] But this concept is not just an advertisement. The Marines' sense of toughness permeates the Corps' lore as well as its reality. To recall an illustrative story, a soldier is trudging through the muck in the midst of a downpour with a 60-pound rucksack on his back. This is tough, he thinks to himself. Just ahead of him trudges an Army Ranger with an 80-pound pack on his back. This is really tough, he thinks. And ahead of him is a Marine with a 90-pound pack on, and he thinks to himself, I love how tough this is. [laughter, applause] Then, of course, 30,000 feet above them—[laughter]—30,000 feet above them an Air Force pilot flips aside his ponytail. [laughter, applause] Now—I'm sorry. I don't know how that got in there—[laughter]—I know they haven't had ponytails in a year or two—[laughter]—and looks down at them through his cockpit as he flies over. "Boy," he radios his wingman, "it must be tough down there." [laughter][6]

The bane of the air force is its name. When the US Army Air Corps was established in 1946 as its own branch of service, the rationale was driven more by the rise of nuclear weaponry than airborne weaponry. America fought and won two world wars without needing a separate air arm, so why a separate branch at the conclusion of World

War II? Why call it the *air* force? Astute observers note that this is the only branch named after a particular type of platform, and oddly it is a platform used by every other service. The navy has jets and helicopters, as does the Marines Corps. The army has thousands of helicopters for combat, transportation, and surveillance. Would there be identity confusion if it were named the Nuclear Force?

In fact, the origin of the air force is rooted not in the sky or in the atom but in a rebellious attitude against the status quo of the existing military way of war. The heart and soul of the air force is innovation, and I would say it goes so far as "creative destruction" in the Schumpeterian sense. Unfortunately, the air force was named the *air* force, a name that burdens it with an identity that is miscast. If it had been named the Innovation Force, the acceleration of information technologies wouldn't have been such a shock. If it had been named the Remote Force, the evolution of battle control further and further away from the front lines would have felt more natural. Both of these qualities—remoteness and innovation—illuminate why the personnel system needs to be flexible, a case that will make more sense if we think back across military history.

ACCELERATIONS IN MILITARY AFFAIRS

The Soviets began thinking seriously about the patterns of technological change in the 1960s, and the rest of the world picked up on the same trends, which became known as the *Revolutions in Military Affairs* or RMA. Military historian Max Boot's book *War Made New* uses the lens of RMA to explore the past. "Technology alone rarely confers an insurmountable military edge," he writes. "Tactics, organization, training, leadership, and other products of an effective bureaucracy are necessary to realize the full potential of new inventions."[7] During World War II, both the Japanese and Germans enjoyed technological advantages—in blitzkrieg, rocketry, industrial management, and aircraft design, to name just a few—but were not able to maintain the same degree of innovative energy in war tactics that America and the allies displayed.

We can speculate that their failures mirrored the mistakes of other centralized empires such as the Ottomans in the nineteenth century and the Ming Chinese in the fifteenth century. When the crossbow became common, it was the death knell of mounted knights in armor, a democratizing weapon. Once gunpowder was invented, mounted cavalry lost much of their advantage. Technology tends to be an equalizer while, at the same time, more open societies tend to develop technology faster.

Another of Boot's themes is that "innovation has been speeding up." The four distinct military revolutions he demarcates took increasingly shorter time spans to mature: two hundred years for the Gunpowder revolution (1500–1700), one hundred years for the First Industrial Revolution (1750–1850), forty years for the Second Industrial Revolution (1900–1940), and thirty years for the Information Revolution (1970–2000). The implication is that America risks falling behind the revolutionary curve because "keeping up with the pace of change is getting harder than ever."[8] Few economists would quibble with his theme. The growth rate of 2 percent per year in the twentieth century took income and productivity levels in the United States to new heights, especially considering that the growth rate in 1820 was nearly zero. If the historical pace continues, flexibility on the part of the military becomes even more essential.

Though the trend is clear, the lesson it has for the armed forces is hard to know. Some RMA advocates argue that old platforms are irrelevant—that is, big ships, expensive fighters, and armored tanks. To be sure, there are visible technologies that pose new threats, round pegs that don't fit into old, square holes. Cybersecurity and robotics are two of the most prominent. The armed forces can rightly counter that those threats are on their radar screens, and more importantly, the experience of counterinsurgency in Iraq confirms the constancy of personal combat with the enemy. The US Army has adapted to the insurgency and its radio-controlled roadside bombs admirably, using new weapons and new jamming techniques.

The point here is that seeking to cut obsolete platforms is not the great lesson of RMA; rather, it is to maintain an innovative spirit among the troops and officers. Boot warns: "Successful adaptation to major technological shifts requires changing the kinds of people who are rewarded within a military culture."[9] A corollary is that the major branches of the US armed forces should be focused on missions, not preserving platforms and old hierarchies. Both the army and the navy treated engineers as second-class officers in the nineteenth century until the advent of railroads and steam power made their talents necessary, and even then the culture took decades to change. In the decades ahead, DOPMA-based (*Defense Officer Personnel Management Act*) personnel systems will be challenged to keep pace, while the scientific frontier is moving much faster.

RISE OF THE REMOTENESS

A battlefield general loves technologies that make his troops stronger, faster, lighter, and better integrated, but a defining theme of military technology is the capacity to kill at distance. Catapults, cannons, tanks, battleships, aircraft carriers, and nukes all shared the common quality of extending the range of the commander, and for every step forward, there was a gnashing of teeth. Author P. W. Singer recounts that when "Hiero, the ancient king of Syracuse, hired the great Archimedes to build him a catapult, the king was said to have cried when he saw the result."[10] It signaled to him the end of the era of traditional warriors, who would be replaced by engineers. That's the same sentiment that leads Marines to laugh at jokes about the air force—fear of being replaced or made irrelevant by changes in technology.

Another gripe common to all the services is that the military seems so wasteful. Many critics point to the tooth-to-tail ratio, which is the number of warriors in uniform compared to the number of support personnel in uniform. The army and Marines have a tooth-to-tail ratio of 1:12, compared to 1:15 for the navy, and 1:32 for the air force. A ratio closer to 1:1 means more tooth, seen as a good thing, while a smaller ratio is perceived as a sign of lower efficiency within the branch of service. Should the air force really be trying to get more tooth and less tail though?

I have to confess that this statistic has always puzzled me, maybe because I heard about it when I was on active duty decades ago and the air force compared "unfavorably" back then. If the goal is to make the tooth—also called the "tip of the spear"—more lethal or effective, doesn't that mean having more tail is okay, even preferable? Technology will almost always be applied to the tail, not the tooth, and Archimedes's catapult is a case in point. The logic of labor-saving technology will also lead to fewer and fewer combat casualties, one of the advantages of a smaller tooth-to-tail ratio.

Remotely-piloted drones are pushing these gaps even wider, though there are signs that robotics may actually have a greater effect on the ground forces in the next decade. Before the Iraq War, few people knew the military even had any UAVs, but the inventory grew by an astounding 4,000 percent between 2002 and 2010. Today, the Congressional Research Service reports that roughly one in three US warplanes is unmanned. There are more than 7,500 UAVs, including roughly 5,000 Ravens used by the army, compared to 10,800 manned jets and helicopters. In dollar terms, the overall Department of Defense (DOD) budget for UAVs "increased from $284 million in FY2000 to $3.3 billion in FY2010" (even as 92 percent of the air force procurement budget remains dedicated to manned systems).[11] As for the ground forces, Joint Forces Command projections in 2005 anticipated a robotic battlefield within two decades, including one plan for a detachment with a mere 150 soldiers and 2,000 robots.[12]

CASE STUDY #1: THE DRONE FORCE

The "rise of robots" in the US arsenal is similar to the rise of nukes in the late 1940s. On the surface, the technology appears to be a sudden momentous development, but the development was rich both before and after it appeared to the public. Drones of one kind or another have been on the drawing board since tanks and aircraft began operating nearly a century ago. The now-ubiquitous UAVs have been under serious development by the Central Intelligence Agency (CIA) and DOD for 30 years. The well-known Predator was initially developed under a 1994 contract with a San Diego-based company called, somewhat ironically, General Atomics.

Each Predator system comes with four aircraft and a single, controlling ground station. The air vehicle, which costs roughly one million dollars on its own, is 27 feet in length with long, narrow wings spanning 49 feet. It is powered by a 4-cylinder, 115-horsepower engine with a rear-mounted propeller that allows it to sustain 24 hours of flight time and a range of nearly 700 miles. The unarmed initial units, designated as RQ-1, were successful in testing and deployed operationally in a surveillance role to the Balkans in 1995.

Initially, it wasn't clear which branch of service would manage the Predator, and in fact, its reassignment by the secretary of defense from the army to the air force wasn't official until 1996. For the next five years, the RQ-1 proved incredibly effective in a reconnaissance role, but the lag between actionable imagery and subsequent armed engagement by others resulted in many missed opportunities. Advocates within the CIA pushed for an armed version of the "Pred," which was tested and made operational in 2001, specifically to target al Qaeda leaders. Designated the MQ-1A, the new version was capable of carrying Hellfire air-to-ground missiles and Stinger air-to-air missiles.

The weaponized Predators have been used extensively in the fight against al Qaeda in Afghanistan and Pakistan since 2002, with hundreds of active combat missions. In late 2002, six suspected terrorists—including Qaed Salim Sinan al-Harethi, an associate of Osama bin Laden—were killed by the Predator in Yemen with pre-approval from the Yemen government. Predators were also used in Iraq, enforcing no-fly zones prior to the 2003 invasion and helping with the counterterrorism mission afterward. Predator sorties were also flown in Libya, in Somalia, and even along the southern US border. Needless to say, many of the systems have been lost to weather, accidents, and enemy fire, but with more than 200 RQ-1 and MQ-1 systems in the inventory, the USAF took delivery of its final Predator vehicle in March of 2011. The reason? Even better systems had been developed, notably the $30 million MQ-9 Reaper, which was introduced in 2007, and the stealthy $15 million Avenger/Sea Avenger.

In popular culture, the air force embodies the technological edge of warfare and has held that role since its birth. There is an irony, however, in the unpreparedness of the personnel culture of the US Air Force for this new kind of unmanned flying. In many ways, the air force developed a stricter hierarchy (of career specialties) and pecking order than other services. Pilots were the equivalent of army commanders atop the hierarchy. They had higher rates of promotion and were given command slots of nearly all organizations in the service. It might make sense to have a career pilot command a maintenance squadron, but a logistics unit? An intelligence group? A nuclear missile training wing? Yet, for more than half a century, the air force has maintained a strict line of separation between its flying officers and "nonrated" officers. Rightly so or not, pilots lord over all other officers, fighter pilots lord over all other pilots, and command and promotions unabashedly favor those groups.

That caste system started to crack as soon as the Predator came online in 1994. Put simply, robotics are reinventing the role and self-image of the fighter pilot. The Top Gun culture is being transformed. In 2001, before the war in Iraq, pilots tapped for Predator duty could refuse the assignment and leave the air force, with seven days to make their decision. "They lose a lot of pilots like that," one explained, because many pilots didn't want to fly a desk.[13] To entice more rated officers to take the two-year UAV stint, each pilot was promised the dream follow-on job of his or her choice (a quasi-flexible response from a usually inflexible HR system). Far from being driven by duty, the service had to bribe its officers with gray-market incentives. Nevertheless, once the war kicked off and demand for more drone drivers rose, pilots were simply ordered abruptly out of the cockpit. Captain David Blair was flying AC-130 Gunship missions on his third deployment when he got the news:

> I was very much under the impression that I was going to be in Gunships and at Hurlburt Field for quite some time. I confidently assumed things were stable and secure—perhaps I had forgotten that the one constant in the fog and friction of warfare is that there are no constants.
>
> I found out I was transferring to the Predator mission right before a step brief for a combat mission, in the form of a Post-it note. There was no preferences worksheet, no input, and, being downrange, no ability to make a case one way or another. I think the conversation went something along the lines of, "We had to give them a name, and it was you. Sorry."[14]

The cultural rift only widened once the UAV drivers racked up more combat time than fighter pilots, but initially these hours did not count as rated flying time, another policy that has since changed. The desk jockeys (as pilots sometimes refer to them) in air-conditioned remote terminals at Creech Air Force Base in the Nevada desert flew thousands of sorties every month over Iraq, while the "best of the best" fighter jocks found themselves with a limited operational role during a decade of war. For example, there were an estimated nine hundred thousand total flight hours for the Predator alone. To be sure, old-school pilots maintain significant legacy advantages in the culture, but there are precious few dogfights in the war on terror. Meanwhile, other air force officers found themselves deployed alongside army and marine ground units. As one nonrated officer explained to me: "It's awfully hard for a guy or gal with wings to be arrogant about the old pecking order when nonrated USAF officers are wearing ribbons for hazardous duty in Kabul and Baghdad, and they aren't." The fact is that plenty of rated officers have those ribbons from serving in nonflying roles as well, but the result is that the simple hierarchy of the last half century has been upended in the post-9/11 military.

To put the HR issue in perspective, consider the workforce requirements for a drone mission. Not only does a Predator, Reaper, or Avenger require the ground based pilot but a real-time sensor operator as well. This count obscures the demand for hundreds of technicians that maintain the UAVs and electronics, and for many more to conduct the intelligence analysis during and after the mission. In total, a 24-hour mission by a single Predator UAV requires the efforts of 168 people.[15] This tells us that the tooth-to-tail ratio is shrinking rapidly, but it also raises questions about how the air force is able to adapt its mix of people.

"Our No. 1 manning problem in the Air Force is manning our unmanned platforms,"[16] said General Philip M. Breedlove, Air Force vice chief of staff, in late 2011. The challenge is imagery analysis, because the capacity to handle the flood of raw intelligence dwarfs the available workforce. As the *Los Angeles Times* reported in 2011: "The Air Force is short of ground-based pilots and crews to fly the drones, intelligence analysts to scrutinize nonstop video and surveillance feeds, and technicians and mechanics to maintain the heavily used aircraft."[17] If the Air Force Personnel Center (AFPC) were using the total volunteer force (TVF) approach, with its greater flexibility for hiring and occupational specialization, there would be no bottleneck.

The bureaucracy has not been the sole impediment. Secretary of Defense Robert Gates became a strong advocate of UAVs early in his tenure based purely on their performance in Iraq and Afghanistan. Unfortunately, he felt the air force was dragging its feet in producing more assets to perform the recon and combat missions. He wanted to double and eventually quadruple the number of CAPs (combat air patrols)—there were less than a dozen in the skies of Iraq at the time—and ultimately fired the top air force leaders because of their reluctance to make the needed changes. US Air Force secretary Michael Wynne and Chief of Staff General Michael Moseley were axed on June 5, 2008. "I've been wrestling for months to get more intelligence, surveillance and reconnaissance assets into the theatre," said Gates, pointing to resistance from military leaders "stuck in old ways of doing business."[18]

Decisive leadership such as that exercised by Gates echoed the bold top-level moves made by the great wartime leaders of World War II,

George Marshall and Dwight Eisenhower, who cleaned out the top ranks and installed true change agents. Unfortunately, today's HR system makes progress in the midranks impossible. In short, the DOPMA-driven system is unprepared for the current labor demand for just about every kind of job associated with unmanned vehicles.

We could charitably say the surge in this new technology was unforeseen by the AFPC, even though it was more than a decade in the making. This is beside the point. Inability to adapt to new innovations and changing situations is exactly the weakness of the current HR approach to career designations versus the open TVF approach. Four years after the Gates firings, Michael Donley, the current secretary of the air force, conceded to reporters that its undersupply of necessary personnel caused it to pull back from growing the UAV mission regardless of demand. In February 2012, the USAF made a surprising announcement to scale back drone acquisitions to a target of 65 CAPs. The reason, as Donley made clear in his April 2012 announcement, is that the USAF simply doesn't have the analytical capacity to meet demand. The unstated reason is that the USAF doesn't have a dynamic workforce system with the ability to scale accordingly. The number of CAPs has grown from a handful in 2001 to 20 in 2007, 40 in 2009, and 60 in 2011. "If we fill out the capability underneath it, adequately man that force, adequately provide the processing exploitation capabilities underneath that," Donley said, "we'll be able to surge to 85 CAPs."[19]

No matter how many smart, well-intentioned, change-oriented personnel officers are assigned to manage the careers of the air force officer corps, they cannot anticipate the labor demand or labor supply of the UAV workforce in three years, let alone ten years. They cannot know the operational demands of the next defense secretary or commander in chief. The exact same dilemma faces the army, navy, and Marine Corps. As Singer explains in *Wired for War*, the rise of robots is hardly limited to aerial vehicles. As the technology for remote control is perfected (and secured), it begs questions about the need for manned tanks, manned helicopters, and manned submarines. The truly revolutionary change will be the need for manned infantry, which still seems too fanciful to imagine for the typical reader and the typical HR professional, but not for Defense Advanced Research Projects Administration project managers, White House policymakers, and entrepreneurial generals and admirals who see the future is now.

CASE STUDY #2: CYBER WAR

President Barack Obama has declared that the "cyber threat is one of the most serious economic and national security challenges we face as a nation" and that "America's economic prosperity in the twenty-first century will depend on cybersecurity."[20] Interestingly, the president had some difficulty filling the job of "Cyber Czar." Obama's initial czar, Melissa Hathaway, resigned nearly a year after her election, and three other candidates for the job reportedly turned it down before Howard Schmidt accepted in 2009. The difficulty reflected the same problems the Bush White House had in keeping someone in the job. Amit Yoran, a West Point graduate and successful security software entrepreneur, served in the job for just a year before resigning abruptly in 2004. Like Hathaway, he grew frustrated with the bureaucratic turf wars. For example, the czar reports to both the National Security Council and the National Economic Council. While more attention and budget share is being given to cybersecurity than ever before, critics argue that the organizational effort has been a shambles. In 2012, Schmidt began championing guidelines for new cyber legislation. With the top of the cyber hierarchy so difficult to organize, what hope is there for coherence operationally?

US Army lieutenant colonel Scott Halter's essay cites cyberwarfare as an example of one of the primary shortcomings in the army's human-capital management system. The issue is career management and the classification of job requirements, notably the army's failure to adapt and respond quickly in staffing new cyber warfare jobs. "The Army is still struggling to assess, develop, and employ the cyber talent it needs more than two years since it established Cyber Command."[21]

When the GAO looked into the government's handling of the emerging cyber workforce in 2011, it reported dismal results.

Five of eight agencies, including the largest, the Department of Defense, have established cybersecurity workforce plans or other agencywide activities addressing cybersecurity workforce planning. However, all of the agencies GAO reviewed faced challenges determining the size of their cybersecurity workforce because of variations in how work is defined and *the lack of an occupational series specific to cybersecurity.*[22]

What the GAO did next is even more revealing about how the federal government responds to a workforce problem. It recommended "better" bureaucracy: "better planning, coordination, and evaluation of governmentwide activities. Agencies concurred with the majority of GAO's recommendations and outlined steps to address them."[23] Planning, coordination, and evaluation? Those are code words for bigger, centralized budgets. The alternative, not to belabor the point, is less planning and more local authority for hiring whatever skills are needed by operating authorities.

On the supply side, the military hasn't been any better. Not only did the military fail, in hindsight, to retain Amit Yoran in uniform, but it encouraged the early retirement of numerous talented West Point professors in the 1990s who were happily working in the computer science and electrical engineering departments. The army had encouraged and paid for their PhDs in those fields, but then was unsure how to employ the officers. Yoran, a former USAF officer and 1993 West Point graduate, founded the security software company RipTech in 1998, which was acquired by Symantec four years later for $145 million. His story echoes the departure of a half dozen USAF intelligence officers and enlistees in 1994 and 1995 who formed the computer security firm Wheelgroup, which was quickly acquired by Cisco in 1998 for $124 million. Clearly, the military had some superstars with human capital that produced solid value, but it was value recognized by the private sector and invisible to the Pentagon.

WHAT NOW?

IBM offers a compelling case study for the armed forces in how a large organization founded on a primary technology can reinvent itself when faced with an existential crisis. IBM was well established in the 1970s as the largest, most successful computer company in the world, but its focus was entirely on business computing. The company was not prepared for the sudden demand for personal computers and famously lost control. It lost the software standard to Microsoft, the hardware standard to Intel Corporation, and then the production monopoly to dozens of IBM-clone manufacturers and other platforms such as Apple and Sun. Technological change undercut the traditional IBM business model, and the company was quickly fading in the late 1980s. In 1993, its board of directors reached outside the insular company and hired

Lou Gerstner, former CEO of RJR Nabisco, a consumer nondurables conglomerate. Gerstner repositioned the firm as an information technology (IT) service provider and made the fateful decision to keep the various pieces unified under one brand. The air force might similarly shift to cyberwarfare and robotic control as means to better perform its mission of air superiority, transport, and support rather than focusing on one dimension of the battlefield (aerospace). But is there any possibility that the air force will hire the civilian CEO of General Atomics to manage it for the next few years?

The DOPMA-based management of officers balances the needs of the military branches with the careers of its people. The army, for example, tries to give as many junior officers as possible a turn in a branch-qualifying job, which is a necessary box to check for the next promotion. While this practice arguably hurts unit cohesion, risks lives, and raises costs, it is one of the many trade-offs forced by a centrally managed HR hierarchy. The alternative is chaos. And that is not a bad thing. Chaos is an alternative that would allow labor supply and demand to meet. By trying to manage careers by defining every step, forecasting the future, and forcing officers to fill slots nobody wants, the DOPMA model ends up lurching from dramatic talent oversupply to talent shortages across hundreds of occupational categories. Compared to the status quo of how HRC manages careers, the labor market in the private sector isn't chaos. Rather, it's a smooth ocean. Less bureaucracy, more stability.

The TVF would "manage" careers the same way it manages job assignments, which is to say by not managing them. Dispersed HR officers would help counsel officers about choices, advising not categorizing. A midcareer artillery captain might, for example, choose to attend a logistics training course that would qualify him or her with a skill, but the old system of hard-coding him or her with a career field (also known as MOS) would become a certification rather than a constraint. If a division commander felt the need to hire another cyber expert, he could hire an active-duty captain with formal professional military education (PME) training and a master's degree, or he could hire a former lieutenant with hands-on experience as the antivirus software program manager at Symantec. Résumés would define career potential and capability, not central databases.

CHAPTER 9

MEASURING MERIT

To understand how the U.S. could face defeat at the hands of a weaker insurgent enemy for the second time in a generation, we must look at the structural influences that produce our general officer corps.[1]

—Lieutenant Colonel Paul Yingling

THERE'S A WAR STORY TOLD AT THE AIR FORCE Academy about the importance of tradition. A US Air Force pilot was shot down over North Vietnam, but was able to parachute from his doomed aircraft and radio for a rescue evacuation—if the locals didn't capture him first. Soon, a US helicopter arrived over the jungle canopy. Via radio, the helicopter issued the challenge/response, changed daily and briefed before every mission. For example, the rescue team would say "Spaghetti" and the response had to be "Meatballs" to authenticate the evacuee's radio call was not an enemy trap. Unfortunately, the downed pilot could not remember the response. He was in shock. As the helicopter hovered, the North Vietnamese raced up the hill toward the sound of the rotors. Again, the rescue team radioed the challenge. Frustrated, the pilot yelled, "I'm an Air Force Academy grad, for God's sake! Pick me up!" Overhead, the helo pilot, also a grad, radioed back, "Try this challenge. 'Fast Neat Average!'" and the downed pilot shot back, "Friendly Good Good!" Thumbs up. They dropped a rescue line down to the forest floor, hooked him up, and pulled him to safety.

"Fast Neat Average Friendly Good Good" is a traditional phrase at the US Air Force Academy. Those six words are the routine response checkboxes marked on the Academy's meal rating paperwork, the Form O-96. A blank form is set out on each of the four hundred tables for cadets to complete after every morning and noon meal. The first section of the form says "Service of Food (Check one)" with a small checkbox next to three options "slow, average, and fast." Soon after the Academy was established in 1955, it became common for cadets to routinely check the box next to "fast" on that first section, "neat" on the next, and so on. The fact that rating of the meal had no relation to the quality of the meal was irrelevant, and in that sense was perfect training for how the military conducts formal evaluations.

Many of the reforms under a new personnel system introduced in this book under the total volunteer force (TVF) concept call for less, not more, guidance. In most aspects of human resources (HR) management, fewer or no rules can be more efficient, but there are exceptions to that principle.

A critical exception is the need for performance evaluations. Accurate evaluations are essential for two different human resource functions—promotions and mentoring. Any promotion system that aspires to reward merit needs an evaluation system that effectively measures merit. And any leadership development system that aspires to improve performance relies on a detailed evaluation that will help leaders understand their individual strengths, weaknesses, and ways to improve. The army uses a single form called the officer evaluation report (OER), or DA Form 67 series, which is generated annually on each individual. The OER is used for both functions, promotion and development.

In the air force, the form is called the officer performance report (OPR), and the same kind of form under different names is used by each service. Supervisors (known as "raters") generate evaluation paperwork once a year, which is often complicated due to the high rate of turnover. For most services, a "senior rater"—the rater's immediate supervisor in the army—also provides an independent evaluation on the same report. Unfortunately, most of the military branches have suffered from an inflation of performance evaluations since the 1970s. To be fair, there are exceptions to that rule—the Marine Corps evaluation includes the rater's average score for all ratees—but frustrations with the forms are a common experience.

In my survey of 250 West Point graduates, only 37 percent gave the evaluation system a grade of A or B, compared to 33 percent who gave it a D, and 18 percent who gave it an F. A focus-group study written in early 2001 by Lieutenant Colonel Marvin Williams at the Command and General Staff College examined the root problems regarding the deep dissatisfaction of army captains with the OER. Its inability to distinguish unique skills or even to recognize merit outside of the command-track jobs were the main findings. That is, the OER has become so inflated and bland through a series of revisions since the 1970s that it fails as mentoring tool and a vitae. While limiting the ability of noncommand talent to be recognized, or skills to be highlighted, the flip-side problem is arguably worse because the OER is perceived to enable toxic leaders to continue in uniform. "The Army needs to look at their officers and cull the bottom 10% every year," one of my survey respondents wrote. "There are lots of bad officers who stay in the Army because it's 'easy' and you never really get fired, just moved around."

I was surprised to learn the phrase "toxic leader" is actually part of the Pentagon lexicon. For example, a recent article by staff writer Michelle Tan in *Army Times* titled "Rooting Out Toxic Leaders" described an internal survey of 22,630 soldiers from the rank of E-5 to O-6, in which 20 percent of respondents see their superior as "toxic and unethical."[2] This is a known problem, which, for whatever reason, top generals have allowed to fester for decades. To be sure, there have been many reforms over the years, all carefully considered by the top generals, but all incremental in nature with predictably tepid results. The TVF evaluation system would embrace a much deeper reform based on the kind of clear signals that exist in open markets.

A PEERLESS EVALUATION SYSTEM

Since good information is vital to any labor market, fixing the inflated evaluation system was something I highlighted in my *Atlantic* essay. When that piece caught the attention of top brass at the Pentagon, *ARMY* magazine asked General Frederick J. Kroesen, former vice chief of staff of the army, to pen a response in its March 2011 issue. His essay was "circulated as a rejoinder to the Atlantic article," according to a friend and senior officer then working at the Pentagon, so it is worth considering carefully what his counterarguments are. He wrote:

No organization in the world has spent more intellectual time and effort trying to create objective, unbiased evaluation and promotion systems than the U.S. Army, recognizing that the search for the fully qualified, then the best qualified, is critical for guaranteeing leadership that has no peer in the world.

... No other profession employs boards of officers to consider reports covering years of service and the evaluations of numbers of raters to approve promotions of the fully qualified (and then to find the truly outstanding).

... Mistakes are almost always the fault of an unusual series of inattentive and unaware rating officers, not the system being employed.[3]

There is absolutely no question that General Kroesen is a heroic soldier, patriot, and leader, but to claim again and again that this system is not only effective but without peer "in the world" suggests he was unaware of much of the world for too long. This is actually one of the fundamental problems with an organization that bars lateral entry. Officers, rarely assigned to work outside the military, and almost never outside the government, lack a comparative world experience to inform a better HR system.

Make no mistake, Kroesen's view is also informed by decades of good reform ideas crashing against the unyielding walls of federal law. The *Defense Officer Personnel Management Act* (DOPMA) is the root of all evil in this ecosystem, and his metapoint is that the army has done the best it can given the constraints handed down by (as he named them) Robert McNamara and the legislative branch. He's right, but this is little solace to junior and midranking officers, those who leave in frustration and those who stay in even greater frustration. The recent Falk-Rogers survey summarized attitudes this way: "[A]ll four services largely fail to distinguish between officers with unique skill-sets or who have chosen non-traditional career paths in assignments and performance evaluations.... For example, the Army relies heavily on the [OER]—a standardized form that emphasizes command ability—for promotions, despite the fact that only 12% of senior military billets are command positions."[4] And as Marvin Williams describes, the army has had to change the OER three times since the 1970s in response to a virtual arms race of inflation among raters, most acutely during the drawdown of the 1990s when the active-duty army force was cut from 730,000 to 485,000.[5] Despite the design of central managers, human nature decides how the evaluations are actually completed. According to G. I. Wilson and Donald Vandergriff: "The OER has always been prone to inflation by officers wanting to project their officers as the best, or because the raters or senior raters did not have the moral courage to face their officers with average or below average OERs that would destroy their careers."[6] In the end, "the 67–8 became inflated and virtually useless," Williams says.[7]

In 1997, a revised OER form was introduced coinciding with the officer professional management system (OPMS) XXI revision. Ratings by peers as well as subordinates were considered, but were a bridge too far for the traditionalists, so those ideas were shelved. This new OER had three categories for the overall assessment of an officer relative to peers—above center of mass (ACOM), center of mass (COM), or the rarely used below center of mass (BCOM). Raters are not allowed to place more than 49 percent of their officers in the ACOM block. What the army calls "block rating" is termed a "forced distribution" in management theory. The problem with the army approach is that the ACOM restraint is the mildest version of a forced distribution possible because it allows weak performers to avoid scrutiny. A prescient 1998 article by then-colonel Walter F. Ulmer Jr. essentially predicted the design would "compromise its potential as a developmental tool by highlighting a competition for simplistic numerical ratings."[8] Soon after its introduction, a cultural norm was established whereby ACOMs were automatically given to officers in branch-qualifying jobs (e.g., company commanders, executive officers) and COMs to staff officers. This norm evens out on average if everyone takes his or her "turn" rotating through key jobs, but the vagaries of lucky timing hurt many good officers and reward many undeserving ones. More to the point, the norm has delinked merit from the measure of merit.

Despite their similarities, each of the services uses different evaluation forms and processes—different for officers and enlisted, different from one another, and with nearly constant adjustments. For example, navy and Marine evaluations address the inflation problem by reporting the rater's average marks alongside the rated officer's marks. The army had hoped its 1997 version of the OER would bring in just the right amount of forced distribution to stymie inflation, but internal studies concluded the COM approach was arguably the root cause of the retention problem that began almost immediately after it was introduced. One official panel reported to the army in 2000 that "the

OER is a source of mistrust and anxiety."[9] Block rating was suspended by the army for nonsenior ranks in 2005.

Unfortunately, the inflation of quantitative measures in OERs and OPRs pushed raters during the last four decades to distinguish their subordinates using the written assessment—a small empty block of white space to summarize work, performance, and potential. The write-ups were soon filled with code words, which evolved in each service and tribe, suffering their own inflation over the years. "Extraordinary" might mean "normal," and "one of my best" officers could be code for "one of my worst." Veterans cynically mock the standardized verbatim comments necessary to enhance an OER. For example, simply saying someone is "one of" the best is considered far inferior to a numbered ranking like "the number one out of sixteen combat officer in the battalion," which is inferior to "the top overall officer in the battalion."

Remember that each officer file is considered for one–two minutes by promotion-board members, typically scanning the OER's first line of written assessment, the last line, the block rating, and bulleted accomplishments. Consider some of the implications. Because careers hinge on the writing ability of supervisors, pity the young officer with a gruff commander focused on simply fighting the enemy. On the other hand, supervisors who worry that their prose may not be very good frequently allow subordinates to draft their own written assessment. This may seem unethical, but it is a rational response to a broken system. Officers across the US military are nudged into a moral gray area, pretending to write objective assessments that are actually amplified self-promotional advertisements.

Perhaps the greatest indictment of the evaluation system is what we might call the integrity critique. As a cornerstone of the supposedly values-driven, service-above-self culture, the US military's performance evaluations in truth pressure officers to sell out their integrity by making dishonest assessments of subordinates. Even minor distortions are difficult to accept for young officers who have been disciplined by strict honor codes during Academy and basic training. Integrity, however, has a steep price when the cultural norm means that honest assessments of subordinates will ruin all of their careers.

Ultimately, the history of the OER proves one thing: no matter how it has been tweaked, behavior of the raters and officers has shifted to inflate the final product and make it meaningless. This hurts morale, and yet reforming the OER during downsizings has also hurt morale.

Everything that I have discovered about this topic confirms that the US military is stymied by evaluations and badly needs a new vision.

FIREWALL FIVES

In early 2010, the USAF announced the promotion results for over one thousand master sergeants, selected from a pool of over ten thousand staff sergeants up for consideration. Each of the selectees had a truly perfect performance report. In the air force, this is known as "firewall fives," meaning a rating of five points out of five possible given in every performance category, 135 out of 135 possible points. Such high scores signified—according to the formal evaluation guidelines—that these 1,269 individuals were "truly among the best" in all 27 ways there are to measure. Surprisingly, perfection was rampant in the air force that year. There were a "mind-boggling" 11,502 individuals who were *not* selected for promotion who also had the maximum evaluation score: 135 out of 135.[10]

The inflation of formal evaluations inside the military has reached a level of excess that is beyond parody and defies understanding. Identical patterns of inflation are rampant among officer and enlisted evaluations at all ranks. The navy, coast guard, army and Marines have similar issues, but the army and air force problems seem most severe. Suspension of the army's block rating is particularly devastating: a bureaucratic system that was driving many of its most talented officers out for its failure to recognize merit was made even less meritorious in order to stem the talent bleed. The US military profession really needs to bite the bullet and look for best practices elsewhere about how to measure talent.

The medical profession doesn't have the military's problems. Nor does the legal profession. Nor even the law enforcement profession. Those labor forces are managed by markets, not hermetically sealed monopsonies. Rather than using bureaucratic and centralized boards to review formal evaluations, other professions use open and informal processes—résumés and letters of recommendation. And it's not as if other professions, say, medicine, for example, are wild, free, unregulated markets. Quite the opposite. Medical professionals must be licensed and certified, and they are subject to review, by professional bodies *as well as* the market. Why such simple and standard practices are not used by the military is certainly the product of path dependency.

Unfortunately, the options for reform are muddled. Some critics, like Don Vandergriff, argue for scrapping competitive evaluations altogether, one of the few areas where I disagree with his analysis. Others are traditionalists who defend the system as the best of all possible worlds. However, numerous critics argue in favor of expanding evaluations to include peer and subordinate input, as well as making the forced distribution more bell shaped, which is what most surveys of active and retired troops seem to support. More detailed and strictly distributed evaluations are common in for-profit American companies, so let's turn there for rich lessons in how to manage talent. There is one company and one man in particular that may be much closer role models than many active-duty soldiers realize.

THE WARRIOR CEO

Bob McDonald is the chief executive officer of Procter & Gamble (P&G), a global commercial-product giant with annual revenues of nearly 80 billion dollars. The firm is headquartered in Cincinnati, Ohio, and employs over one hundred thousand people worldwide. In addition to producing many of the leading consumer goods and services in modern times, P&G is also famous for its world-class leadership system. And as the CEO, McDonald is like nearly every other senior manager at the company, a lifelong employee. But in his case, there was one exception at the start of his career: five years in the US Army.

In 1964, young McDonald committed himself to following in his dad's footsteps by joining the US Army. Being an idealist, dreaming of making a difference in the world, he knew the one place to go would be the United States Military Academy at West Point. He submitted an application to the local congressman's office in the thirteenth district of Illinois, and was given an appointment for an interview like other young men from around the district. The young congressman had decided that the fairest way to allot service-academy appointments was by letting young students compete on a rigorous civics test that they could take in his office. The difference between Bob McDonald and the other young men who showed up for their appointments was that the former was eleven years old in 1964.

"To his credit, my congressman allowed me to take his civics exam that year and to retake it every year until I was 18," McDonald remembers. "He said that he would accept my best score. So that's what I did, every year for seven years, I studied and took that test, and was eventually nominated by him in 1971. Actually, the congressman is someone you may know. He wasn't famous then, but his name is Don Rumsfeld."

After graduation from West Point in 1975, McDonald was assigned to the Eighty-Second Airborne Division and served in uniform for five years, primarily in the Eighty-Second Airborne. Upon leaving the military, he received the Meritorious Service Medal, and was recruited to join P&G in 1980. Like most competitive executives, he served as a brand manager relatively quickly, running Tide (the laundry detergent brand) in the mid-1980s. After 29 years working exclusively for P&G, with particular success helping the company expand internationally, the board tapped him to become CEO in 2009.

Soon after taking the CEO reins, McDonald decided to take his senior executives for a retreat to a new location. It was a place where he had learned his first and deepest lessons about leadership, and it meant a great deal to him to share his sense of values-based leadership that he'd internalized there. West Point. The team stayed at the legendary Thayer Hotel on campus with its renovated leadership conference facilities overlooking the Hudson.

As the CEO of one of America's great companies, with over one hundred thousand employees and billions of dollars in revenue every year, McDonald is often asked about his leadership principles. He keeps a two-page document handy—WHAT I BELIEVE IN—that explains the ten most important principles that guide him. West Point is mentioned in number 1 (a purpose-driven life) and number 5 (character is a leader's most important attribute), but what caught my eye was principle 4, which says: "Putting people in the right jobs is one of the most important jobs of the leader." This is a lesson the army should learn from its protégé.

MANAGING TALENT

McDonald was kind enough to spend some time with me for this book during a series of interviews in early April, 2011, though he cautioned that he doesn't want to be associated with any criticisms of the military or the troops. What we discussed is P&G and how it manages talent.

So, how does P&G evaluate its massive workforce and conduct job assignments? Before we get to that, consider the parallels between the private sector multinational corporation and the US

Army. "In general, P&G hires at the entry level, and higher positions are filled from the inside," McDonald reminds me. The company's corporate culture is famous for growing its own leaders, just like the Pentagon, as well as its core values, particularly the camaraderie mixed with competitiveness among ambitious brand managers. The pay is good but not spectacular compared to other Fortune 500 companies. Still, a P&G job is coveted by business-school graduates every year because it is without peer in the fierce world of consumer marketing. If the fight for profits among companies can be likened to war, then P&G is the analog to the Pentagon.

"Actually, it is easier for my firm to match talent with jobs than the army, since we only have 127,000 employees," McDonald says. "It's the job of management to have a personal relationship with its people, and we keep a leadership profile of each person in the company. We use it to identify best opportunities for training and work, and that drives how we match people with jobs. In my case, I was sent to the Philippines in 1991, which led to a decade of leadership opportunities in Asia. I would have never seen how important global business would become to P&G, but P&G knew that, and knew it would need its future senior leaders to have global experience. That same challenge faces me today in Africa."

I challenged McDonald to explain what he meant by being sent. Did he have a choice? That's an important distinction, and yes, employees at P&G can choose to accept opportunities or look for alternatives. The biggest difference between P&G and the military is that hiring is done locally, not centrally. McDonald continued:

> "People at P&G have a large say in where they ultimately go, and the local manager has the authority to select and hire among candidates, but HR also has a role in identifying good candidates for openings. Also, frankly, there is one major exception to the rule on hiring authority. I've put in a top-down system to make sure diverse candidates get opportunities for the best jobs."

Inside hiring is the norm at P&G, as it is in the military: "[W]e also look at outside hiring as a failure of strong succession planning inside." McDonald contrasted this with military practice. Like General Electric, P&G operates its organization like a real-time leadership factory, so that every manager at top levels is constantly grooming three or more replacements. McDonald emphasizes that this is different from treating managers as fungible.

Because the organization is at some point like a pyramid, talent needs to be managed in a way that gives people opportunities to move laterally within the company, rather than just up or out. Think of it as up or sideways. By random chance, another military veteran I spoke with at P&G was ranked much lower than McDonald but was also a few years older. This individual was given the freedom to specialize away from the command track in order to stay in one geographic location for two decades: "For more than half my career, I worked for younger bosses who made lower salaries." As for career management, this employee remarked: "At P&G, HR doesn't manage your career. You manage your own career."

Like any large organization, P&G uses regular performance reviews, and uses them for multiple purposes. First, performance feedback is a management tool to help guide employees in real-time job performance with the overlapping purpose of developing the employee's talent. The P&G evaluation is also saved for reference during internal job matching.

The key to the P&G review is "relative ratings"—the company's term for a forced distribution—which requires managers to identify a top 15 percent and bottom 10 percent within common pools of similar workers. Pools are ten people or more. P&G started relative performance rating in 1999. New employees dislike it somewhat early in their career because it naturally creates anxiety, but senior executives love it, both for feedback and for internal hiring. "It draws out genuine and diverse information on the mix of talents each person has," says McDonald, by highlighting certain skill strengths and certain skill weaknesses, not just the overall score off a too-simplistic system.

"What we learned is that a three-tier rating works best, and we use a 1, 2, 3. More than three becomes cumbersome. When we tried a 1 through 5 system, it led to splitting hairs. But without a relative rating system, organizations will become stagnant for the simple reason that people are not fungible. Jobs are not fungible. Understanding unique skills leads to better job matches, performance, and job satisfaction."

McDonald authorized me to speak with the company's global chief of human resources, Moheet Nagrath. "We have this approach we call 'Build From Within,' which aims to develop all senior leaders in the company from the recruits who enter at the beginning of their careers. This makes the P&G model hard to replicate at other firms, but it's very similar to the military structure," said Nagrath. "We find the key to making talented managers stay is to give them the right job."[11]

P&G reviews use two scorecards for each employee. The objective scorecard for performance flows out of objective numbers: profits, market share, and so forth. The second scorecard is a more subjective rating that measures how well a manager has built up the capabilities of his or her organization: strategy, culture, and systems. This is provided after conversations between the manager and their supervisor. Finally, the review includes an innovative supplemental feedback rating to assess the worker's potential, a measure that is distinct from current performance. This was instituted because the company's operating rule is to promote quickly. "The reward for getting a 1 is to be promoted to a harder job. But what happens is the first year in that job, everyone tends to get a 2 rating," explained McDonald. Getting less than perfect in a review is natural, but P&G wanted to supplement that with additional feedback.

P&G believes peer rating is absolutely essential. This provides feedback to employees as well as helps supervisors identify their top performers. "We use a computerized system so that each manager is evaluated electronically by roughly ten peers," Nagrath says. The peers are chosen by the ratee and supervisor together. The frequency of peer reviews is once every two years, on average. The software used for the process is homegrown, but was developed by incorporating practices from other firms. "P&G is constantly open to new and better management ideas," McDonald says.

Nagrath also described P&G's integrated job-assignments process. While local managers have principal hiring authority, it is not absolute, nor is it chaotic. For one, the company maintains a unified, global database of all employees so that local managers have a trusted resource to assess all candidates. Likewise, the HR system works together globally to recommend candidates and help conduct internal searches when there are unique talent needs in the dispersed and rapidly changing environment. In the early 1980s, P&G had no presence in China (no company did), but now China is a major focus for growth with a dedicated P&G workforce in the country. The job-matching process is conducted daily, and Nagrath's organization is constantly assigning people to new positions. Just like the armed forces, the matching process is long, but it is not complicated by a separate promotion process that obscures available candidates. Employees work closely with their immediate supervisors to plan their careers so that HR is aware of geographic preferences and other ambitions. But there is also an active open-market process called the "Open Job Posting" on the company intranet where junior executives can volunteer for positions and post their résumés as well. By the time a manager makes it to senior ranks, the opportunities become much more carefully managed and interpersonal, with input from the front office as well as the board.

The impression I got from Nagrath is that managing talent is a "delicate balance" between what are pretty well-established career paths for different specialties (manufacturing versus sales, for example). Each path has key jobs that are essential experiences, and the employees are encouraged to express interests, but no employee has complete freedom to demand or expect whatever job s/he wants. Once a new job is matched, the employee is expected to work in it for three years minimum. A final feature of the P&G approach is that local HR directors assist regional and brand managers in hiring and counseling the team. In sum, the P&G experience is a powerful case study showing how a large, semisealed professional organization can be effectively managed using decentralized HR techniques that engage employees by aligning institutional and individual needs. It can be done.

360 DEGREES

The army has so far resisted doing 360-degree reviews because of concerns that it is antithetical to a highly disciplined mission. Lieutenant Colonel Stephen Gerras argued in a May 2002 paper for the Army War College that "[l]eaders who who send soldiers into combat need to make many tough decisions that oftentimes are not pleasing to their subordinates. If we directly tie promotion decisions to subordinate and peer ratings, leaders may stop focusing on emphasizing tough, realistic training."[12] That essay was published the same year that Lieutenant Colonel Tim Reese argued in his War College thesis that a "360-degree leadership assessment of officer effectiveness, using peer and subordinate input, should be used as a formal part of the officer evaluation system."[13] Ulmer pressed the army for 360-degree reviews in his 1998 essay in *Parameters*, but the storm of interest passed, and the G-1 held firm with its top-down model. The entire army was soon overwhelmed by the more pressing issues of manning two wars, so is just now reconsidering the idea.

The larger question is one of design. To be sure, there are bad ways to design evaluation by peers and subordinates. There are also good ways. Let's start with the observation that "popularity contests" already exist in the current HR structure, but it is dominated by a top-down hierarchy, so that officers have only one audience for seeking popularity—their immediate supervisors—at the expense of everyone else. Colonel Ulmer made the point in his 1998 *Parameters* essay that more information—for promotions, assignments, and especially development—is good information. "The more closely we scrutinize either theory or practice, the more inadequate the exclusively top-down assessment of performance and potential appear."[14]

The real irony is that peer performance reviews are already deeply embedded in military culture. US Army Ranger training, for example, involves peer ratings to determine who passes and fails. Instructors notice, and that input affects who is tapped as the distinguished graduate. Here are Ulmer's fuller thoughts:

> Peer and subordinate evaluations have been used by commanders especially interested in leader development in some Army schools, in selected pre-commissioning programs, in some special training situations, and in a few units. And while they are apparently used routinely in the military services of some other nations, they appear to remain broadly unacceptable to the US Army general officer corps. It is difficult to dispute the reality that in order to promote individuals who are in fact good leaders we must somehow measure their style of leadership. Only followers know for certain the leader's moral courage, consideration for others, and commitment to unit above self. This is the indisputably crucial element in leader assessment and development systems. If in fact we prize these values and want to ensure that we promote those who have routinely demonstrated them, some form of input from subordinates is required. Again, the concept and technology are available to handle such inputs without organizationally dysfunctional side effects.[15]

THE NEW EVALUATION

I had heard whispers while writing this book that the army had been quietly working on some major reforms to its HR system during 2011. That is good news. The institution finally has a chance to catch its breath after a decade of war. While wholesale, radical reform like a TVF might be too much to expect in the short term, the "Green Pages" experiment gave reason to hope. But buzz about a new OER was steady, and in September 2011, HRC announced that a new Form 67–9 was being implemented. To my pleasant surprise, it included a 360-degree evaluation. Beginning on November 1, 2011, seven years after it had been eliminated, the army once again required block rating of all officers, with no more than 49 percent of officers allowed in the ACOM block by each senior rater.

Yet disappointingly, upon closer inspection, the reforms seem evolutionary, not revolutionary. It is a first step, but unfortunately it is so minor that advocates of the peer and subordinate review clearly lost to the old guard, yielding a symbolic change that will likely prove nothing and probably just linger for a decade. Here is what the new system actually requires, according to the HRC press release:

> The rater will include a comment that the rated officer has completed or initiated a 360/Multi-Source Assessment Feedback *within the last three years*. The new OER form will eventually have a yes/no box check for 360 completion. The MSAF provides input from peers, superiors and subordinates which will help the rated officer develop as a self-aware and adaptable leader. Officers can access the "360 Assessment" at https://msaf.army.mil. Results of the feedback will still *remain confidential* and *only be available to the rated officer* and used for self development not evaluative purposes.[16]

A quasi-optional rating with private feedback from hand-picked peers and subordinates would be tepid enough, but the new review form isn't even required. All that is required is that the officer has initiated a review, not completed it. It's even harder to understand how this is developmentally useful if results are kept secret from the commander. Sorry, but the reformers lost this battle.

The soldiers are not being protected by keeping peer input out of the promotion process. Far from it. Soldiers and junior officers are the ones advocating for a broader evaluation process because they feel the brunt of toxic leaders. No, it seems clear that the incumbent senior officers running the top-down evaluation, promotion, and assignment system are preserving the idea of a central control.

If and when the day comes that a handful of generals can join forces with the right legislators on the Senate and House Armed Services Committees, making the case for the genuine 360-degree review, the military will change profoundly.

FINAL THOUGHTS

This book has provided an overview of the military's broken leadership system. The examples of George Patton and Dwight Eisenhower being threatened with court-martial as junior officers because they understood the potential of armored warfare before their commanding generals should stay with us, especially because the army has only become less forgiving of mavericks in the last half century. To be sure, many great leaders such as Patton, Eisenhower, David Petraeus, and H. R. McMaster stay in uniform and overcome the bureaucratic flaws, but the existence of patriotism in a few is no excuse for institutional inefficiency.

Survey after survey of active-duty troops—in wartime and peacetime—reveal decades of frustration with HR policies that remain in place. Bleeding talent through retention is only the superficial symptom seen by the media and public, but active-duty troops know that internal bleeding of mismanaged talent is even worse. Innovative, outspoken, and high-integrity officers are too often kneecapped by a set of rules that rewards careerism and risk aversion instead.

At the heart of the book, I recommend the total volunteer force that takes advantage of market-driven incentives and personal autonomy rather than coercion. To truly empower the men and women in uniform to realize full productivity, we need to find ways to end coercion *after* the first day they take the oath of office.

Personnel economics is a dull phrase, yet it is a subject of daily conversation by soldiers, sailors, airmen, and Marines whenever they talk about compensation, retirement, assignments, lousy and great commanders, stop-loss, optempo, or evaluations. I was in the air force for over five years (nearly ten counting my cadet days), and I never saw the holistic way a centrally planned bureaucracy drove all of these elements because I never imagined there could be an alternative. Hopefully this book changes that perspective, even for those who disagree that coercion and central planning should be neutered in the US military.

But let me say to those who disagree: My proposed TVF concept is one of many that could improve the legacy system enshrined in DOPMA laws and OPMS regulations, and I happily accept there are better concepts to be found. What no reader should accept is the false dilemma between military service and the TVF's "mercenary" values. There is no productive outcome when we force a soldier to choose between the family's best interest and the nation's best interest. A smart reform will align both interests in the same direction, and eschew the coercive mentality altogether.

As a final note, let me admit that I shared a rough draft of this manuscript with my old friend, John Nagl. We spoke the other day and he said, "Two things. Love the ideas. Never going to happen." I had to laugh. John is probably right that the Pentagon bureaucracy will outlast memories of me and this book. Certainly it has outlasted wiser advocates and smarter proposals. I am happy, though, for playing my part as an ideas man, since I haven't done what John and other ground troops have done: carrying a weapon into combat and fighting the good fight. If all I can do is make the case for the revolutionary reform that is too idealistic to be realized, so be it. As we said at my school: Aim High.

APPENDIX

SURVEY OF WEST POINT GRADUATES

An initial survey (Part One) of West Point graduates from six classes (1989, 1991, 1995, 2000, 2001, and 2004) was conducted between late August through mid-September of 2010 using an online survey website.[1] An email solicitation was sent to members of each class from the class scribe/president. A total of 250 individuals responded by completing the survey. Of the respondents 78 (31 percent) were on active duty at the time. A follow-up survey (Part Two) was created based on comments and feedback, sent to the initial 250 respondents in mid-September, and completed by 126 of them by the October deadline.

Note that in most cases, percentages are reported as whole numbers, which may not sum to 100 percent due to rounding. Percentages for each result are calculated based on the number of responses to individual questions.

PART ONE

The instructions to the survey respondents included a few sentences defining key terminology as follows: "For the purpose of the survey, define 'entrepreneurial' as (1) independent, (2) creative/unorthodox, and (3) willing to take risks. These are traits the US armed forces recognize as vital for success in many fields. Therefore, do not think of entrepreneurial as irresponsible, disobedient, etc."

The first question (tables A.1 and A.2) asks whether the best officers leave the military early rather than serving a full career, and by design does not define "best" or "early." This decision was made in an effort

Table A.1 Do the best officers leave the military early rather than serving a full career?

	Total Percent	Total Count (N=248)	Active Duty Percent (N=78)
Yes, almost all of the best leave	3	8	1
Yes, MOST of the best leave, some stay	45	111	33
Partly, about half the best leave	45	111	47
No, a FEW of the best leave, most stay	7	17	17
No, the second best leave	0	1	1

Table A.2 Results by class

	1989	1991	1995	2000	2001	2004
Yes, almost all of the best leave (%)	3	2	5	0	5	17
Yes, MOST of the best leave, some stay (%)	39	41	42	67	48	42
Partly, about half the best leave (%)	48	47	50	30	43	42
No, a FEW of the best leave, most stay (%)	9	9	3	4	5	0
No, the second best leave (%)	0	1	0	0	0	0
Number of respondents	34	109	39	27	21	12

to ensure that respondents would not bracket the question in terms of entrepreneurial leadership or any other defined criteria.

Only 7 percent of West Point graduates believe that most of the best officers stay in the military. Among the active-duty respondents (78), only 17 percent believe that most of the best officers are staying in the military. Younger graduates were less optimistic, as seen in the responses from the 27 members of the class of 2000 (of which 13 remain on active duty).

Still, nearly half of the respondents took the middle option recognizing that "about half" of the best officers leave and half stay. And respondents reported in comments that the army retains some great leaders.

Comments from Respondents

- "Good leaders, those with entrepreneurial tendencies, are crushed by the military in spirit and in deed. I think this type of leader is attracted to the military, and during their personal growth stage, do well. But they soon 'outsmart' the norm and become frustrated by the confines of their senior leaderships' boundaries."

- "I believe that a lot of quality/best officers have departed earlier for a variety of reasons; however, many quality officers willing to make daily sacrifices continue to serve. This has always been the case."
- "The best junior officers have spent 8 years doing more work for the same pay as their peers who contribute only the bare minimum. There is no system to reward the best officers prior to the BZ Major board at 8 years of service."

Responses in table A.3 suggest a perception that the military is far less meritocratic than the private sector, and more pointedly that the military is not a meritocracy at all. Two-thirds of the full panel reported that the military leans more toward seniority than merit, and the average score (with 10 representing a promotion system based 100 percent on seniority) is 6.8. For the private sector, the average score is 4.0. This view holds, albeit less strongly, when the sample is limited to active-duty officers. Younger cohorts tend to view the military as less of a meritocracy, but all cohorts give the private sector similar scores on average.

Comments from Respondents

- "Because promotions are based on a strict timetable and because they are near-automatic given the high rates through LTC [lieutenant colonel], it's almost solely based on seniority. Anymore, it's not 'good' merit that gets you promoted but it's 'bad' merit that will not get you promoted."

Table A.3 Any promotion system balances seniority against merit. If 1 is all merit and 10 is all seniority, how do you rate the US military's promotion system in comparison to the private sector?

	US Military (%)	Private Sector (%)
1	0	2
2	3	16
3	7	26
4	9	20
5	8	17
6	8	10
7	18	5
8	26	3
9	19	1
10	2	0

- "I feel the military strongly promotes based on merit and ability; however, the military in the past few years has suffered a loss of officers at the junior level so therefore have had to increase their promotion rates regardless of merit and performance to fill the higher ranks."
- "In the civilian world, my performance is all that matters. There are no year groups. For the most part, a promotion is based on talent, not seniority. The year group system is one of the most asinine things the Army uses."
- "There is a third, hidden factor in the officer promotion system, that of demonstrated personal loyalty to the rater, the Commander and the US Army as a whole. It is entirely possible to be a highly motivated officer who achieves excellent results yet still receives average ratings and relatively slow promotions."

The question shown in table A.4 asks respondents to assign letter grades to 14 different aspects of the military in terms of fostering

Table A.4 Grade the following aspects of the military at fostering innovative and entrepreneurial leadership (A = excellent, C = neutral, F = fail)

	A & B (%)	A (%)	B (%)	C (%)	D (%)	F (%)
Experience in the field	89	43	46	7	4	4
Service academies	86	42	44	8	5	2
Junior officer training (years 3–10)	58	9	48	27	15	6
Recruiting talented people	55	12	42	28	17	7
War colleges	53	19	35	44	3	22
Military doctrine	49	11	38	31	19	9
Senior officer training (years 11+)	48	11	36	43	10	24
Initial training (year 1)	45	10	35	30	25	10
Evaluation system	32	5	27	36	33	18
Job assignment system	28	4	24	35	37	18
Promotion system	27	4	22	33	41	21
Retirement structure	26	11	14	44	30	15
Hierarchical culture	25	7	19	31	43	16
Compensation system	20	3	17	35	45	34

"innovative and entrepreneurial" leadership. As a benchmark, the raw talent (recruitment) received 55 percent As and Bs, the fourth highest. The other aspects can be understood in terms of this ratio as either improving or degrading the initial entrepreneurial talent. In general, formal training programs received average marks, including everything from service academies and war colleges to initial through senior officer training. Even doctrine received good marks.

The weaknesses in fostering innovative and entrepreneurial leadership according to West Point graduates falls heavily on the personnel system: evaluations (with a letter grade ratio AB/DF of 0.6), job assignments (0.5), promotions (0.4), and compensation (0.3). For example, only 8 out of 250 respondents gave the job assignment system an A grade, compared to 39 who gave it an F. While these various personnel systems may serve other army missions, they are perceived as failing to promote entrepreneurial leadership.

Comments from Respondents

- "We need leaders that are balanced between the art and science of actually sending bullets down range and the art and science of leadership, global economy, global security, and leadership. Our eval and promotion system are heavily weighted toward 'experience in the field.' [Many noncombat commanders] develop skills and abilities that commanders of traditional O6/Colonel level commands never achieve. Yet, the 'experience on the "battlefield"' is outweighing the 'experience in the management field' and they are leaving at the end of their commands."
- "Gov and military greatest benefit are job security and retirement pension. The way to jeopardize that is to rock the boat. That philosophy retards military innovation."
- "I feel like before I separated in 2007, the Army was in the midst of a cultural shift, particularly with its company and junior field grade officers, due to gained experience from multiple deployments in OIF/OEF [Operation Iraqi Freedom/Operation Enduring Freedom]. From a doctrinal and educational perspective, I felt the Army was starting to become more entrepreneurial, but like any large bureaucracy, it takes time for innovations to diffuse."

Table A.5 Agree or disagree: Creative thinking and new ideas are (were) valued in your military units.

	Total Percent (%)	Total Count (N = 242)
Strongly agree	18	43
Agree	51	124
Disagree	24	59
Strongly disagree	7	16

- "Retirement structure of the Army was terrible. The army's assumption was every officer does 20 years and therefore earns a government retirement. There was no 401k equivalent when I was in the military, which eliminated an opportunity to invest a significant amount of pretax dollars for retirement."
- "The military leadership 'gets' that innovation is important, but the seniority structure prevents execution except in leadership laboratories (West Point, War College, etc.) or in actual combat when boots on ground execute as needed. Good innovation is rewarded with mission accomplishment."

To assess opinions regarding the level of creative thinking, we asked if such thinking was valued (table A.5). Two-thirds of respondents reported that "creative thinking and new ideas" are or were valued in their experience. Only 7 percent strongly disagreed. These data suggest that entrepreneurial leadership is ongoing at the tactical/cultural level, regardless of the level of support at the institutional level.

Comments from Respondents

- "A majority of the missions I conducted/led/participated in during 27 months of combat service in Iraq were based in creative thinking and new ideas vs. any type of Army doctrine. Simply put, operations were ahead of doctrine (meaning that the doctrine had not yet been written). Conversely, the rigidity and lack of creative thinking ability and a tendency on the part of senior NCOs (1SGs/SGMs/CSMs) to rely on the 'this is how we've always done it' method often times created much conflict in the planning/execution of missions."
- "Army units were entrepreneurial; the Army was not."

- "Both conventional Infantry organization and in Special Operations units—the more an entrepreneurial mindset is valued, the more successful the organization (and the better the experience)."
- "Depends on the unit and the senior leadership. My first unit challenged and mentored the junior officers. My second unit of assignment just wanted me to do as I was told."
- "For the most part, creative thinking is valued, but there is only so much leeway given the crushing hand of the Army Regulatory

Table A. 6 To improve entrepreneurial leadership, the US military should…

	Strongly Agree (%)	Agree (%)	Disagree (%)	Strongly Disagree (%)	Active Duty Cohort: Agree & Strongly Agree (%)
Allow greater specialization rather than track everyone for flag officer	39	51	10	0	87
Expand early promotion opportunities	40	47	12	1	77
Allow former officers to rejoin the service (lateral entry)	29	54	15	2	73
Eliminate "year groups" after 10 years	29	49	20	2	67
Use market mechanism to allocate jobs instead of central placement	22	54	22	2	76
Lay off more officers involuntarily	21	41	33	5	62
Force a distribution of top and bottom 10–20% in evaluations	22	41	32	6	66
Allow former soldiers to use GI Bill money as startup loans instead of education	17	43	30	10	51
Expand the academies to include graduate schools	25	28	33	14	54
Reauthorize conscription (draft)	4	10	29	57	14

system and the constant turnover of leadership at all levels. A junior leader is forced to react to 'the new guys' priorities every few months, and no long term progress is ever made. There is an obsession with paperwork and peripheral activities that do little to support the overall wartime mission."

Respondents to the question in table A.6 showed strong support for a variety of policies that might enhance entrepreneurial leadership in the US military. The highest support is for allowing greater specialization (90 percent agree), essentially countering the military's "up or out" philosophy. Expanding early promotion opportunities (87 percent) and eliminating the strict promotion year groups (pools of peers based on common commissioning year) (78 percent) also have strong support.

Comments from Respondents

- "I think the Army doesn't really have a good inventory of the talent/skills of its people and many opportunities are missed and that talent eventually slips away without anyone ever really knowing what they just lost."
- "I know so many officers who were already 'retired' at 15 or 16 years. They did not want to take a battalion command but did want a cushy job and nice retirement. Why are those guys still in? There should be some way to separate them."
- "Allowing lateral entry would encourage people to cross over to the private sector and back. They will learn a ton. They will bring back ideas. They won't stay in the Army just because they are afraid to leave. What does the Army have to lose?"
- "I think the Army needs to look at their officers and cull the bottom 10% every year. There are lots of bad officers who stay in the Army because its 'easy' and you never really get fired, just moved around."
- "Instead of expanding the military academies to include graduate schools (a terrible idea), the military should instead focus on sending more (all?) officers to civilian or already established military graduate schools."
- "Market mechanism to allow officer placement in areas of greater specialization is especially important starting at O4 and above."

- "Need to remove all bias and inflation from performance evaluation system and ensure that creativity and risk-taking are values to strive for in the organization."
- "There needs to be more 360 degree feedback in evaluations, especially commander evaluations. I think my BDE CDR [Brigade Commander] (and in turn DIV CDR [Division Commander]) was completely oblivious to what was actually happening as a result of my BN CDR [Battalion Commander] command culture. However, he got a glowing OER, promotion to O-6, and choice assignment. Because my BN CDR wasn't around long enough to reap the harvest of the terrible seed he sowed, he left a complete mess for the follow on BN CDR. To make the Army more entrepreneurial, let leaders stay long enough to actually be a part of the process they create. The Army's job placement system sweeps everyone away too quickly."

This question (table A.7) aims to identify whether, from the army's perspective, other military branches are more entrepreneurial. While the advanced high-tech systems of the air force and the low-tech systems of the Marines are widely recognized, leadership is another matter. And on that score, the panel believed the army's leadership to be as or more entrepreneurial than every other service. Civilians serve in large numbers within many military units, both in command units and at lower levels. While they may be diligent, civilian workers in the military are not perceived to exhibit more entrepreneurial leadership on average.

Four reasons stand out as the most frequently cited by officers in explaining why they left the ranks (table A.8). High op tempo during war, other life goals, and family income all play a role. But the top reason for leaving the military cited by this panel is frustration with military

Table A.7 In your experience, do the officers of the following branches have more entrepreneurial leadership than the US Army?

	More (%)	Less (%)
US Marine Corps	17	27
US Air Force	24	25
US Navy	7	24
US military civilians	9	56

Table A.8 What were the reasons you left the military? Agree or disagree if they were important reasons for your decision (Skip if you never served or remain on active duty)

	Strongly Agree (%)	Agree (%)	Disagree (%)	Strongly Disagree (%)
Frustration with military bureaucracy	50	32	16	2
Family	57	24	15	5
Other life goals	35	45	15	5
Higher potential income	45	35	14	4
Frequent deployments	31	32	30	4
Limited opportunity in military	17	40	32	10
Pace of military promotions	22	31	39	7
Weak role models/commanders	24	22	35	19
Higher education	20	25	45	9
Better leadership opportunity	7	25	53	14
Retirement age (20 years+)	5	6	44	44
Medical discharge	2	4	25	68

bureaucracy, with 82 percent agreeing that it was one of their reasons for leaving.

Weak role models were cited by 46 percent of respondents. This factor would ideally be much lower, but it is notably not among the top half of all reasons cited. The fact that higher education is cited by a relatively large number is also troubling, especially because the army has made great strides in making graduate education more available (indeed, it is essentially a requirement for senior rank). Again, these data point to a lack of flexibility in individual career management.

Notably, officers are not departing in order to pursue a "better leadership opportunity." A casual explanation for the high rate of ex-military leaders in the private sector is that such opportunities draw talent away from the service. This survey response suggests that story is less significant than commonly perceived.

PART TWO

Part Two of the survey was developed in response to feedback based on private presentations of the initial results. A few weeks after

Table A.9 Which of the following statements do you agree with? (Check all that apply.) The current military personnel system...

	Percent (%)	Active Duty Percent (%)
...does a good job weeding out the weakest leaders.	26	18
...does a good job retaining the best leaders.	6	5
...does a good job matching talents with jobs.	16	18
...does a good job promoting the right officers to general.	28	38
...promotes and incentivizes entrepreneurial leaders.	5	8
...should be radically reformed.	55	55

Part One concluded, a message with an Internet link to Part Two was emailed directly to the initial respondents, and 126 of those individuals responded.

Feedback from Part One focused largely on whether an entrepreneurial military culture was desirable. A handful of counterarguments were frequently made in response to the proposed meritocratic and entrepreneurial reforms. The US military has a well-deserved pride in its culture, and has a track record of tremendous achievements in recent decades. In addition, the military remains a very highly respected institution in the United States. Naturally then, changes along the lines suggested in Part One are viewed by some as a risk to what has been on balance a successful institution. All of these factors helped develop the following questions.

The first question in Part 2 of the survey (table A.9) explores some of the specific harms and weaknesses of the current military personnel system. The first two options ask about opposite ends of the leadership spectrum: promoting the best and culling the weakest leaders. In both areas, less than one-third of respondents agree that the military is doing a good job. Only one-sixth of respondents (17 percent) think the military does a good job matching talents with jobs. The final option asks whether the personnel system should be radically reformed, something we asked to contrast with common calls for incremental change, and 59 percent of respondents agree.

Two additional questions (tables A.10 and A.11) attempt to make an unequivocal assessment of the impact of the current retention of officers in the US military. Typical responses in conversations about military retention are that high turnover is normal in the contemporary US economy and that high attrition rates are normal in the "up or out" military

Table A.10 Does the current exit rate of the military's best young officers harm national security?

	Percent (%)	Active Duty Percent (%)
Yes, strongly agree	19	23
Yes, agree	59	55
No, disagree	20	23
No, strongly disagree	2	0

Table A.11 Does the current exit rate of the military's best young officers lead to a less competent general officer corps?

	Percent (%)	Active Duty Percent (%)
Yes, strongly agree	23	20
Yes, agree	43	48
No, disagree	31	30
No, strongly disagree	4	3

rank structure. While turnover may be high, turnover of top talent is the issue under scrutiny in this survey. Hence, these two questions asked for an assessment with respect to national security and general officer corps' competence. In both cases, strong majorities agree that there are negative consequences. Of all respondents 78 percent (and 78 percent of active-duty respondents) agree that the current exit rate of the best officers harms national security, while 65 percent (68 percent among active duty) agree that it leads to a less competent general officer corps.

The results in table A.12 reflect my effort to identify which reforms might cause more of the best officers to stay.

A common belief is that most exiting officers were likely to leave regardless of military personnel policies. Simply put, the opportunity for higher income, security, and stability are too strong to resist. Also, many believe that most officers find the military less appealing once they reach midcareer and see the stress on family life caused by active-duty service. Surprisingly, only 31 percent of respondents believe that the best officers would leave regardless of reforms.

The reform that most respondents agreed would increase retention of top officers is "if the military was more of a meritocracy," with 90 percent agreement. Two other reforms garnered nearly 90 percent agreement: a more entrepreneurial personnel system and a job-matching system that was driven by a market mechanism.

Table A.12 Do you agree or disagree with the following statements? Many of the best officers who leave the service would…

	Strongly Agree	Agree	Disagree	Strongly Disagree
…stay if the military was more of a meritocracy.	37.3% (47)	52.4% (66)	8.7% (11)	1.6% (2)
…stay if they could remain in a job as long as they and their commander wanted (and change jobs whenever they wanted).	30.4% (38)	40.8% (51)	28.0% (35)	0.8% (1)
…stay if the pay was based on performance instead of time-in-service.	31.0% (39)	38.9% (49)	28.6% (36)	1.6% (2)
…stay if job assignments were matched with a market mechanism rather than central planning.	24.2% (30)	62.9% (78)	12.9% (16)	0.0% (0)
…stay if the military had a more entrepreneurial personnel system.	21.8% (27)	66.1% (82)	12.1% (15)	0.0% (0)
…stay if they did not have to attend so many mandatory training courses.	9.6% (12)	20.8% (26)	58.4% (73)	11.2% (14)
…stay if they were not obligated to pursue higher rank.	10.4% (13)	32.8% (41)	51.2% (64)	5.6% (7)
…leave regardless of reforms to the personnel system.	4.8% (6)	25.8% (32)	62.9% (78)	6.5% (8)

More control over job tenure had 70 percent agreement, as did a compensation based more on performance instead of time-in-service.

A majority disagreed that two other reforms would keep the best officers from leaving. Reducing mandatory training was not seen as a major retention incentive by 68 percent of respondents. Requiring promotions to higher rank was not seen as a retention disincentive by 57 percent.

Skepticism about radical and specific policy changes is expected, often expressed as assertions about what the troops really want. The next question (table A.13) put these counterarguments to the test. For instance, when the all-volunteer force (AVF) replaced the draft in the early 1970s, many observers felt it would create a mercenary culture. That same argument is often heard in defense of the status quo; despite its imperfections, the current personnel system goes hand in hand with core values of teamwork and a sense of equality. Another common

Table A.13 Do you agree or disagree with the following arguments against changing the US military?

	Strongly Agree	Agree	Disagree	Strongly Disagree
Encouraging entrepreneurship will lead to excessive risk taking and loss of life.	0.8% (1)	1.6% (2)	70.4% (88)	27.2% (34)
Core values such as service-above-self will be eroded by an entrepreneurial personnel system.	0.8% (1)	11.2% (14)	60.0% (75)	28.0% (35)
Competency to command in the military requires much longer experience than nonmilitary professions.	7.2% (9)	47.2% (59)	35.2% (44)	10.4% (13)
Increasing meritocracy in the military will lead to a more mercenary culture.	0.8% (1)	12.0% (15)	56.8% (71)	30.4% (38)

argument is that the slow pace of promotions relative to civilian professions is due to the life-and-death nature of the profession of arms.

Will encouraging entrepreneurship in the military lead to excessive risk taking and loss of life? Only 2.4 percent of respondents agree it will. This result is in line with the current innovative spirit encouraged by Pentagon leaders and practiced at the unit level (as described earlier).

Regarding core values, 88 percent of respondents disagree that an entrepreneurial personnel system will erode core values such as service above self. Likewise, 87 percent disagree that increasing meritocracy will lead to a more mercenary culture.

The lone counterargument that showed substantive agreement among respondents was that competency to command in the military requires much longer experience than nonmilitary professions, with over half the respondents (54 percent) agreeing. Only 10 percent disagreed strongly.

Finally, I asked about performance evaluations (table A.14). The current system of performance evaluations is different across services, so the results here reflect primarily on the US Army. Commanders evaluate subordinates using a simple distributional classification and written summary. Seventy-four percent of respondents agree that requiring commanders to utilize a top 10 percent and bottom

Table A.14 What reforms to military performance evaluations would yield better, more entrepreneurial leadership?

	Strongly Agree	Agree	Disagree	Strongly Disagree
Require commanders to identify the top 10% and bottom 10% of officers.	29.6% (37)	44.8% (56)	21.6% (27)	4.0% (5)
Include evaluations from peers.	22.2% (28)	56.3% (71)	21.4% (27)	0.0% (0)
Include evaluations from subordinates.	26.4% (33)	44.0% (55)	28.0% (35)	1.6% (2)
Promotion recommendations remain in officer's permanent record, not stricken from review by future promotion boards.	19.5% (24)	50.4% (62)	28.5% (35)	1.6% (2)

10 percent distribution would yield better, more entrepreneurial leadership.

Respondents also support using evaluations from peers (79 percent) and subordinates (72 percent) in assessing performance of officers. Finally, in response to reports that an officer's record is often partially hidden in some situations, 70 percent of respondents agree that making all promotion recommendations part of an officer's performance record would be beneficial.

Methodology and Panel Selection

The panel included 250 respondents who are all graduates of the United States Military Academy (USMA), located in West Point, New York. Data were collected electronically over the Internet using a survey website.

Sample Selection

The goal of the survey was to sample a representative group of army officers across a broad range of career experiences. Initial consideration was given to sampling students at various professional military schools, such as the Army War College or Command and General Staff College; however, those groups would primarily include members who are currently active-duty officers. Therefore, I utilized a channel that included both current and former officers, and was neutral in recruitment of the sample.

Each graduating class from West Point has a set of class officers, one of whom is the class scribe, tasked with coordinating messages from classmates for quarterly newsletters and news summaries in the alumni magazine. Scribes tend to have widely varying levels of contact with their classmates, and each class tends to be responsive to different degrees. Regardless, my goal was to get the support of one or more scribes for each half decade (i.e., 1990, 1995, 2000, and 2005). I chose to draw the line at the class of 1989 and no earlier, so that responses focused on more recent personnel practices of the army.

I contacted the first two scribes via email introduction through two individuals whom I know personally (from the classes of 1989 and 1991 respectively). I explained the survey project in an email to those scribes. They pointed me to the website, west-point.org, which is described as "a 501(c)(3) organization connecting almost 30,000 USMA grads, parents, and friends of West Point. Since its inception in 1996, WP-ORG (westpoint.org) has been funded by the generosity of member contributions and is governed and run independently from USMA and the Association of Graduates." Utilizing the scribe contact list at WP-ORG, I reached out to numerous scribes across the years 1992–2005.

Although I never met any of the scribes personally, a total of six scribes agreed to forward the message to their respective classes. These were for the classes of 1989, 1991, 1995, 2000, 2001, and 2004. I sent the following email text, which was forwarded (or posted) to the respective class lists:

> *Tim Kane (cc line), is a USAFA '90 grad and economist, and he needs our help. Tim is asking for you to take a short survey about leadership in the Army in the **next 3–4 days**. The link is....*
>
> *Tim's current project is to help the Army get better at retaining more of the amazingly talented officers that they have. He promises to send us the results.*

Members of the class of 2004 were advised to contact me directly if they wished to participate, and those who did were then given the link to the online address.

The online survey was kept open until mid-September. In addition to the 242 respondents from the target lists, the survey link was shared by some recipients with other graduates from USMA (e.g., spouses in many instances) in adjoining classes. The sample therefore includes one respondent from each of the following classes: 1985, 1987, 1988, 1990, 1992, 2003, 2005, 2007, and 2010. No respondents were screened before or after participating in the survey for any reason.

In summary, recruitment to the survey was done in a neutral and unbiased fashion. Potential respondents were given enough information to know that the survey was being done by a credible researcher. Participants who went to the online survey website were welcomed with the following text:

> *This survey seeks to assess innovative and entrepreneurial leadership in the U.S. military. The results will be published with summary data made publicly available. For the purpose of the survey, define "entrepreneurial" as (1) independent, (2) creative/unorthodox, and (3) willing to take risks. These are traits the U.S. armed forces recognize as vital for success in many fields. Therefore, do not think of entrepreneurial as irresponsible, disobedient, etc. All questions are optional, and individual replies will be kept anonymous. Thank you for participating.*
>
> *Tim Kane, Ph.D., Study Director*
> *The Kauffman Foundation*

Fortunately, the respondent sample (table A.15) was well balanced in terms of the overall population of West Point graduates. Fully a third of the respondents were on active duty at the time of the survey, and no class appeared to be an outlier in any category. In a recent paper, the retention rate for the USMA class of 1996 was roughly 40 percent at the eight-year point (i.e., in 2004), which indicates that the retention

Table A.15   Results by class

	1989	1991	1995	2000	2001	2004
Number of respondents	34	109	39	27	21	12
Years active duty (avg.)	7.1	9.9	9.3	7.7	7.2	6.2
Active duty (current) (%)	12	26	36	48	38	50
MBA (%)	32	37	44	22	43	17
Entrepreneur (current or former) (%)	35	27	23	11	29	8

(active-duty) rates of the survey sample here appear to be above the norm.

The heavily represented class of 1991 is approaching its 20-year retirement mark, so having 26 percent of the sample from that class on active duty is a good sign (compared to the 12 percent for the retirement-eligible class of 1989, which was also subject to more early-out opportunities during the "peace dividend" drawdown of the early 1990s).

The following table (A.16) shows a predictable rank distribution, especially from the class of 1991 (which includes 37 current and former officers who have achieved the rank of lieutenant colonel). All of this suggests the respondent pool is not composed of disgruntled ex-officers who achieved lower rank and/or resigned their commissions.

Table A.16 Highest rank, by class year

	1989	1991	1995	2000	2001	2004
Number of respondents	34	109	39	27	21	12
2LT	4	10	2	–	–	–
CPT	22	55	21	13	20	12
MAJ	3	6	15	14	–	–
LTC	3	37	–	–	1	–
COL	2	–	1	–	–	–
N/A	–	1	–	–	–	–

NOTES

INTRODUCTION

1. Lydia Saad, "Congress Ranks Last in Confidence in Institutions," *Gallup Politics* (July 22, 2010), http://www.gallup.com/poll/141512/congress-ranks-last-confidence-institutions.aspx.

1 A CAUTIONARY TALE

1. "History and the Movie '300,'" Victor Davis Hanson's private papers, http://www.victorhanson.com/articles/hanson101106.html (accessed July 12, 2012).
2. Originally cited in Lieutenant Colonel Scott M. Halter's "What is an Army but the Soldiers?—A Critical Performance Assessment of the U.S. Army's Human Capital Management System," *MILITARY REVIEW* (January-February 2012), 16, which referenced Volney Warner, *General Officer Survey on Army Title X Activities* (Washington DC: Center for Army Analysis, 2011).
3. Ibid.
4. Casey Wardynski, David S. Lyle, and Michael J. Colarusso, "Towards A U.S. Army Officer Corps Strategy For Success: Retaining Talent," *Strategic Studies Institute (SSI)* (January 2010), http://www.strategicstudies institute.army.mil/pdffiles/PUB965.pdf (accessed May 7, 2010).
5. Robert M. Gates, Speech, West Point, NY, Friday, February 25, 2011, http://www.defense.gov/speeches/speech.aspx?speechid=1539 (accessed February 26, 2011).
6. Ibid.
7. Fred Kaplan, "An Officer and a Family Man," *Slate.com* (January 16, 2008), http://www.slate.com/articles/news_and_politics/war_stories/2008/01/an_officer_and_a_family_man.html (accessed July 12, 2012).
8. See Tim Kane, "Why Our Best Officers Are Leaving," *The Atlantic* (January/February 2011).
9. Mark Moyar, *A Question of Command* (New Haven, CT: Yale University Press, 2009), 7.

10. Ibid., 3.
11. Ibid., 259–261.
12. Ibid., 268–274.
13. Ibid., 271.
14. Ibid., 215.
15. Andrew Tilghman, "The Army's Other Crisis: Why the Best and Brightest Young Officers Are Leaving," *Washington Monthly* (December 2007), http://www.washingtonmonthly.com/features/2007/0712.tilghman.html (accessed October 15, 2009).
16. Tim Kane, "Who Are the Recruits? The Demographic Characteristics of U.S. Military Enlistment, 2003–2005," Heritage Foundation Center for Data Analysis Report #06–09 (October 27, 2006), http://www.heritage.org/research/reports/2006/10/who-are-the-recruits-the-demographic-characteristics-of-us-military-enlistment-2003–2005 (accessed October 15, 2009).
17. Moyar, 219.
18. Arthur Hadley, *The Straw Giant* (New York: Random House, 1971), 22.
19. Ibid, 27.
20. Ibid, 294.
21. Leonard Wong, "Fashion Tips For The Field Grade," *Strategic Studies Institute* (October 4, 2006), 2. http://www.strategicstudiesinstitute.army.mil/pdffiles/pub731.pdf (accessed June 7, 2011).
22. Leonard Wong, "Developing Adaptive Leaders: The Crucible Experience Of Operation Iraqi Freedom," *The Strategic Studies Institute* (July 2004, 20), http://www.strategicstudiesinstitute.army.mil/pdffiles/PUB411.pdf (accessed March 3, 2010).
23. Renny McPherson, "The Next Petraeus: What Makes a Visionary Commander, and Why the Military Isn't Producing More of Them," *The Boston Globe* (September 26, 2010), http://www.boston.com/bostonglobe/ideas/articles/2010/09/26/the_next_petraeus/?page=1 (accessed October 10, 2010).
24. Tim Duffy, *Military Experience & CEOs: Is There a Link?*, Korn/Ferry International (June 16, 2006). Available at http://www.kornferry.com/PressRelease/3392.
25. Warren Bennis, *Still Surprised: A Memoir of a Life in Leadership* Jossey-Bass, (San Francisco, CA: Jossey-Bass, 2010), 13.
26. Bernard Rostker and K. C. Yeh, *I Want You! The Evolution of the All-Volunteer Force* (Santa Monica: RAND Corporation, 2006), 66.
27. Gates Commission Report, Letter of Transmittal from Thomas S. Gates to the President (February 20, 1970).
28. Milton Friedman, "Why Not a Volunteer Army?" in *New Individualist Review*, edited by Ralph Raico (Indianapolis: Liberty Fund, 1981), 825.
29. Bernard D. Rostker, Harry J. Thie, James L. Lacy, Jennifer H. Kawata, and Susanna W. Purnell, "The Defense Officer Personnel

Management Act of 1980: A Retrospective Assessment" (RAND Corporation, 1992), www.rand.org/pubs/reports/R4246.html.

30. *Enhancing Adaptability of U.S. Military Forces*, Report of the Defense Science Board (January 2011), 139.

31. *Military Pay Tables—1949–2012*, The Defense Finance and Accounting Service, last updated January 18, 2012, http://www.dfas .mil/militarymembers/payentitlements/militarypaytables.html.

32. Wikipedia has a useful summary at "United States Military Pay," http://en.wikipedia.org/wiki/United_States_Military_Pay (accessed October 20, 2011); and the US Department of Defense offers extensive details at the defense.gov website *Military Compensation*, http://militarypay.defense.gov/pay/index.html (accessed October 20, 2011).

2 THE PARADOX OF MILITARY LEADERSHIP

1. Warren Bennis, *Still Surprised: A Memoir of a Life in Leadership* (San Francisco: Jossey-Bass, 2010), 13.

2. Brian O'Keefe, "Battle-Tested: From Soldier to Business Leader," *Fortune Magazine* (March 8, 2010), http://money.cnn.com/2010/03/04 /news/companies/military_business_leaders.fortune/. *Fortune* revisited the story on July 13, 2011: "In the last few years, many of the most desirable employers in banking, consulting and technology have gone out of their way to attract these servicemen and women, according to campus veterans organizations and some employers, inviting them to celebrity-packed recruiting events, hosting veterans-only events on campus, and creating affinity groups that allow employees who served in the military to reach out to prospectives." Rouen, Ethan Rouen, "Military Vets: MBA Job Recruiters' Dream Candidates?," http://management.fortune.cnn.com/2011/07/13/military-vets-mba-job -recruiter%E2%80%99s-dream-candidates/.

3. O'Keefe, Battle-Tested.

4. Ibid.

5. Anne Marlowe, "The Truth About Those Who Fight For Us," *Wall Street Journal* (September 27, 2011), http://online.wsj.com/article /SB100014 24053111903791504576587244025371456.html (accessed October 5, 2012).

6. Tim Kane, "Stupid Soldiers: The Left's Worldview," *Human Events* (November 3, 2006), http://www.humanevents.com/2006/11/03/stupid -soldiers-the-lefts-worldview/ (accessed October 29, 2011).

7. Tony Perry, "Whites Account for Most of Military's Fatalities," *Los Angeles Times* (September 24, 2005), http://articles.latimes.com/2005 /sep/24/nation/na-dead24 (accessed July 18, 2012).

8. Ann Scott Tyson, "Youths in Rural U.S. are Drawn to Military," *The Washington Post* (November 4, 2005), http://www.washingtonpost .com/wp-dyn/content/article/2005/11/03/AR2005110302528.html, (accessed July 18, 2012).

9. Michael Moore, director *Fahrenheit 9/11*, DVD (United States: Lions Gate Films, 2004).

10. Oliver North, "They're Heroes to Me" (April 29, 2004), http://www.military.com/NewContent1/0,14361,FreedomAlliance_042904,00.htm (accessed July 18, 2012).

11. Tim Kane, "Who Bears the Burden? Demographic Characteristics of U.S. Military Recruits Before and After 9/11," *Heritage Foundation Center for Data Analysis* Report No. CDA05–08, November 7, 2005, at http://www.heritage.org/research/nationalsecurity/cda05–08.cfm; and "Who Are the Recruits? The Demographic Characteristics of U.S. Military Enlistment, 2003–2005," Heritage Foundation Center for Data Analysis Report No. CDA06–09 (October 26, 2006), at http://www.heritage.org/Research/NationalSecurity/cda06–09.cfm.

12. Shanea J. Watkins and James Sherk, "Who Serves in the U.S. Military? Demographic Characteristics of Enlisted Troops and Officers," Heritage Foundation Center for Data Analysis (August 21, 2008), 7.

13. Beth J. Asch, James R. Hosek, and John T. Warner, "New Economics of Manpower in the Post-Cold War Era," in *Handbook of Defense Economics* 2, edited by Todd Sandler and Keith Hartley (Amsterdam, The Netherlands, and Oxford, UK: Elsevier, 2007), 1075–1138, (http://www.sciencedirect.com/science/article/pii/S1574001306020321).

14. Congressional Budget Office, "The All-Volunteer Military: Issues and Performance," Pub. No. 2960, July 2007, www.cbo.gov/ftpdocs/83xx/doc8313/07–19-MilitaryVol.pdf (accessed July 19, 2007).

15. Watkins and Sherk, "Who Serves in the U.S. Military."

16. See "Class of 2003," West Point: The United States Military Academy, http://www.usma.edu/class/2002/profile.asp for the profile of the class of 2003, which entered West Point in the summer of 1999 (accessed October 2, 2011).

17. See United States Census Bureau, "Statistics About Business Size," http://www.census.gov/econ/smallbus.html (accessed October 28, 2011).

18. See "Department of Defense Active Duty Military Personnel by Rank/Grade (Women Only)," Department of Defense Personnel and Procurement Statistics (September 30, 2009), http://siadapp.dmdc.osd.mil/personnel/MILITARY/rg0909f.pdf (accessed October 27, 2011); and "Army Demographics: FY11 Army Profile," Army Human Resources Policy Directorate, September 30, 2011, http://www.armyg1.army.mil/hr/docs/demographics/FY11_ARMY_PROFILE.pdf (accessed October 28).

19. "Top Companies: Biggest," last modified May 23, 2011, http://money.cnn.com/magazines/fortune/fortune500/2011/performers/companies/biggest/employees.html.

20. See Tim Duffy's *Military Experience & CEOs: Is There a Link?*, Korn/Ferry International (June 16, 2006). Available at http://www.kornferry.com/PressRelease/3392.

21. Ibid.
22. US Census Bureau, *Educational Attainment in theUnited States: 2007, January 2009*, http://www.census.gov/prod/2009pubs/p20–560.pdf.
23. Duffy, *Military Experience & CEOs*.
24. Efraim Benmelech and Carola Frydman, "Military CEOs," unpublished manuscript. University of California, Berkeley, Haas School (November 2009), 28. http://www.haas.berkeley.edu/groups/finance /military 11 10 09.pdf (accessed July 29, 2012).
25. John Keegan, *A History of Warfare* (New York: Vintage Books, 1993), 8.
26. Tom Kloditz, "Why the Military Produces Great Leaders," *Harvard Business Review* (February 6, 2009), http://blogs.hbr.org/frontline-leadership/2009/02/why-the-military-produces-grea.html.
27. Bill Coleman, interview, Palo Alto, California, July 2010.
28. Ibid.
29. Bennis, *Still Surprised*. He further writes, "It is no accident that the war produced so many authentic leaders in the second half of the 20th century. Nobody who has to make choices that result in the deaths of others takes leadership lightly" (24).
30. *The Wealth of Nations* has five major sections, or books, and the first of three parts of book V is a discussion of military issues. Smith wrote in section V.1.18, "If the state has recourse to the first of those two expedients, its military force is said to consist in a militia; if to the second, it is said to consist in a standing army. The practice of military exercises is the sole or principal occupation of the soldiers of a standing army, and the maintenance or pay which the state affords them is the principal and ordinary fund of their subsistence. The practice of military exercises is only the occasional occupation of the soldiers of a militia, and they derive the principal and ordinary fund of their subsistence from some other occupation. In a militia, the character of the labourer, artificer, or tradesman, predominates over that of the soldier; in a standing army, that of the soldier predominates over every other character: and in this distinction seems to consist the essential difference between those two different species of military force." Adam Smith, *An Inquiry into the Nature and Causes of the Wealth of Nations,* originally published in 1776, available free online at the Library of Economics and Liberty, http://www.econlib.org /library/Smith/smWN.html (accessed July 29, 2012).
31. "Bugle Notes: Learn This!" West Point, http://www.west-point.org /academy/malo-wa/inspirations/buglenotes.html (accessed July 18, 2012).
32. Headquarters Department of the Army, *Field Manual 7.21–13* (October 2003), 5–6.
33. Bennis, *Still Surprised*, 12.
34. United States Army, "2010 Army Posture Statement," From the 2010 Army Posture Statement, Addendum F (AFORGEN), https://

secureweb2.hqda.pentagon.mil/vdas_armyposturestatement/2010 /aps_toc.asp (accessed October 12, 2011).

35. Keegan, *History of Warfare*, 8.

36. Michelle Malkin, "Romney and McCain: The GOP Frenemies Club," *The Washington Examiner*, January 11, 2012 (accessed July 18, 2012), http://washingtonexaminer.com/article/157015.

37. The Quotations Page, "Harry S. Truman Quotes," http://thinkexist.com /quotation/i_learned_that_a_great_leader_is_a_man_who_has/186396 .html (accessed July 18, 2012).

38. William Shakespeare, *Twelfth Night* (London: Penguin Books, 1995), II, v, 156–159.

39. Interested readers are directed to Matt Ridley's book, *Nature via Nurture* (2005).

40. Benmelech and Frydman, "Military CEOs," 23.

41. Donald F. Kuratko and Richard M. Hodgetts, *Entrepreneurship: A Contemporary Approach*, 4th ed. (Fort Worth, TX: Dryden Press, 1998), 5.

42. See United States Small Business Administration, "Owner Demographic Economic Research," http://archive.sba.gov/advo/research/demographic .html (accessed October 4, 2011).

43. "Henry W. Bloch," H&R Block, 2011, http://www.hrblock.com/press /hbloch_bio.jsp(accessed October 23, 2011).

44. National Endowment for the Humanities, "Changing the Channel: A Conversation with Brian Lamb" *Humanities*, 24 (2) (March/April 2003), 14.

45. See "America's Best Leaders: Q&A with Brian Lamb, President and CEO of C-SPAN," *U.S. News and World Report* (October 22, 2005), http://www.usnews.com/usnews/news/articles/051022/22lamb_print. htm (accessed July 18, 2012).

46. Ibid.

47. See Leonard Wong, "Developing Adaptive Leaders in Iraq and Afghanistan," *Harvard Business Review* (January 23, 2009), http:// blogs.hbr.org/frontline-leadership/2009/01/developing-adaptive -leaders.html#c041184 (accessed October 2, 2011).

48. Leonard Wong, "Developing Adaptive Leaders," Strategic Studies Institute (2004), http://www.strategicstudiesinstitute.army.mil/pdffiles /PUB411.pdf (accessed October 28, 2011).

49. See Schoomaker's 2006 comments at Sara Wood, "Soldiers Must Be Adaptive for Future, Army Chief Says," US Department of Defense, Februrary 21, 2006, www.defense.gov/news/newsarticle. aspx?id=14799 (accessed October 7, 2011).

50. Leonard Wong, *Developing Adaptive Leaders: The Crucible Experience of Operation Iraqi Freedom* (Carlisle, PA: Strategic Studies Institute, US Army War College, 2004), 18.

51. See Martin E. Dempsey, "Building Critical Thinkers: Leader Development Must Be the Army's Top Priority," *Armed Forces Journal*

(February, 2011), http://armedforcesjournal.com/2011/02/5663450 (accessed October 23, 2011).

52. Del Jones, "A Vanishing Breed: CEOs Seasoned by Military Combat," *USA Today* (January 18, 2005), http://www.usatoday.com /money/companies/management/2005–01-18-war-ceo_x.htm (accessed July 18, 2012).

53. See the Survey Documentation and Analysis (SDA) website hosted by UC Berkeley at http://sda.berkeley.edu/cgi-bin/hsda?harcsda+gss10 using the variable VETYEARS and the control YEAR to get time series data from the GSS.

54. Bob McDonald, phone interview, July 10, 2011.

3   ENTREPRENEURS IN UNIFORM

1. *Contrails, United States Air Force Academy Cadet Handbook* (Colorado Springs, CO: United States Air Force Academy, Cadet Wing Training, 1990).

2. Joseph A. Schumpeter, *Essays Of J. A. Schumpeter (1951)* (Whitefish, MT: Kessinger Publishing, 2010).

3. Peter G. Klein, Joseph T. Mahoney, Anita M. McGahan, and Christos N. Pitelis, "Toward a Theory of Public Entrepreneurship," *European Management Review* 7 (2010): 1–15.

4. Donald F. Kuratko and Richard M. Hodgetts, *Entrepreneurship: A Contemporary Approach*, 4th ed., (Forth Worth, Texas: Dryden Press, 1998).

5. Peter G. Klein, Joseph T. Mahoney, Anita M. McGahan, and Christos N. Pitelis, "Toward a Theory of Public Entrepreneurship," *European Management Review* 7 (2010): 1–15.

6. David McCullough, *American History* (New York: Simon & Schuster, 2001).

7. John Berlau, "Founding Father," *The American Spectator* (February 15, 2010), http://spectator.org/archives/2010/02/15/founding-father (accssed July 17, 2012).

8. Richard Holmes, *Battlefield: Decisive Conflicts in History* (Oxford: Oxford University Press, 2006), 290.

9. Max Hastings, *Warrior: Extraordinary Tales from the Battlefield* (New York: Harper Collins, 2005).

10. "Line officer" is a term to distinguish those officers who serve in combat command. Though it sounds like a reference to "front line," the expression may be traced to the formations of the warships of the British Royal Navy.

11. John Keegan, *The American Civil War* (New York: Knopf, 2009), 272.

12. Philip A. Crowl, "Alfred Thayer Mahan: The Naval Historian," in *Makers of Modern Strategy*, edited by Peter Paret (Princeton: Princeton University Press, 1986), 444–480.

13. Ibid., 445.
14. Ibid., 444.
15. Michael Lee Lanning, *The Military 100: A Ranking of the Most Influential Military Leaders of All Time* (New York: Barnes and Noble, 1999), 228.
16. Seth Shulman, *Unlocking the Sky: Glenn Hammond Curtiss and the Race to Invent the Airplane* (New York: Harper Collins, 2003), 1.
17. Richard Hallion, *Taking Flight: Inventing the Aerial Age from Antiquity through the First World War* (New York: Oxford University Press, 2003), 153.
18. Arthur Herman, interview by the author, October 10, 2011.
19. Rebecca Maksel, "The Billy Mitchell Court-Martial: Courtroom Sketches from Aviation's Trial of the Century," *Air & Space magazine* (July 2009), http://www.airspacemag.com/history-of-flight/The-Billy -Mitchell-Court-Martial.html.
20. Ibid.
21. Ibid.
22. Robert Coram, *Boyd: The Fighter Pilot Who Changed The Art of War* (New York: Hachette Book Group, 2002).
23. Ibid.
24. Ibid.
25. Ibid.
26. Ibid.
27. Ibid.
28. Mike Haynie, interview by the author, Fall 2011.
29. Jeff Peterson, interview by the author, Spring 2010.
30. Creighton Abrams entry at http://www.arlingtoncemetery.net /abrams.htm (accessed July 29, 2012).
31. Max Hastings, *Warrior: Extraordinary Tales from the Battlefield* (New York: Harper Collins, 2005).
32. John Wukovits, *Eisenhower* (New York: Palgrave Macmillan, 2006).
33. Ibid.
34. Ibid.
35. Ibid.
36. Nathan Rosenberg, *Inside the Blackbox: Technology and Economics* (Cambridge: Cambridge University Press, 1982).
37. Charles Jones, "Growth and Ideas," in *The Handbook of Economic Growth*, edited by Philippe Aghion and Steven Durlauf, 1st ed., vol. 1B (Amsterdam: Elsevier, 2005), 1107.

4 EXODUS

1. Dwight D. Eisenhower, "Special Message to the Congress on Career Incentives for Military Personnel, January 13, 1955." The American Presidency Project, by Gerhard Peters and John T. Woolley, http://www.presidency.ucsb.edu/ws/?pid=10265 (accessed July 17, 2012).

2. Thom Shanker, "Young Officers Leaving Army at a High Rate," *New York Times* (April 10, 2006), http://www.nytimes.com/2006/04/10/washington/10army.html.

3. Casey Wardynski, David S. Lyle, and Michael J. Colarusso, "Towards a U.S. Army Officer Corps Strategy for Success: Retaining Talent," The Official Homepage of The United States Army, January 28, 2010, http://www.army.mil/article/33628/ (accessed July 17, 2012).

4. Andrew Tilghman, "The Army's Other Crisis: Why the Best and Brightest Young Officers Are Leaving," *Washington Monthly* (December 2007), http://www.washingtonmonthly.com/features/2007/0712.tilghman.html (accessed July 17, 2012).

5. Wayne Grigsby, personal interview with the author, February 2010.

6. Tom Vanden Brook, "Officer Shortage Looming in the Army," *USA Today* (March 12, 2007), http://www.usatoday.com/news/washington/2007–03-12-officer-shortage_N.htm.

7. Wardynski, Lyle, and Colarusso, "Toward a U.S. Army Officer."

8. Ibid.

9. United States Government Accountability Office, "Military Personnel: Strategic Plan Needed to Address Army's Emerging Officer Accession and Retention Challenges," Report to the Committee on Armed Services, House of Representative (January 2007).

10. Tilghman, "The Army's Other Crisis."

11. Jeff Peterson, interview with the author, Spring 2010.

12. James R. Hosek and Beth J. Asch, "Changing Air Force Compensation: A Consideration of Some Options," in the 9th Quadrennial Review of Military Compensation, 2002, http://prhome.defense.gov/rfm/mpp/qrmc/Vol4/v4c4.pdf (accessed March 7, 2011).

13. Wardynski, Lyle, and Colarusso, "Toward a U.S. Army Officer," 11.

14. According Arthur Coumbe: "Officer attrition is a problem that has intermittently afflicted the Officer Corps since the conclusion of World War II. Over this period, the Army has frequently struggled to retain not only the requisite number of officers but 'talented' officers as well. The retention of junior officers has posed a particularly difficult challenge." See Arthur T. Coumbe, *Army Officer Development: Historical Context* (Carlisle, PA: Strategic Studies Institute, April 2010).

15. David McCormick describes poorly executed demobilizations after World War II, Korea, and Vietnam in his book about the post–Cold War "downsizing [that] has compromised the army's institutional health…" He writes: "The quality of the officer corps in each case suffered as the army lost some its brightest young officers." *The Downsized Warrior: America's Army in Transition* (New York: NYU Press, 2008), 7.

16. Coumbe, *Army Officer Development*.

17. James Hosek, "Deployment, Stress, and Intention to Stay in the Military," RAND Corporation, 2006, http://www.rand.org/content/dam/rand/pubs/research_briefs/2006/RAND_RB9150.pdf.

18. The full results of the survey were published in a paper on the Social Science Research Network (SSRN) and are abridged in this volume's appendix. Note that in most cases, percentages are reported as whole numbers, which may not total 100 percent because of rounding. Percentages for each result are calculated based on the number of responses to individual questions. See Tim J. Kane, "The Entrepreneurial Army: A Survey of West Point Graduates," *Social Science Research Network* (January 4, 2011), http://papers.ssrn.com /sol3/papers.cfm?abstract_id=1734594.

19. Small Wars Journal blog, http://smallwarsjournal.com/blog/2011/01 /why-our-best-officers-are-leav/ on January 5.

20. US Naval Institute blog http://blog.usni.org/2011/01/07/why-our-best -officers-are-leaving/ on January 7, 2011.

21. See Eric Tegler, "The Officer Market," February 25, 2011, http:// www.defensemedianetwork.com/stories/the-officer-market/.

22. A related statistic that Fowler's textbook spends much more time on is the response rate, which is the percentage of people who actually respond to one's survey request. If I ask one hundred people a question, and only ten answer, are the results valid? On the other hand, one could inflate the response rate by taking a survey of three people, getting three responses, and declaring a perfect rate. My sample frame was a list of roughly thirty-one hundred individual email addresses. I do not know how many of those received, opened, and read the email, but let's assume all of them did. This yields a response rate of just under 8 percent. In theory, a low response rate can yield biased results. But the relationship between response rate and actual survey error isn't linear. The potential for bias decreases exponentially with each extra respondent. Recent studies by Allyson Holbrook of the University of Illinois and her colleagues challenge the empirical effect of lower response rates. For example, a 2007 study of Holbrook's reviewed 81 national surveys with response rates varying from 5 to 54 percent, and reported that lower rate surveys were marginally less accurate. See Allyson Holbrook, Jon Krosnick, and Alison Pfent, "The Causes and Consequences of Response Rates in Surveys by the News Media and Government Contractor Survey Research Firms," in *Advances in Telephone Survey Methodology*, edited by James M. Lepkowski, N. Clyde Tucker, J. Michael Brick, Edith D. De Leeuw, Lilli Japec, Paul J. Lavrakas, Michael W. Link, and Roberta L. Sangster (New York: Wiley, 2007). Following numerous such studies, the American Association for Public Opinion Research (AAPOR) stated that response rates "do not necessarily differentiate reliably between accurate and inaccurate data." See "Response Rate—An Overview," http://www.aapor.org/Response_Rates_An _Overview1.htm (accessed January 23, 2012). Perhaps the 8-percent respondent sample in my survey included a large number of disgruntled ex-officers with an axe to grind? That's possible. This is especially

possible given that the survey was voluntary. However, I took the precaution of using neutral language in the solicitation message that invited participants to the survey. Also, the demographics of the respondents matched the larger population, particularly the fact that the proportion of active-duty respondents was one-third of the sample, which is higher than if we had just randomly selected graduates or even the larger officer population.

23. Charles Levinson, "As War Grows Longer, Troops' Patience Is Shorter," *Christian Science Monitor* (May 2006). Reprinted at http://seattletimes.nwsource.com/html/nationworld/2002898832 _troops30.html (accessed July 20, 2012).

24. Regarding the survey statistics: "Approximately, 22,500 Army leaders participated, with a response rate of 16.1%. This participation provides an overall sampling error of approximately +/- 0.6%. Essentially, this means that 95 times out of 100 the percentage reported will be within 1% of the true percentage (of perceptions)."

25. Sayce Falk, and Sasha Rogers, "Junior Military Officer Rretention: Challenges & Opportunities," Policy Analysis Exercise, John F. Kennedy School of Government, Harvard University, March 2011.

26. Ibid., 15.

27. Ibid., 27; emphasis in the original.

28. Ibid., 4.

29. Ibid., 4.

30. Ibid., 4.

31. Wardynski, Lyle, and Colarusso, "Toward a U.S. Army Officer."

32. Ibid. 18.

33. See Jim Tice, "Army Scaling Back Officer Promotion Rates," *ArmyTimes. com* (January 23, 2012), http://www.armytimes.com/news/2012/01/army -scaling-back-officer-promotion-013012w/ and various GAO studies, "Strategic Plan Needed to Address Army's Emerging Officer Accession and Retention Challenges," notably GAO-07–224 (January 19, 2007), http://www.gao.gov/new.items/d07224.pdf.

34. Doug Webster, personal interview with the author, Summer 2011.

5 IT'S NOT BUSINESS, IT'S PERSONNEL

1. Adam Smith, *An Inquiry into the Nature and Causes of the Wealth of Nations*, originally published in 1776, available free online at the Library of Economics and Liberty, http://www.econlib.org/library /Smith/smWN.html (accessed July 29, 2012).

2. See Rick Hampson, "Afghanistan: America's Longest War," *USA Today* (May 28, 2010), http://www.usatoday.com/news/military/2010–05 -27-longest-war-afghanistan_N.htm.

3. H. R. McMaster, *Dereliction of Duty: Lyndon Johnson, Robert McNamara, The Joint Chiefs of Staff, and the Lies That Led to Vietnam* (New York: Harper Collins, 1997), 28. The highly regulated systems

that McNamara put in place would eventually abolish the direct commissioning of midrank officers like he had been during World War II.

4. Department of Defense, "Robert S. McNamera," http://www.defense. gov/specials/secdef_histories/bios/mcnamara.htm (accessed June 28, 2012).

5. The Federalist Papers, "James Madison Quotes," http://www .thefederalistpapers.org/founders/james-madison-quotes (accessed May 1, 2012).

6. John T. Nelson, "General George C. Marshall: Strategic Leadership and the Challenges of Reconstituting the Army, 1939–1941," Strategic Studies Institute (February 1993), last modified September 14, 2011, http://www.strategicstudiesinstitute.army.mil/pubs/summary.cfm? q=358.

7. Richard W. Stewart, ed., *American Military History, Vol. 1, The United States Army and The Forging of a Nation, 1775–1917* (Washington, DC.: Center of Military History, United States Army, 2005). Available at http://www.history.army.mil/books/AMH-V1/ch16.htm.

8. Ibid.

9. "Department of Defense," *Training for Future Conflicts* (Washington, DC: 2003), http://www.au.af.mil/au/awc/awcgate/dod/dsb_tfc.pdf.

10. This is from Wilson and Vandergriff's essay "Leading the Human Dimensions out of a Legacy of Failure," in *America's Defense Meltdown* (Stanford: Stanford University Press, 2008), 56. The book is available free online at http://pogoarchives.org/labyrinth/11/02.pdf (accessed July 31, 2012).

11. Casey Wardynski, David S. Lyle, and Michael J. Colarusso, *Talent: Implications for a US Army Officer Corps Strategy*, Volume 2, in a monograph series by the Strategic Studies Institute (November 2009).

12. Paul Yingling, "A Failure in Generalship" *Armed Forces Journal*, http:// www.armedforcesjournal.com/2007/05/2635198/ (accessed July 18, 2012).

13. US Army War College, *How the Army Runs: A Senior Leader Reference Handbook*, 2011–2012 (Carlisle: USAWC, 2011), http://www.carlisle. army.mil/usawc/dclm/htar.cfm, 8.

14. Ibid., 9.

15. Ibid., 10.

16. These are infantry, armor, field artillery, air defense, aviation, Special Forces, engineers, military intelligence, military police, signal corps, adjutant general, finance, ordnance, transportation, quartermaster, and chemical corps.

17. Alexandra Newman and Dan Shrimpton, "The US Army Uses a Network Optimization Model to Designate Career Fields for Officers," *Interfaces* vol. 35, no. 3 (May/June 2005) 230–237.

18. It should be noted that in 2011 the army started experimenting with a market-based reform for rebranching midcareer, which may lead to further reforms in initial branching and assignments as well. See DesiRee Pavlick, "Voluntary Transfer Incentive Program Now Accepting Applications for Branch Transfer," US Army (August 26, 2011), http://www.army.mil/article/64386/.

19. Joseph Bruhl, "Gardener Leaders: A New Paradigm for Developing Adaptive, Creative, and Humble Leaders." *Military Review* XCII, no. 4 (July-August 2012).

20. US Army War College, "Study on Military Professionalism" (June 30, 1970), http://www.dtic.mil/cgi-bin/GetTRDoc?AD=ADA063748 (accessed July 30, 2012).

21. Donald Vandergriff, *Raising the Bar: Creating and Nurturing Adaptability to Deal with the Changing Face of War* (Washington, DC: Center for Defense Information Press, 2006), 58.

22. US Arm Field Manual 1–0, *Human Resources Support* (April 16, 2010), Chapter 1, 1–17.

23. Much of this analysis comes from the masterful 2006 study by RAND scholars Peter Schirmer, Harry J. Thie, Margaret C. Harrell, and Michael Tseng, *Challenging Time in DOPMA* (Santa Monica: RAND Corporation, 2006), http://www.rand.org/pubs/monographs/MG451.html.

24. Ibid., xiv.

25. From Scott Halter's "What Is an Army, But the Soldiers?—A Critical Performance Assessment of the US Army's Human Capital," *Military Review* vol. 92 (2012): 16–23. Issue 1, accessed April 13, 2012, http://usacac.army.mil/CAC2/MilitaryReview/Archives/English/MilitaryReview_20120229_art007.pdf.

26. Ibid.

27. *The Fourth Star: Four Generals and the Epic Struggle For the Future* by Greg Jaffe was published in late 2009. It recounts the biographies of four generals who led the army after the 9/11 attacks.

28. Schirmer, et al. *Challenging Time in DOPMA*, xiv.

29. James Kitfield, "Army Chief Struggles To Transform Service During War," *Government Executive* (October 29, 2004), http://www.govexec.com/federal-news/2004/10/army-chief-struggles-to-transform-service-during-war/17929/ (accessed July 18, 2012).

30. Wardynski, et al., *Talent.*

31. Vandergriff's 2006 book *Raising the Bar* emphasized a wholesale reform of the army's officer development model. He personally pointed me to the effect of Elihu Root and the industrial labor model that army manpower used as a foundation.

32. Wilson and Vandergriff, "Leading the Human Dimensions," 53.

33. Edward Lazear, interview with the author, April 2011.

34. Friedrich Hayek, "The Use of Knowledge in Society." *American Economic Review* XXXV, no. 4. pp. 519–30.
35. Wardynski, et al., *Talent*, 60.
36. Ibid.
37. Ibid.; emphasis in the original.
38. Ibid.
39. Sayce Falk and Sasha Rogers, "Junior Military Officer Retention: Challenges and Opportunities," Harvard University (Cambridge: JFK School of Government, March 2011), 38.
40. Ibid., 40.

6 WINNING BATTLES, LOSING WARS

1. Testimony of Gen. George C. Marshall, Chief of Staff, United States Army, Hearings before a Special Committee Investigating the National Defense Program, United States Senate, Seventy-Seventh Congress (Washington, DC: United States Government Printing Office 311932, April 15–25, 1941), http://www.marshall foundation.org/MarshallonLeadership.htm (accessed on March 13, 2012).
2. Mark Moyar, *A Question of Command: Counterinsurgency from the Civil War to Iraq* (New Have, CT: Yale University Press, 2009), 15–16.
3. James Q. Wilson, *Bureaucracy: What Government Agencies Do and Why They Do It* (New York: Basic Books, 1989), 223.
4. John F. Kennedy, "Remarks at West Point to the Graduating Class of the U.S. Military Academy, June 6, 1962," in *The American Presidency Project*, edited by Gerhard Peters and John T. Woolley, http://www.presidency.ucsb.edu/ws/index.php?pid=8695 (accessed July 19, 2012).
5. Obituary: General William Westmoreland, *The Telegraph* (July 20, 2005), http://www.telegraph.co.uk/news/obituaries/1494380/General -William-Westmoreland.html (accessed July 19, 2012).
6. Moyar, *A Question*, 158.
7. Ibid., 158–159.
8. These figures come from Fred Kaplan, "Challenging the Generals," *New York Times* (August 26, 2007).
9. Thomas A. Ricks, *Fiasco: The American Military Adventure in Iraq* (New York: The Penguin Press, 2006), 40.
10. Ibid., 75.
11. Ibid., 97.
12. Alyssa Fetini, "Obama's White House: Secretary of Veterans Affirs: Eric Shinseki," *Time* (December 2, 2008), http://www.time.com/time /specials/packages/article/0,28804,1863062_1863058_1865215,00. html (accessed July 19, 2012).
13. Ibid.
14. Ricks, *Fiasco*, 163.

15. Moyar, *A Question*, 219.
16. Ricks, *Fiasco*, 173.
17. Paul Yingling, "A Failure In Generalship," *Armed Forces Journal* (May 2007), http://www.armedforcesjournal.com/2007/05/2635198/ (accessed July 19, 2012); emphasis added.
18. Department of the Army, Pamphlet 600–3, *Commissioned Officer Professional Development and Career Management* (Washington, DC: US Army, February 2010), 36–37.
19. Scott Wuestner, interview by the author, March 28, 2012.
20. Cindy Williams, "The U.S. Army," *The American Interest* vol. 3, no. 4 (March/April 2008), http://www.the-american-interest.com/article.cfm?piece=399 (accessed March 22, 2012).
21. Ricks, *Fiasco*, 422–423.
22. Fred Kaplan, "Annual General Meeting: Finally, the Army Is Promoting the Right Officers," *Slate* (August 4, 2008), http://www.slate.com/articles/news_and_politics/war_stories/2008/08/annual_general_meeting.html (accessed July 19, 2012).
23. Ibid.
24. Andrew Tilghman, "The Army's Other Crisis: Why the Best and Brightest Young Officers Are Leaving," *Washington Monthly* (December 2007), http://www.washingtonmonthly.com/features/2007/0712.tilghman.html (accessed July 19, 2012).
25. Kaplan, Annual General Meeting.
26. John Nagl, interview with the author, February 2012.
27. I have never interviewed or met McMaster, but other sources in the army tell me he has held two one-star jobs to date, though neither was a deputy division commander role, the qualifying job necessary for highest rank. He has been selected for major general.

7 COERCION

1. David Warsh, "A Very Short History of the Volunteer Army," (July 20, 2003), http://www.economicprincipals.com/issues/2003.07.20/284.html (accessed February 12, 2012).
2. Thomas Aquinas wrote in *Summa Theologica* (1273): "For we call that violent which is against the inclination of a thing.... [A] thing is called voluntary because it is according to the inclination of the will. Therefore, just as it is impossible for a thing to be at the same time violent and natural, so it is impossible for a thing to be absolutely coerced or violent, and voluntary," (Thomas Aquinas, *Summa Theologica: Volume 1, part 1* [New York: Cosimo, 2007], 413).
3. James Q. Wilson, *Bureaucracy: What Government Agencies Do and Why They Do It* (New York: Basic Books, 1989), 149.
4. John Keegan, *A History of Warfare* (New York: Vintage Books, 1993), 32.
5. Eric Tegler, "The Officer Market; The Army Responds," *Defense Media Network* (February 27, 2011), http://www.defensemedianetwork.com

/stories/the-officer-market-the-army-responds/ (accessed Febrary 2, 2012).

6. Paul Yingling, "The Founders' Wisdom," *Armed Forces Journal* (February 2010), http://www.armedforcesjournal.com/2010/02/4384885/ (accessed February 23, 2012).

7. These quotes are from Milton and Rose Friedman's *Two Lucky People* (Chicago: University of Chicago Press), 377–381.

8. Charles Patrick Neimeyer, *America Goes to War: A Social History of the Continental Army* (New York: New York University Press, 1996), 128.

9. Alexis de Tocqueville, *Democracy in America* (Chicago: University of Chicago Press, 2000), Book 1 (1835), Chapter 13.

10. "All-Volunteer Armed Force Seen as 'Unrealistic' by Pentagon," *The Robesonian* (January 5, 1970), http://newspaperarchive.com /robesonian/1970–01-05/ (accessed February 7, 2012).

11. This is cited from Bernard Rostker and K. C. Yeh, *I Want You! The Evolution of the All-Volunteer Force* (Santa Monica: RAND Corporation, 2006), 31–32, but Rumsfeld's interest in the issue is thoroughly discussed in Bradley Graham's Rumsfeld biography *By His Own Rules* (2009).

12. Bernard Rostker, *I Want You!: The Evolution of the All-Volunteer Force* (Santa Monica: RAND Corporation, 2006), 35.

13. Associated Press, August 26, 1970.

14. Milton and Rose Friedman, *Two Lucky People*, page 380.

15. David R. Henderson "The Role of Economists in Ending the Draft." *Econ Journal Watch* vol. 2, no. 2 (August 2005), 369.

16. Tim Kane, "Why Our Best Officers are Leaving," *The Atlantic* (January-February 2011).

17. See Thomas E. Ricks, "No, Our Best Officers Are Not Running Off; 4 Officers Respond to that Atlantic Article," *Foreign Policy* (March 23, 2011), http://ricks.foreignpolicy.com/posts/2011/03/23/no_our _best_officers_are_not_running_off_4_officers_respond_to_that _atlantic_articl (accessed April 5, 2011).

18. Ibid.

19. Tegler, "The Officer Market."

20. See Philip Carter and Owen West, "Dismissed! We Won't Solve the Military Manpower Crisis by Retaining Our Worst Soldiers," *Slate* (June 2, 2005), http://www.slate.com/articles/news_and_ politics/war_stories/2005/06/dismissed.html (accessed February 24, 2012).

21. Thomas E. Ricks, "Nate Fick: It Is Time to Discard the Military's 20-year Retirement System," *Foreign Policy* (May 6, 2010), http:// ricks.foreignpolicy.com/posts/2010/05/06/nate_fick_it_is_time_ to_discard_the_military_s_20_year_retirement_system (accessed February 27, 2012).

22. Mike Haynie, email and telephone interviews by Tim Kane, January 10–20, 2011.
23. Ibid.

8 WAR MACHINES

1. Inaugural Address of President John F. Kennedy, Washington, DC (January 20, 1961), http://www.jfklibrary.org/Research/Ready-Reference/JFK-Quotations/Inaugural-Address.aspx (accessed August 20, 2011).
2. Lawrence Freedman, *The Evolution of Nuclear Strategy* (New York: Palgrave MacMillan, 2003), 15.
3. P. W. Singer, *Wired for War: The Robotics Revolution and Conflict in the 21st Century* (New York: Penguin, 2009), 434.
4. See, e.g., Andrew Bacevich's *American Empire* (2004), among others.
5. Max Boot, "The Paradox of Military Technology," *The New Atlantis* (Fall 2006), http://www.thenewatlantis.com/publications/the-paradox-of-military-technology (accessed March 4, 2012).
6. "Beyond Outrageous: CENTCOM Boss Takes Mindless Shot at USAF," *Air Force Magazine* (August 19, 2009), http://www.airforce-magazine.com/Features/airpower/Pages/box082009petraeus.aspx (accessed March 23, 2012).
7. Max Boot, *War Made New: Technology, Warfare, and the Course of History, 1500 to Today* (New York: Gotham Books, 2006), 15.
8. Ibid., 16.
9. Ibid.
10. Singer, *Wired*, 331.
11. See Jeremiah Gertler, "U.S. Unmanned Aerial Systems," Congressional Research Service Report 42136 (Washington, DC: January 3, 2012), http://www.fas.org/sgp/crs/natsec/R42136.pdf/ (government document) (accessed March 9, 2012).
12. Singer, *Wired*, 133.
13. Linda Shiner, "Predator: First Watch: Lesson Learned: Never Send a Man to do a Machine's Job," *Air & Space* (May 2001, 5).
14. Blair originally wrote about his transition on the Air University blog, *The Wright Stuff*, which is no longer available. The post was republished at the *Small Wars Journal* blog, dated July 27, 2009, at the link http://www.smallwars.org/blog/back-to-basics.
15. This number is cited by the Congressional Research Service and USAF sources.
16. David S. Cloud, "Civilian Contractors Playing Key Roles in U.S. Drone Operations," *Los Angeles Times* (December 29, 2011), http://articles.latimes.com/2011/dec/29/world/la-fg-drones-civilians-20111230 (accessed March 14, 2012).
17. Boot, *War Made New*.

18. Michael Hoffman, "Task Force to Get More UAVs into War Zones," *Air Force Times* (April 26, 2008), http://www.airforcetimes.com/news/2008 /04 /airforce_uav_callout_042608w/ (accessed March 7, 2012).

19. Michael B. Donley, Hearing Transcript, United States Air Force (April 5, 2012), http://www.airforce-magazine.com/DWG/Documents/2012 /April%202012/040512Donley.pdf (accessed April 17, 2012).

20. "Remarks by the President Securing Our Nation's Cyber Infrastructure," The White House (May 29, 2009), http://www.whitehouse.gov/the -press-office/remarks-president-securing-our-nations-cyber -infrastructure (accessed March 12, 2012).

21. Scott M. Halter, "What is an Army but the Soldiers?: A Critical Assessment of the Army's Human Capital Management System," *Military Review* (January/February 2012), http://usacac.army.mil/CAC2/ MilitaryReview/Archives/English/MilitaryReview_20120229_art007 .pdf (accessed March 13, 2012).

22. Government Accountability Office, "Cybersecurity Human Capital: Initiatives Need Better Planning and Coordination," (Washington, DC, November, 2011); emphasis added.

23. Ibid.

9   MEASURING MERIT

1. Paul Yingling, "Failure in Generalship," *Armed Forces Journal* (May 2007), http://www.armedforcesjournal.com/2007/05/2635198/ (accessed April 23, 2012).

2. Michelle Tan, "Evals Latest Move to Root Out Toxic Leaders," *Army Times* (October 9, 2011), http://www.armytimes.com/news/2011/10 /army-launches-mandatory-360-degree-evals-for-officers-100911w/ (accessed April 9, 2012).

3. Frederick Kroesen, "Losing the 'Best and the Brightest,' Again," *ARMY Magazine* (March 2011), http://www.ausa.org/publications/ armymagazine/archive/2011/3/Documents/FC_Kroesen_0311.pdf (accessed April 11, 2012).

4. Sayce Falk and Sasha Rogers, "Junior Military Officer Retention: Challenges & Opportunities," *Harvard University, JFK School of Government* (March 2011), http://www.foreignpolicy.com/files/ fp_uploaded_documents/Falk-Rogers%20PAE%2003–11%20vF.pdf (accessed April 3, 2012).

5. Marvin W. Williams, "The Relationship of the Officer Evaluation Report to Captain Attrition," School of Advanced Military Studies (May 31, 2001), http://www.dtic.mil/cgi-bin/GetTRDoc?AD=ADA416022 (accessed April 2, 2012).

6. G. I. Wilson and Donald Vandergriff, "Leading the Human Dimensions out of a Legacy of Failure in America's Defense Meltdown," *America's Defense Meldown* (November 2008), 59.

7. Further argument along these lines comes from Lieutenant Colonel Scott Halter's 2012 *Military Review* essay: "The Officer Evaluation Report (OER) is an example of an antiquated tool. Using a non-searchable form with a culturally skewed and inflated narrative that overly focuses on command, this document provides little real utility to determine an individual's potential and actual skills or his intellectual character. Instead, the OER measures short-term performance and accomplishments from the eyes of two or three superiors and is generally inaccurate and unscientific. The 2009 Army Research Institute survey found that 88 percent of officers self-evaluated themselves to be in the top 25 percent of their peer group—an indicator of the Army's inability to use a developmental tool like the OER to review and develop its leaders. This poor mechanism for evaluating future leaders has many consequences. Chiefly, it robs the Army of the ability to clearly see what skills, behaviors, and experiences its people possess," (19). See "What Is an Army, But the Soldiers?—A Critical Performance Assessment of the US Army's Human Capital," *Military Review*, January-February 2012, 16–23.

8. Walter F. Ulmer, "Military Leadership in the 21st Century: Another 'Bridge Too Far'?," *Parameters* (Spring 1998), 4–25, http://www.carlisle.army.mil/USAWC/parameters/Articles/98spring/ulmer.htm (accessed April 7, 2012).

9. Quoted in Lieutenant Colonel Timothy R. Reese's Army War College paper, and originally published in the 2000 *Army Training and Leader Development Panel Officer Study, Report to the Army*, United States Army (October 2000), http://www.au.af.mil/au/awc/awcgate/army/atld-panel/off_report.pdf.

10. See Bruce Rolfson, "Airmen to Chief: Fix Evals Now" *Air Force Times* (March 26, 2010), http://www.airforcetimes.com/news/2010/03/airforce_epr_032610w (accessed April 20, 2012).

11. Moheet Nagrath, inteview with via phone and email, April 15, 2011.

12. Stephen J. Gerras, "The Army as a Learning Organization," US Army War College, May 2002, 17.

13. Tim Reese, "Transforming the Officer Evaluation System: Using a 360-Degree Feedback Model," US Army War College (April 9, 2002), http://oai.dtic.mil/oai/oai?verb=getRecord&metadataPrefix=html&identifier=ADA401643 (accessed April 12, 2012).

14. Walter F. Ulmer, "Military Leadership in the 21st Century: Another 'Bridge Too Far'?," *Parameters* (Spring 1998), 4–25, http://www.carlisle.army.mil/USAWC/parameters/Articles/98spring/ulmer.htm (accessed April 7, 2012).

15. Ibid.

16. See Mark Edwards, "Army Implements Officer Evaluation Report Policy Changes," US Army, Media Release (Fort Knox: September 16,

2011), http://www.jbmhh.army.mil/inc/OERModificationsPressRele
aseFINAL-16Sep.pdf (accessed April 28, 2012); emphasis added.

APPENDIX: SURVEY OF WEST POINT GRADUATES

1. Questions for the initial survey were designed during May–August
2010 with input and advice from many individuals, including James
Carafano, William Casebeer, Scott Clemenson, Kyle Davis, Anthony
DeToto, Dean Dorman, Jason Dempsey, Guy Filipelli, Alyse Freilich,
Grover Harms, Warren Hearnes, Steve Kiser, Beau Laskey, Robert
Litan, John Nagl, Shawn Olds, Kelly Perdew, Jeff Peterson, Carl
Schramm, Troy Thomas, Josh Weed, and Elad Yoran.

SELECTED BIBLIOGRAPHY

Ackerman, Spencer. "Air Force Chief: It'll Be 'Years' Before We Catch Up on Drone Data."

Ambrose, Stephen E. *The Victors. Eisenhower and His Boys: The Men of World War II*. New York: Simon and Schuster, 1998.

Asch, Beth J., James R. Hosek, and John T. Warner. "New Economics of Manpower in the Post—Cold War Era." *Handbook of Defense Economics*. Elsevier, 2007.

Berlau, John. "Founding Father, Entrepreneur: The Overlooked Business Career Of George Washington," *Reason*, February 12, 2009. http://reason.com/archives/2009/02/12/founding-father-entrepreneur.

Blount, Roy Jr. *Robert E. Lee*. New York: Viking, 2003.

Boot, Max. *War Made New: Technology, Warfare the Course of History 1500 to Today*. New York: Gotham Books, 2006.

Brett, Joan F., and Leanne E. Atwater. "360 Degree Feedback: Accuracy, Reactions, and Perceptions of Usefulness." *Journal of Applied Psychology* vol. 86, no. 5 (2001): 930–942.

Carlson, Kenneth D. "A Deliberate Process: Developing Strategic Leaders in the United States Air Force, United States Army War College, Strategy Research Project. Carlisle, PA: March 30, 2007. http://www.dtic.mil/cgi-bin/GetTRDoc?AD=ADA469621.

Carter, Philipp, and Owen West. "Dismissed!" *Slate.com*, June 2, 2005. http://www.slate.com/articles/news_and_politics/war_stories/2005/06/dismissed.html.

Cloud, David S. "Civilian Contractors Playing Key Roles in U.S. Drone Operations." *Los Angeles Times*, December 29, 2011. http://articles.latimes.com/2011/dec/29/world/la-fg-drones-civilians-20111230.

Congressional Budget Office, "The All-Volunteer Military: Issues and Performance." Pub. No. 2960, July 19, 2007. www.cbo.gov/ftpdocs/83xx/doc8313/07–19-MilitaryVol.pdf.

Coram, Robert. *Boyd: The Fighter Pilot Who Changed The Art of War*. New York: Hachette Book Group, 2002.

Coumbe, Arthur T. *Army Officer Development: Historical Context*. Carlisle, PA: Strategic Studies Institute, 2010.

Cowley, Robert, and Geoffrey Parker. *The Reader's Companion to Military History*. New York: Houghton Mifflin, 1996.

Crowl, Philip A. "Alfred Thayer Mahan: The Naval Historian." In *Makers of Modern Strategy*, edited by Peter Paret, Gordon A. Craig, and Felix Gilbert. Princeton, NJ: University Press, 1986, 444–477.

"Cybersecurity Human Capital: Initiatives Need Better Planning and Coordination." GAO-12-8. November 29, 2011. http://www.gao.gov /products/GAO-12-8.

Danger Room. WIRED.com. April 5, 2012. http://www.wired.com /dangerroom/2012/04/air-force-drone-data/#more-77781

Defense Science Board. *Enhancing Adaptability of U.S. Military Forces*, January 2011. http://www.acq.osd.mil/dsb/reports/EnhancingAdapt abilityOfUSMilitaryForcesB.pdf.

Dempsey, Martin E. "Building Critical Thinkers: Leader Development Must Be the Army's Top Priority." *Armed Forces Journal*, February 2011. http://armedforcesjournal.com/2011/02/5663450.

Department of the Army. "Commissioned Officer Professional Development and Career Management." Pamphlet, February 1, 2010, 600–603.

Doubler, Michael D. *Closing with the Enemy. How GIs Fought the War in Europe, 1944–1945*. Lawrence: University Press of Kansas, 1994.

Duffy, Tim. *Military Experience & CEOs: Is There a Link?* Korn/Ferry International, 2006.

Entous, Adam, Julian E. Barnes, and Siobhan Gorman. "More Drones, Fewer Troops." *Wall Street Journal*, January 26, 2012. http://online. wsj.com/article/SB1000142405297020462420457718323421679911 6.html.

Falk, Sayce, and Sasha Rogers. "Junior Military Officer Retention: Challenges and Opportunities." John F. Kennedy School of Government, Harvard University, March 2011. http://www.foreignpolicy.com/files /fp_uploaded_documents/Falk-Rogers%20PAE%2003–11%20vF. pdf/.

Fields, William S., and David T. Hardy. "The Third Amendment and the Issue of the Maintenance of Standing Armies: A Legal History." *American Journal of Legal History*, vol. 35 (1991): 393–431.

Formica, Anthony M. "Lost in Transmission: How the Army Has Garbled the Message about the Nature of Its Profession." *Military Review*, vol. 92 (March–April 2012): 44–52.

Fowler Jr., Floyd J. *Survey Research Methods*, 4th edition. Thousand Oaks, CA: SAGE, 2008.

Friedman, Milton, and Rose Friedman. *Two Lucky People*. Chicago: University of Chicago Press, 1998.

———. Why Not a Volunteer Army?" In *New Individualist Review*, edited by Ralph Raico. Indianapolis: Liberty Fund, 1981.

"Cybersecurity Human Capital: Initiatives Need Better Planning and Coordination." GAO-12-8. November 29, 2011. http://www.gao .gov/products/GAO-12-8.

Gerras, Stephen J. "The Army as a Learning Organization." US Army War College, Department of Command, Leadership, and Management, May 2002. http://www.dtic.mil/cgi-bin/GetTRDoc?AD=ADA469631.

Gertler, Jeremiah. "U.S. Unmanned Aerial Systems." Congressional Research Service. Report 42136. January 3, 2012. http://www.fas.org/sgp/crs/natsec/R42136.pdf.

Hadley, Arthur T. *The Straw Giant*. New York: Random House, 1971.

Halter, Scott M. "What Is an Army But the Soldiers?—A Critical Performance Assessment of the US Army's Human Capital." *Military Review* vol. 92, no. 1 (January–February 2012): 16–23.

Hampson, Rick. "Afghanistan: America's Longest War." *USA Today*, May 28, 2010. http://www.usatoday.com/news/military/2010–05-27-longest-war-afghanistan_N.htm.

Hastings, Max. *Warriors: Portraits from the Battlefield*. New York: Alfred A. Knopf, 2005.

Hastings, Michael. "The Runaway General." *Rolling Stone*, June 22, 2010. http://www.rollingstone.com/politics/news/the-runaway-general-20100622.

Haught, David D. *Officer Personnel Management in the Army: Past, Present, and Future*. Carlisle, PA: Army War College, 2003.

Hayek, Friedrich. "The Use of Knowledge in Society." *American Economic Review* vol. 35, no. 4 (September 1945): 519–530.

Henderson, David. R. "The Role of Economists in Ending the Draft." *Econ Journal Watch* vol. 2, no. 2 (August 2005): 362–376.

Holbrook, Allyson, Jon Krosnick, and Alison Pfent. "The Causes and Consequences of Response Rates in Surveys by the News Media and Government Contractor Survey Research Firms." In *Advances in Telephone Survey Methodology*, edited by James M. Lepkowski, N. Clyde Tucker, J. Michael Brick, Edith D. De Leeuw, Lilli Japec, Paul J. Lavrakas, Michael W. Link, and Roberta L. Sangster. New York: Wiley, 2007.

Holmes, Richard. *Battlefield: Decisive Conflicts in History*. New York: Oxford University Press, 2006.

Hosek, James. "Deployment, Stress, and Intention to Stay in the Military." Santa Monica: RAND Corporation, 2006. http://www.rand.org/content/dam/rand/pubs/research_briefs/2006/RAND_RB9150.pdf.

Hosek, James, and Beth Asch. "Air Force Compensation: Considering Some Options for Change." Santa Monica: RAND Corporation, 2002. http://www.rand.org/pubs/monograph_reports/MR1566-1.html.

Huntington, Samuel P. *The Soldier and the State: The Theory and Politics of Civil-Military Relations*. Cambridge: The Belknap Press of Harvard University Press, 1957.

Jaffe, Greg. *The Fourth Star: Four Generals and the Epic Struggle For the Future*. New York: Crown Publishers, 2009.

Jones, Charles. "Growth and Ideas." In *The Handbook of Economic Growth*, edited by Philippe Aghion and Steven Durlauf. 1st ed. Vol. 1B (Amsterdam: Elsevier, 2005), 1063–1111.

Kane, Tim. "Who Are the Recruits? The Demographic Characteristics of U.S. Military Enlistment, 2003–2005." Heritage Foundation, Center for Data Analysis Report #06–09, October 27, 2006.

———. "Who Bears the Burden? Demographic Characteristics of U.S. Military Recruits Before and After 9/11." Heritage Foundation, Center for Data Analysis Report #05–08, November 7, 2005.

———. "Why Our Best Officers Are Leaving." The Atlantic, January /February 2011.

Keegan, John. A History of Warfare. New York: Vintage Books, 1993.

Kaplan, Fred. "Annual General Meeting: Finally, the Army Is Promoting the Right Officers." Slate, August 4, 2008. http://www.slate.com /articles/news_and_politics/war_stories/2008/08/annual_general _meeting.html.

———. "Challenging the Generals." New York Times, August 26, 2007. http://www.nytimes.com/2007/08/26/magazine/26military-t. html?pagewanted=all.

———. "An Officer and a Family Man." Slate.com, January 16, 2008. http:// www.slate.com/articles/news_and_politics/war_stories/2008/01/an _officer_and_a_family_man.html (accessed July 12, 2012).

Kilcullen, David. The Accidental Guerrilla. New York: Oxford University Press, 2009.

Kitfield, James. Prodigal Soldiers. New York: Simon & Schuster, 1995.

Klein, Peter G., Joseph T. Mahoney, Anita M. McGahan, and Christos N. Pitelis. "Toward a Theory of Public Entrepreneurship," European Management Review 7 (2010): 1–15.

Kroesen, Frederick J. "Losing the 'Best and the Brightest,' Again." ARMY magazine, March 2011. http://www.ausa.org/publications/armymagazine /archive/2011/3/Documents/FC_Kroesen_0311.pdf.

Luvaas, Jay. Lee and the Operational Art: The Right Place, The Right Time. Carlilse, PA: US Army War College, 1992.

Maksel, Rebecca. "The Billy Mitchell Court-Martial." Air & Space Magazine, July 1, 2009. http://www.airspacemag.com/history-of-flight/The-Billy -Mitchell-Court-Martial.html.

Manning, Michael Lee. The Military 100. Secaucus, NJ: Citadel Press, 1996.

McCormick, David. The Downsized Warrior: America's Army in Transition. New York: NYU Press, 2008.

McCullough, David. 1776. New York: Simon and Schuster, 2005.

McDonald, Robert A. Personal interviews via phone and email with the author, Spring 2011.

McMaster, H. R. Dereliction of Duty: Lyndon Johnson, Robert McNamara, The Joint Chiefs of Staff, and the Lies That Led to Vietnam. New York: Harper Collins, 1997.

McPhereson, Renny. "The Next Petraeus: What Makes a Visionary Commander, and Why the Military Isn't Producing More of Them."

Boston Globe, September 26, 2010. http://www.boston.com/bostonglobe/ideas/articles/2010/09/26/the_next_petraeus/.

Moore, Michael, dir. *Fahrenheit 9/11*. DVD, United States: Lions Gate Films, 2004.

Moyar, Mark. *A Question of Command: Counterinsurgency from the Civil War to Iraq*. New Haven, CT: Yale University Press, 2009.

Nagl, John. *Learning to Eat Soup with a Knife*. Chicago: Praeger, 2002.

Nagrath, Moheet. Personal interviews via phone and email with the author, Spring 2011.

O'Donnely, Sally B. "Criticism Mounts of U.S. Generals in Iraq." *Time*, October 27, 2006. http://www.time.com/time/nation/article/0,8599,1551801,00.html.

O'Keefe, Brian. "Battle-Tested: from Soldier to Business Leader." *Fortune*, March 8, 2010. http://money.cnn.com/2010/03/04/news/companies/military_business_leaders.fortune/.

Paret, Peter, ed. *Makers of Modern Strategy, from Machiavelli to the Nuclear Age*. Princeton, NJ: Princeton University Press, 1986.

Reese, Timothy R. "Transforming the Officer Evaluation System: Using a 360-Degree Feedback Model." US Army War College Strategic Research Project, April 2002. http://www.dtic.mil/cgi-bin/GetTRDoc?AD=ADA401643.

Ricks, Thomas E. *Fiasco: The American Military Adventure in Iraq*. New York: Penguin, 2006.

———. *The Gamble: General David Petraeus and the American Military Adventure in Iraq, 2006–2008*. New York: Penguin Press, 2009.

Rolfsen, Bruce. "Airmen to Chief: Fix Evals Now." *AirForceTimes.com*, March 26, 2010. http://www.airforcetimes.com/news/2010/03/airforce_epr_032610w/.

Rostker, Bernard. *I Want You! The Evolution of the All-Volunteer Force*. Santa Monica: RAND Corporation, 2006.

Rostker, Bernard D., Harry J. Thie, James L. Lacy, Jennifer H. Kawata, and Susanna W. Purnell. "The Defense Officer Personnel Management Act of 1980: A Retrospective Assessment." Santa Monica: RAND Corporation, 1992. http://www.rand.org/pubs/reports/R4246.html.

Roth-douquet, Kathy, and Frank Schaeffer. *AWOL: The Unexcused Absence of America's Upper Classes from Military Service and How It Hurts Our Country*. New York: Harper Collins, 2006.

Schirmer, Peter, Harry J. Thie, Margaret C. Harrell, and Michael Tseng. *Challenging Time in DOPMA*. Santa Monica: RAND Corporation, 2006.

Schumpeter, Joseph A. *Essays Of J. A. Schumpeter (1951)*, edited by Richard V. Clemence, Whitefish, MT: Kessinger Publishing, 2010.

Shanker, Thom. "Young Officers Leaving the Army at a High Rate." *New York Times*, April 10, 2006. http://www.nytimes.com/2006/04/10/washington/10army.html?pagewanted=all.

Sherk, James, and Shanea J. Watkins. "Who Serves in the U.S. Military? Demographic Characteristics of Enlisted Troops and Officers." Center for Data Analysis, *The Heritage Foundation*, August 21, 2008.

Shiner, Linda. "Predator: First Watch." *Air & Space Magazine*, May 2001. http://www.airspacemag.com/military-aviation/predator.html.

Shrimpton, Dan, and Alexandra M. Newman. "The US Army Uses a Network Optimization Model to Designate Career Fields for Officers." *Interfaces* vol. 35, no. 3 (2005): 230–237.

Singer, P. W. *Wired for War: The Robotics Revolution and Conflict in the 21st Century*. New York: Penguin, 2009.

Smith, Adam. *An Inquiry into the Nature and Causes of the Wealth of Nations*. Originally published in 1776, available free online at the Library of Economics and Liberty. http://www.econlib.org/library/Smith/smWN.html (accessed July 29, 2012).

Sorley, Lewis. *A Better War: The Unexamined Victories and Final Tragedy of America's Last Years in Vietnam*. Orlando: Houghton Mifflin Harcourt, 1999.

Steele, John P. *2010 Center For Army Leadership Annual Survey of Army Leadership (CASAL): Volume 1, Executive Summary*. The Center for Army Leadership, U.S. Army Combined Arms Center, May 2011. http://usacac.army.mil/CAC2/Repository/CASAL_TechReport2011-1_V1.pdf.

Tan, Michelle. "Rooting Out Toxic Leaders." *ArmyTimes.com*, October 9, 2011. http://www.armytimes.com/news/2011/10/army-launches-mandatory-360-degree-evals-for-officers-100911w/.

Tegler, Eric. "The Officer Market." *Defense Media Network*, February 25, 2011. http://www.defensemedianetwork.com/stories/the-officer-market/.

Tice, Jim. "Army Scaling Back Officer Promotion Rrates." *ArmyTimes.com*, January 23, 2012. http://www.armytimes.com/news/2012/01/army-scaling-back-officer-promotion-013012w/.

Tilghman, Andrew. "The Army's Other Crisis: Why the Best and Brightest Young Officers are Leaving." *Washington Monthly*, December 2007. http://www.washingtonmonthly.com/features/2007/0712.tilghman.html.

Tocqueville, Alexis de. *Democracy in America*, 1835. http://xroads.virginia.edu/~HYPER/DETOC/home.html (accessed January 20, 2012).

Ulmer, Walter F. "Military Leadership into the 21st Century: Another 'Bridge Too Far'?" *Parameters* vol. 38 (Spring 1998): 135–155.

Unger, Harlow Giles. *The Unexpected George Washington: His Private Life*. Hoboken: John Wiley & Sons, 2006.

United States Army, Counterinsurgency Field Manual, FM No. 3–24. Chicago: University of Chicago Press, 2007.

US Government Accountability Office. "Military Personnel: Strategic Plan Needed to Address Army's Emerging Officer Accession and Retention Challenges." GAO-07-224, January 19, 2007. http://www.gao.gov/new.items/d07224.pdf.

Vandergriff, Donald. *Raising the Bar: Creating and Nurturing Adaptability to Deal with the Changing Face of War* (Washington, DC: Center for Defense Information Press, 2006).

Wardynski, Casey, David S. Lyle, and Michael J. Colarusso. "Towards a U.S. Army Officer Corps Strategy for Success: Retaining Talent." Strategic Studies Institute. US Army War College, January 2010. http://www.strategicstudiesinstitute.army.mil/pubs/display.cfm?pubID=965.

Warsh, David. "A Very Short History of the Volunteer Army." *EconomicPrincipals.com*, July 20, 2003. http://www.economicprincipals.com/issues/2003.07.20/284.html.

Wayland, Bradley A. "The Current Officer Evaluation and Promotion System." *Air & Space Power Journal*, December 2002. http://www.airpower.maxwell.af.mil/airchronicles/cc/wayland.html.

Williams, Cindy. "The U.S. Army." *The American Interest* vol. 3, no. 4 (March/April 2008): 26–30.

Williams, Marvin W. "The Relationship of the Officer Evaluation Report to Captain Attrition." School of Advanced Military Studies ('Fort Leavenworth, May 31, 2001). http://www.dtic.mil/cgi-bin/GetTRDoc?AD=ADA416022.

Wilson, G. I., and Donald Vandergriff. "Leading the Human Dimensions out of a Legacy of Failure." In *America's Defense Meltdown*, edited by Winslow Wheeler. Stanford: Stanford University Press, 2008, 53–79.

Wilson, James Q. *Bureaucracy: What Government Agencies Do and Why They Do It*. New York: Basic Books, 1989.

Wong, Leonard. "Developing Adaptive Leaders: The Crucible Experience of Operation Iraqi Freedom." Strategic Studies Institute, July 2004. http://www.strategicstudiesinstitute.army.mil/pdffiles/PUB411.pdf.

———. "Fashion Tips for the Field Grade." Strategic Studies Institute, October 4, 2006. http://www.strategicstudiesinstitute.army.mil/pubs/display.cfm?pubID=731.

———. "Developing Adaptive Leaders in Iraq and Afghanistan." *Harvard Business Review*, January 23, 2009. http://blogs.hbr.org/frontline-leadership/2009/01/developing-adaptive-leaders.

Wukovitz, John. *Eisenhower*. New York: Palgrave Macmillan, 2006.

Yingling, Paul. "A Failure in Generalship." *Armed Forces Journal*, May 2007. http://www.armedforcesjournal.com/2007/05/2635198.

———. "The Founders' Wisdom." *Armed Forces Journal*, February 2010. http://www.armedforcesjournal.com/2010/02/4384885/.

INDEX

Mahan, Alfred Thayer, 34, 70–1
Maksel, Rebecca, 74
Malone, Mike, 122
Marines. *See* United States Marine
  Corps
market versus military dichotomy, 51
Marlowe, Ann, 37
Marshall, George C., 48–9, 80,
  112, 131, 143, 148, 195
Mattis, James, 153
McCain, John, 50, 166
McChrystal, Stanley, 24, 159
McClellan, George, 67, 148
McCormick, Dave, 3, 243n15
McCullough, David, 63
McDonald, Bob, 25, 57, 206–10
McFarland, Sean, 159
McKinley, William, 112
McMaster, H. R., 20, 23, 111,
  157–61, 214, 249n27
McNamara, Robert, 110–11, 123,
  148, 173, 202
McPherson, Renny, 24
Meade, George, 68, 80
Melville, George, 72
military civilian gap, 56–8
Military Occupation Specialty
  (MOS), 30, 155, 185, 198
Military Personnel Command
  (MPC), 12, 105
Mill, John Stuart, 164
Miller, James, 177
Mises, Ludwig von, 127
"mission first," 77
Mission Ventures, 2–3
Mitchell, Bill, 59, 73–5, 85
Moore, Michael, 20, 38, 58
Moseley, Michael, 194
Moulton, Harold, 94
Moyar, Mark, 16–17, 20, 147, 153
Myers, Richard, 153

Nagl, John, 9, 12–13, 18–21, 23,
  143–4, 159, 215
Nagrath, Moheet, 210–11

Napoleon, 34, 59, 65
nation-building, 54–5, 149
navy. *See* United States Navy
NeocorTech, 1
NetRanger, 106
Newcomb, Simon, 72
Newman, Alexandra, 120
Nimitz, Chester, 71, 85
9/11, 7, 19, 86–8, 93, 109, 120,
  149, 194
Nixon, Richard, 26–7, 131–2,
  173–6
North Atlantic Treaty
  Organization (NATO),
  144, 151, 185
Nozick, Robert, 164
nuclear weapons, 111, 119, 145–7,
  166, 183–4, 187–8

Obama, Barack, 10–11, 56,
  109, 196
Odierno, Raymond T., 43
Officer Career Satisfaction
  Program (OCSP), 104
officer evaluations, 22–3, 32, 125,
  128, 200–4, 213–14, 225,
  253n7
officer professional management
  system (OPMS), 120, 122,
  129, 138, 203, 215
Oi, Walter, 5, 132, 171, 173
Omar, Mullah, 109
One Bullet Away (Fick), 181
OODA (Observe, Orient, Decide
  and Act) loop theory, 76
Operation Desert Storm, 20, 76,
  149, 158–9, 187
Operation Enduring Freedom, 54.
  See also Afghanistan War
Operation Iraqi Freedom (OIF),
  23, 39, 221. *See also* Iraq War
organization capital, 30

Pace, Peter, 153
Page, Larry, 60

270 I BLEEDING TALENT